FACING THE PLANETARY

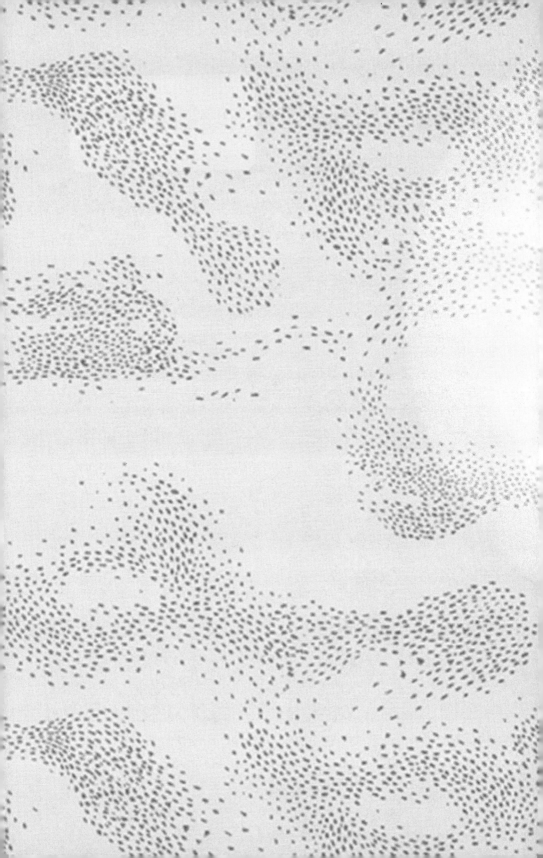

FACING THE PLANETARY

ENTANGLED HUMANISM

AND THE POLITICS OF SWARMING

WILLIAM E. CONNOLLY

DUKE UNIVERSITY PRESS
Durham and London 2017

Library of Congress Cataloging-in-Publication Data
Names: Connolly, William E., author.
Title: Facing the planetary : entangled humanism and the politics of
    swarming / William E. Connolly.
Description: Durham : Duke University Press, 2017. |
    Includes bibliographical references and index.
Identifiers: LCCN 2016034894 (print) | LCCN 2016036388 (ebook)|
ISBN 9780822363309 (hardcover : alk. paper)
ISBN 9780822363415 (pbk. : alk. paper)
ISBN 9780822373254 (e-book)
Subjects: LCSH: Global environmental change—Political aspects. |
    Climate change mitigation—Citizen participation. | Climatic
    changes—Effect of human beings on. | Human ecology.
Classification: LCC GE149 .C665 2017 (print) | LCC GE149 (ebook) |
    DDC 322.4—dc23
LC record available at https://lccn.loc.gov/2016034894

Chapter 2 was previously published as "Species Evolution and
Cultural Freedom" in *Political Research Quarterly* (June 2014): 441–
52 and is reprinted with permission of the publisher. The postlude,
an interview with Bradley MacDonald, was previously published
as "Confronting the Anthropocene and Contesting Neoliberalism:
An Interview with William E. Connolly" in *New Political Science: A
Journal of Politics and Culture* 37, no. 2 (2015): 279–75 and is reprinted
with permission of the publisher.

Cover art: A murmuration in winter, Rome, Italy. Rolf Nussbaumer
Photography / Alamy Stock Photo.

For James, Katherine,
Cameron, William, Jesse,
Charles, and Julian

CONTENTS

PRELUDE: **MYTH AND THE PLANETARY**

I

Does the mythic today express that which circulates below the threshold of official expression? Do we tend to treat myth as a wild dream when things are going well and as a portent when official stories lose the aura of credibility? Perhaps such a switch in status is under way today, as some old myths now feel revelatory and several official narratives lurch closer to nightmares. The turn to myth is a turn toward an insurrection of voices straining to be heard beneath the clamor of dominant stories.

To test these suggestions, let us turn briefly to the Book of Job. Some scholars suggest that it was once a pagan story, crossing into Judaism and later into Christianity, crossings fueled by the singular power of its poetry. I consult a translation by Stephen Mitchell, in part because of its poetic power, in part because it resists being encapsulated too quickly or completely into any of the three traditions it traversed, in part because students respond to it intensely when I teach it every now and then at Hopkins.[1]

Job, apparently, is a noble gentile in a land in which he belongs to a minority. He is respected as decent. But he then suffers immensely: he loses his sheep, his sons and daughters are killed, and boils sprout all over his body. Some friends arrive to comfort him, but this comforting also involves judging him according to the system of judgment in play. Suffering, consolation, judgment: Job is neither the first nor the last to encounter that fraught combination.

Job had shared the cosmic view of the friends. Now he contests it, to make them see and feel its effects upon him. He says he is innocent and does not deserve what has happened to him. God is supposed to punish only those who are guilty. Eliphaz, the Temanite, will have none of that. He says, "You are lucky that God has scolded you; so take his lesson to heart. For he wounds, but then binds up; he injures but then he heals. When disaster strikes, he will rescue you and never let evil touch you."[2]

Eliphaz's reduction of Job's suffering to a "scolding" by God adds insult to his injuries. Job is called upon to admit his infractions. But he cannot identify any rule he has flouted. He hasn't stolen anything, slept with another man's wife, nor exploited those who work for him. He is even "kind" to his slaves, an institution of the day. The friends suggest that he is lying about his innocence. But they too are unable to identify a norm he has broken. He must have disobeyed nonetheless; otherwise he would not suffer. The give-and-take between Job and his interlocutors becomes increasingly intense and filled with accusations. In fact, however, the friends subsist as *minor voices* within Job, and his cries tap strains of *doubt* in them about the equivalence between human suffering and divine punishment. He senses how the growing intensity of their accusations reflects tremors of existential fear in them. Otherwise they could just walk away, leaving him to stew in his own juices. He roars:

> You have turned against me;
> my wretchedness fills you with fear.
> Have I ever asked you to help me or begged you to pay my ransom . . .
> Look me straight in the eye: Is this how a liar would face you?
> Can't I tell right from wrong? If I sinned wouldn't I know it?[3]

"My wretchedness fills you with fear." A strange statement at first hearing, perhaps. But Job sees that if they were to admit that he does not deserve to be wretched they would also jeopardize the comforting equivalence of their own well-being and the desert for it they project onto the cosmos. Their comfort would no longer be a reliable sign of their virtue. His suffering thus hurts him *and* assaults their sense of existential security. Do they fear that they might suffer a similar fate if they relinquish their judgment of Job during this trial? Job's threat to their image of the cosmos is too much to take, existentially.

So the stakes of the debate keep ratcheting upward. The accusers must continue to accuse, even if the accusations render Job's suffering more acute. Indeed this trauma—and the existential uncertainties it opens—presses them to intensify commitment to a story of human uniqueness in the eyes of God to suppress doubts about whether such a story detracts from the grandeur of both God and the world. This is a familiar response to crisis, when live alternatives to the system in which it occurs are in short supply. It was discernible in the intensification of support for neoliberal ideology after it produced the economic meltdown of 2008. Or consider the intensity of climate denialism today in the face of the massive evidence supporting climate change.

II

Job rebels against this logic of intensification, albeit with ambivalence. But his rebellion takes the form of contesting the accusations by ratcheting up his own intensity. Job and his friends have forged a chiasmic relation in which a minor voice in Job whispers things they assert with shows of confidence, and minor voices in them pose doubts against their own views. The stage is set for a showdown.

A thoughtful party among the accusers tries to resolve the impasse. We cannot know how God orders the world morally, he says; we only know that he does do so and that human suffering serves a higher purpose that is mysterious to us. The hope is that this theological subtlety will settle Job down and also reassure the accusers—er, friends. Such an existential orientation—call it the "complex image of a morally ordered universe"—saves the benevolence to humans of an all-powerful God by counseling those who suffer to confess faith in a higher purpose they cannot fathom. That faith bears a close resemblance to one of the two stories about evil Augustine tells later. Variants of it have also been advanced in capitalist and communist states to justify the suffering of minorities and classes that do not deserve the ugly historical fate bestowed upon them. Show trials and the slow, often hidden violence accompanying the pursuit of progress: the myth of progress itself must not be called into question. At any rate the complex moral story has provided a dominant reading of the Book of Job. That reading is perhaps reinforced by the narrative epilogue appended to the poem.[4]

I wonder, though, whether Job himself actually accepts such a story after his encounter with the Nameless One, the One he so boldly and desperately called upon to explain himself. Is it possible that the demand for existential reassurance many readers impose on the story makes them miss the conversion Job actually undergoes? I wonder too whether the theme of a complex moral order is the wisest story to embrace during an era when hegemonic nature/culture bifurcations, secular/sacred divisions, life/nonlife dichotomies, center/periphery relations, and science/faith struggles historically inscribed in Euro-American life are rattled by the advent of the Anthropocene.

By "the planetary" I mean a series of temporal force fields, such as climate patterns, drought zones, the ocean conveyor system, species evolution, glacier flows, and hurricanes that exhibit self-organizing capacities to varying degrees and that impinge upon each other and human life in numerous ways. The Anthropocene is a period of two hundred to four hundred years (depending on who is counting) during which a series of capitalist, communist, technological, militarist, scientific, and Christian practices became major *geological forces* that helped to reshape some of these nonhuman forces. Minor currents in these cultural traditions struggled against those tendencies. The key point to emphasize is that geologists, evolutionists, and others, after mostly denying the point until as late as the 1980s, now concur that several of these planetary forces have been marked by gradual change periodically *punctuated themselves by rather rapid changes*. To face the planetary today is to encounter these processes in their multiple intersections and periods of volatility. To encounter the Anthropocene is to keep in mind that there were rather rapid changes in several of these force fields even before capitalism and the others became geological forces. The combination of capitalist processes and the amplifiers in nonhuman geological forces must be encountered together. Such a combination poses existential issues today of the sort that plagued Job and his "friends" in their day.

The two forces together make the contemporary condition more volatile and dangerous than it would be if only the first were involved. That is why I attend in this study to critiques of the doctrine of gradualism, a doctrine advanced until recently in scientific theories of species evolution, geological change, ocean current shifts, and climate change. Dissonant conjunctions between capital as a geological force and self-organized amplifiers point to irreversible changes that will continue to accelerate after a certain juncture, even if capitalist states do reshape the energy grids and infrastructures of consumption. The real question is: At what juncture?

Capitalist and communist states blindly rushed into this new world while their attentions were focused on a cold war, religious struggles, colonial exploitation, world wars, economic growth, revolutions, available sites for coal and oil extraction, technological advances, a nuclear stalemate, media scandals, electoral competition, space exploration, new frontiers of investment, automobile production, and paving the world. Until recently the dominant regimes did not know quite what they were doing, even though they did know something about class, race, and regional exploitations covered over by competing assumptions about the progression of abundance. Several regions outside the old capitalist centers that have made the least contribution to this new planetary condition now suffer the most from it.

III

Perhaps we can now hear the "questions" the Nameless One bellows to Job in a distinctive way. In a way that seems to flout later Jewish tradition, it does eventually accept Job's demand that it speak. Is this a divine voice above Job or a subdued voice in him that was clamoring for attention? Either way it demands to know where Job was when it invented the world. The Nameless One does not wait for an answer to that question. It continues, as if the answer is obvious. Here are a few other "questions":

> Where were you when I wrapped the oceans in clouds and swaddled the sea in shadows?
>
> Have you seen to the edge of the universe? Speak up if you have such knowledge.
>
> Who cuts a path for the thunderstorms and carves a road for the rain—to water the desolate wasteland, the land where no man lives?
>
> Do you know all the patterns of heaven and how they affect the earth?
>
> Do you deck the ostrich with wings . . . with elegant plumes and feathers?
>
> Do you show the hawk how to fly, stretching his wings on the wind?
>
> Do you teach the vulture to soar . . . ? He sits and scans for prey, from far off his eyes can spot it.[5]

Job becomes spellbound as the questions accumulate. You might too, as you wonder how so many diverse beings, forces, and energies could coexist in the same world and how they could possibly either mesh neatly with us or be predisposed to our deployment. It is a grand, volatile world of multiple forces, perhaps worthy of our admiration even if we now construe ourselves as minor agents in it.

Capitalist, science, and techno forces today jeopardize the existence of ostriches, hawks, and vultures, as well as the lions, antelopes, and buffalo also included in the litany by the Nameless One. They even affect the "patterns of the heavens," though not in ways that vindicate a will to human mastery. Some contemporaries in late capitalist states think, as Job's friends did, that God will provide them with abundance if they obey him; many evangelicals in the United States now insist that God embraces neoliberal capitalism.[6] Those who reject that view used to assume that they could master the world with or without the blessing of a God. In early Euro-American modernity these two stories competed against each other. Today both are dubious.

Job is rattled by the interrogation. But the Voice has merely been warming up:

> Look now: the Beast that I made:
> he eats grass like a bull.
> Look: the power in his thighs,
> the pulsing sinews in his belly.
> His penis stiffens like a pine;
> his testicles bulge with vigor.
> His ribs are bars of bronze,
> his bones iron beams.
> He is the first of the works of God,
> created to be my plaything.
> He lies under the lotus,
> hidden by reeds and shadows.
> He is calm though the river rages,
> though the torrent beats against his mouth.
> Who then will take him by the eyes
> or pierce his nose with a peg . . . ?[7]

The Voice adopts a tone that soars above the debate between Job and the friends. It speaks of a rich, variegated world filled with multifarious life, each mode pursuing distinctive vectors and powers. Even more, these multifarious forces and beings are not designed to serve humanity in the first or last instance. The human estate is entangled with diverse beings and forces following trajectories of their own. No pristine harmony here was spoiled by an original sin. Rather multiple *forces* on the way both enable and exceed a stability of *forms*. This volcano God indeed is closer to a lava flow bubbling along implacably with intense heat and energy than to the unique pattern of granite that eventually becomes consolidated out of it. That slab of granite could melt down again too.

IV

The primacy of forces over forms. This myth does not focus on a primeval human agent who breaks a divine command. Nor does it concentrate on a primordial incest taboo, in the senses played out by Sophocles and Freud. Strange alliances, impersonal collisions, and asymmetrical interdependencies are as important to this world as divine commands, kinship ties, and rulers: the hawk draws drafts of wind to soar above the earth and sight its prey; the nomad draws sustenance from an oasis formed by other forces; the clouds protect the oceans from drying. This world is neither our oyster nor our servant. Rather we inhabit it, and we are inhabited by its multiple stabilities and volatilities.

Is it hubristic to act as if humanity is or could form the pinnacle of things? The hippopotamus "is the *first* of the works of God, created to be my *plaything.*" What about us? Are we cosmic playthings? Well, we have now become playthings of planetary forces, forces that a few regimes have agitated but none controls. The Jobian story I hear contests in advance both a high-tech regime of human mastery and its most popular counterpoint: the image of a world obeying providential patterns of regularity when the human footprint is light. The world is not, in the last analysis, the plaything of investment capital and military regimes, nor is it underneath those forces a pristine wilderness waiting for ecotourists. It is wise to tend and cultivate the oases we encounter, but there is no cosmic guarantee that they will persist.

Indeed the Anthropocene has become the Whirlwind of today, with its implacable flooding of low-lying zones, glacier melts, temperature increases, intense storms, expanding zones of drought, proliferating species extinctions, ocean acidification, threat to monsoons, refugee crises, and potential shifts in the planetary ocean conveyor belt.

V

The repetitions and intensifications bellowed by the Nameless One continue until Job relents. He says, "I know you can do all things, and nothing you wish is impossible.... I had heard of you with my ears but now my eyes have seen you. Therefore I will be quiet, comforted that I am dust."[8] The poetic utterances of the Nameless One have captivated him.

"Nothing you wish is impossible." Patriarchy is assumed and enforced by this Voice and by the poem that precedes it. Little doubt about that. But does the patriarchal Voice—bellowed from a *tornado*, with its deafening winds and massive powers of destruction—really say that the species to which Job belongs is its favorite? Or that obedience to it is the one and only virtue? Why bellow from such an impersonal force field, then, a force that seems to strike targets randomly? Does it really say that if you accept the mystery of an unfathomable moral world order, it will protect you and your progeny in the last instance? Where in the *poem* is such a message delivered? Does the fact that the epilogue assumes a narrative form suggest that it is a later appendage designed to tame the wonder of the poem? Perhaps the poem, and the diverse energies bursting through it, points to human entanglements in a dissonant world of multiple forces that do not carry special entitlements or guarantees for any beings. We inhabit a majestic world with implacable powers that exceed ours. Its energies solicit our embrace in part because we and it are made of the same stuff. Perhaps the freedom of Job consists in his creative rebellion against the punitive stories of his friends, an appreciation of implacable forces, and an emerging *attachment* to a multiplicitous world that exceeds the stories he and his friends shared and contested.

The world is not our special preserve. Richard Alley, a distinguished glaciologist, conveys a Jobian image of the world when he says, "For most of the last 100,000 years a crazily jumping climate has been the rule, not the exception. Slow cooling has been followed by abrupt cooling, centuries of cold, and then abrupt warming, with the abrupt warmings generally about 1500 years apart, although with much variability. At the abrupt jumps, the climate often flickered between warm and cold for a few years before settling down."[9] Glacier flows, oceans, and climate are intercalated, bumpy time machines.

Is Job now comforted because he both embraces a diversity of being and participates in a world without cosmic guarantees? He may embrace this newly minted God, or—though this may be a stretch for the time in which he lives—he may doubt the credibility of any such belief. Either way he seems to me to contest any image that places humans at the top of a ladder of moral desert. There *is* no such ladder in a world of multifarious forces.

Perhaps Job is comforted by a larger, unruly world in which life can be sweet, death sets a condition of life, struggles against suffering must often be renewed, hubris is dangerous, and experimentation is nonetheless essential. I pose such a possibility *as one way to receive Job today*, a way that may allow some who have heretofore been self-identified "secularists" both to work critically upon the Jobian message and to pursue spiritual ties across creedal differences with others moved by different creeds whose passions are also activated by the power of planetary forces. The reading of Job I embrace is a minority report to put into active conversation with other faiths, as several constituencies pursue affinities of *spirituality* across differences in *creed* during a dangerous time.

VI

Job was comforted. The challenges of today solicit both an embrace of this un-ruly world and pursuit of new political assemblages to counter its dangers. Today the urgency of time calls for a new pluralist assemblage organized by multiple minorities drawn from different regions, classes, creeds, age cohorts, sexualities, and states. This is so in part because the effects of the Anthropocene often hit the racialized urban poor, indigenous peoples, and low-lying areas hard, while its historical sources emanate from privileged places that must be challenged from inside and outside simultaneously. Militant citizen alliances across regions are needed to challenge the priorities of investment capital, state hegemony, local cronyisms, international organizations, and frontier mentalities. Some adventurers I will consult already record and pursue such countermovements.

What follows is a series of attempts to face the planetary. Not only to face down denialism about climate change but also to define and counter the "pas-sive nihilism" that readily falls into place after people reject denialism. By pas-sive nihilism I mean, roughly, formal acceptance of the fact of rapid climate change accompanied by a residual, nagging sense that the world ought not to be organized so that capitalism is a destructive geologic force. The "ought not to be" represents the lingering effects of theological and secular doctrines against the idea of culture shaping nature in such a massive way. These doc-trines may have been expunged on the refined registers of thought, but their remainders persist in ways that make a difference. Passive nihilism folds into other encumbrances already in place when people are laden with pressures to make ends meet, pay a mortgage, send kids to school, pay off debts, struggle with racism and gender inequality, and take care of elderly relatives. Or, simi-larly, they may eke out a living in the forest and try to figure how to respond when a logging company rumbles into it. Or, on another register, they may teach students who both want to believe in the future they are preparing to enter and worry whether that lure has itself become a fantasy. The sources of passive nihilism are multiple. Under its sway, as we shall see, many refute cli-mate denialism but slide away from stronger action. That is the contemporary dilemma. Few of us surmount it completely. But perhaps it is both necessary and possible to negotiate its balances better.

VII

Perhaps a brief preview of how the chapters fold into one another will be helpful. Chapter 1 engages diverse tendencies toward "sociocentrism" and the notions of belonging and human exceptionalism that are often associated with them. To be sociocentric in the strongest sense is to act as if cultural interpretation and social explanation can proceed without consulting deeply nonhuman, planetary forces with degrees of autonomy of their own. A second-order tendency is to acknowledge capitalism as a geological force but to minimize the temporal bumpiness of planetary processes before that era and thus to miss some of the synergies in play today. Many scholars are moving away from such dispositions, but these still convey lingering effects, as we shall see again in the last chapter. So I have selected a few classical exemplars of the tendency who disagree with each other radically in other respects. They are Jean-Jacques Rousseau, Isaiah Berlin, Friedrich Hayek, and Karl Marx. The idea is to chart briefly the specific version this tendency finds in each and to delineate the notion of belonging and exceptionalism attached to it. Where pertinent, I note recent breaks in the traditions under review; these breaks engage more robustly the bumpiness of planetary processes. Sociocentrism, traditions of cultural belonging, and human exceptionalism must be considered together because sometimes a transfiguration along one dimension is dragged down by residual attachment to the other two.

Chapter 2 engages a dynamic intersection between a recent turn in theories of species evolution and thinking now available to cultural theorists about the character and import of human creativity. A first step beyond sociocentrism. The idea is that the new biological theories supported by figures such as Lynn Margulis and Terrence Deacon bolster and inform a deeper grasp of creativity in human life rather than, as the older theories of evolution did, compromise those very experiences. This rough congruence, then, provides independent evidence in support of the new theories, since any good theory of evolution must be able to encompass emergence of the human species. This chapter inaugurates a theme that will be underlined in later chapters: the need to foster intersections between the work of the new earth scientists and work in the social sciences and humanities. The mutual allergies between these traditions can no longer be afforded. As the chapter proceeds we see how the proposed confluence between evolutionists and humanists can issue in a theory of human drives as simultaneously purposive, limiting, unconscious, and essential to moments of creativity in cultural life. I introduce the need for such intersections by addressing the admirable recent work of Stuart Nagel on the matter, and then pursue it in a somewhat different way than he proposes. As these issues are defined it also becomes clear how and why "arts of the self" and "micropolitics" are needed to work on purposive dispositions to action (drives) below the reach of reflexive reconfiguration. I also address a now familiar criticism advanced by some radicals against the new biology: that it inevitably binds its practitioners to neoliberal capture of the processes under study.

The relation between culturally incorporated drives and creativity is explored further in chapter 3. There I put the neuroscientist Giacomo Rizzolatti into conversation with Alfred North Whitehead, Herbert Marcuse, and Gilles Deleuze on the subliminal dimensions of human habit, sociality, and creativity. The discussion of drives is now pursued in relation to the question of engendering a critical politics. That chapter closes with a discussion of how some classical modes of belonging reviewed in chapter 1 need to be transfigured into multiple sites of attachment in a world that confounds previous notions of individual autonomy, communal closure, national belonging, and market and state modes of mastery over nature. The idea is that a deeper appreciation of the sources and functions of creativity can help to support multisited practices of attachment that are needed to replace notions of organic belonging today.

With these preliminary explorations under our belt the text now pivots. Chapter 4 reviews several significant, sometimes rapid changes in glaciers, climate, and ocean currents that occurred either prior to the Anthropocene or well before it attained full steam. The point is to review how such temporal bumps proceeded, what cyclical forcings and noncyclical amplifiers were in play, and how civilizations in various times and places were affected. To review such a history of planetary forcings and amplifiers better prepares us to grasp how the capitalist triggers of today interact with climate, ocean, species, microbe, and glacial systems. Along the way I address a philosophical debate that has resurfaced between those who contend that all processes exhibit some degree of feeling and experience (pan-experientialism) and those who say that some temporal bumps were so large that, say, new capacities emerged from couplings that did not previously exhibit them (emergentism). Engaging Whitehead, Arthur Eddington, Eduardo Viveiros de Castro, and others I support the idea that some modes of experience reach far deeper into the biosphere than exceptionalists had imagined, but I hesitate to embrace entirely the theme of panexperientialism. The chapter closes with a critical engagement with the work of the philosopher Colin McGinn, a "mysterian" who insists that we must assume both that nature is composed of blind laws and that humans, magically, are capable of complex practices of agency, freedom, and responsibility. This combination poses, he says, an unsolvable mystery that we must embrace, and it also gives us tremendous power and entitlement over nature. I dissent from McGinn's view and the spirituality attached to it. To project modes of agency and feeling more deeply into being is a first, though insufficient, step on the way to deepening attachment to the earth, accepting a more robust conception of entangled humanism, and exercising greater modesty in relation to nonhuman beings and forces. That discussion looks back to the engagement with the issue of attachment in the previous chapter and forward to engagements that follow. It may be, for instance, that as we tap loose strands of subliminal attachment to the earth already there, even with its volatilities, we can draw upon arts reviewed in earlier chapters to extend those threads.

I turn in chapter 5 to the issue of political action in a world of rapid climate change and dominant political systems resistant to addressing it with the urgency needed. Such a combination means that most of the worst casualties are suffered by people and other species in regions outside the old capitalist centers as well as in depressed urban areas inside them; this is so even though neither constituency has made a major contribution to these effects. Drawing selective sustenance from a series of eco-activists in several regions—including Wangari Maathai, Mahatma Gandhi, Bruno Latour, Eugene Holland, Pope Francis, and Naomi Klein—I explore a politics of swarming across registers of politics that could issue eventually in cross-regional general strikes. I address familiar objections against such actions, supporting a cross-regional pluralist assemblage that presses states, corporations, churches, universities, and the like from inside and outside simultaneously. Along the way I explore the value of enacting a variety of eco-role experiments as part of the swarming strategy; such experiments work precisely on the visceral register of habits and reluctances in need of being moved. It is agreed in advance that such a flurry of cross-regional general strikes is *improbable*. So realists can put that gun back into their holster. But such actions have become an *improbable necessity* today, given the urgency of time.

The last chapter begins with Rob Nixon's lament, in *Slow Violence and the Environmentalism of the Poor*, that until recently postcolonial thought and Euro-American environmentalism had tended to pass each other in the night. I then turn to the work of Anna Tsing, whose creative engagements with eco-movements in Indonesia provide exemplary corrections. Through an appreciative engagement with a key essay by Dipesh Chakrabarty I then make the case that today three-way conversations must be intensified between postcolonial ecology, eco-movements in old capitalist centers, and new practitioners of the earth sciences. The ghosts still haunting the old separation between the humanities and earth sciences must be exorcised. I further support that case by discussing how recent geological explorations of two extinction events, events occurring well before the Anthropocene, can inform and infuse eco-thinking and action today. Two more engagements with bumpy temporality. As the chapter proceeds I reformat Nietzsche's nineteenth-century account of passive nihilism to fit the contemporary condition. It is necessary to rework the visceral register of cultural life on which passive nihilism is set. That discussion is designed to render timely the exploration of drives, arts of the self, role experiments, and macropolitics launched in previous chapters.

I close with a pitch in favor of entangled humanism. That idea is not presented as a creed everybody everywhere should embrace. No cross-regional pluralist assemblage could or should be anchored in such a universal. But it is perhaps an idea that many in the old capitalist centers—still haunted by the ghosts of mastery, sociocentrism, and human exceptionalism—might internalize to better open lines of exchange and agonistic respect with other traditions, some of which are touched upon in the previous three chapters.

The postlude consists of a conversation between Bradley Macdonald and me on the longer trajectory of my work in political theory and ecology. It takes us through the activism promoted by the Caucus for a New Political Science, to early work on environmentalism Michael Best and I did in *The Politicized Economy*, to the idea of capitalism as an "axiomatic," and other things yet. One finding is that Best and I were carriers of one brand of sociocentrism in the approach to environmentalism adopted in *The Politicized Economy*. Another is how the recent work of Maurizio Lazzarato on the disciplinary role of debt in old capitalist states both increases our grasp of how impersonal controls inhabit capitalist societies and secretes a sociocentrism that diverts our critical gaze from the planetary. Another, perhaps, is the need to stretch political theory—the home discipline of both Macdonald and me—into new intellectual domains today, doing so to render more of us worthy of the events we encounter. One compelling event is the intensification of capitalist and planetary imbrications, with what all these intersections mean to our intellectual work and political encounters. It is easy to become distracted from these implacable imbrications as TV scandals, terrorism, action films, economic meltdowns, electoral circuses, and ugly imperial wars draw attention away. I thank Brad for initiating this conversation.

Each chapter in this book starts in the middle of things; none advances to the edge of the universe. I think and hope that they draw sustenance from the spirit of Job.

CHAPTER 1 SOCIOCENTRISM,
THE ANTHROPOCENE, AND THE PLANETARY

Michel Foucault explored the politics of the disciplinary society within enclosed institutions such as monasteries, madhouses, prisons, factories, schools, and localities. Later he began to address the related politics of impersonal control by which the behavior of entire constituencies is channeled in some directions rather than others. From disciplines within closed institutions to impersonal, probabilistic controls distributed across an entire regime.[1] The simplest model of the latter would be an air terminal where people appear to be running around in different directions even as the plane schedules and gate locations pull them into discernible patterns. A street version would be an array of cameras, cops, arrest records, and traffic signs in the inner city that record anonymous movements, regulate trajectories, and create police questioning of "suspicious people." The patterns of control that emerge are probabilistic because they establish general trends while many escape, ignore, bypass, or flout them. I use the word *discipline* to capture both modes of containment: the institutional politics of normalization and the probabilistic processes of impersonal regulation.

I also need to explore diverse models of belonging that have attracted different thinkers and constituencies to this or that mode of discipline. The idea is to discern how diverse practices of belonging, while competing with each other, have often also commonly participated in what I call *sociocentrism*. In its most extreme form, sociocentrism is the propensity to interpret or explain social processes by reference to other social processes alone. It is often connected to perspectives that treat nature as a set of resources to extract. A less dramatic version occurs when you acknowledge that this or that social order is profoundly affected by its climate, fauna, and soil systems but act as if that environment is set on long, slow time. A more attenuated version yet is when you acknowledge that capitalism has become a geologic force exerting profound effects on climate and many other features of the environment but ignore or minimize the self-organizing amplifiers and internal volatilities of planetary processes themselves. Yet another version is to acknowledge modes of self-organization in species evolution but to minimize such capacities—and the periodic volatilities attached to them—with respect to climate, oceans, glacier flows, and the like.

Sociocentrism is often bound to notions of human exceptionalism and nature as a deposit of resources to use and master; in it humans are treated as the only entitled agents in the world. Those themes in turn are often linked to specific visions of freedom and belonging to the world. To dramatize diverse renditions of the connections among sociocentrism, exceptionalism, freedom, and belonging I focus on four classic models that competed for hegemony before the actual and potential ravages of climate change were widely recognized. The affinities across radical difference among Rousseau, Isaiah Berlin, Hayek, and Marx may help us to see how much work must still be done to reconfigure sociocentrism, human exceptionalism, and dominant modes of belonging. Where pertinent, I will note recent work within the relevant traditions that begin to make the needed adjustments.

Belonging to a Free Nation

Foucault, of course, was not the first Western thinker to study discipline in relation to freedom. Rousseau did so when he asked, in *The Government of Poland*, how to lift an entire population in an autocratic setting geographically vulnerable to invasion into a unified, territorial state in which each adult male member could eventually hope to become a qualified citizen of the nation. His goal was to bring a territorial people to a point where their national mode of belonging could set the unreflective background from which the free participation of all could proceed. Freedom through national identification and regimentation, you might say. The goal was to bring freedom, participation, belonging together into the nation.

Because of contingencies of history—which included the large size of the territory, its climate, and its geographic vulnerability to invasion—the Polish people were not yet ready to become citizens of a democratic nation, in Rousseau's judgment. A host of state and local disciplines were needed to lift them gradually to the necessary level of political intelligence, local initiative, and national belonging. Each young male Pole, for instance, was to serve in the militia for a short period. Such service would ensure the defense of the country against predatory powers such as Russia; it would promote male identification with the nation; and the short-term character of the service would curtail the danger a standing military poses to the spirit of the nation.

The leaders of the nation-in-waiting should also set a national style of dress. This would discourage people from becoming attracted to those from other countries and, in general, discourage cross-national travel, sexual intercourse, and marriage. Landholdings should be reduced from their current size, which made land available only to a few, and gradually distributed much more broadly. This feat would decrease the power of the nobility and prepare peasants to become citizens through identification with the nation. Yearly festivals were to be held to dramatize the nation; at these festivals a few members who had demonstrated love of country were to be lifted to full citizenship during a public ceremony. Rousseau loved public ceremonies.

Paper money was to be eliminated because it allows lords and entrepreneurs to transfer holdings outside the territory and because the very mobility of money creates financial bubbles that eventually burst. Rousseau was a smart guy. Get rid of paper money, he said, if you seek to generate probable behavior conducive to formation of an egalitarian nation. Rousseau believed in private property, but he was not a capitalist theorist of endless growth. His *Discourse on Political Economy*, for instance, celebrated small, privately owned farms and campaigned against the fetish of economic growth. The latter project always works against equality.

Men were to be retained as the official head of each family so that internal conflicts within families were curtailed and so that internal family disputes would not spill over into the common life. Even if the innate differences between men and women were minor, Rousseau insisted, the male gender must prevail in order to foster the unity of the family. The power of the Catholic Church—a church Rousseau did not admire—was to be decreased gradually so as to reduce conflicts it might pose to the unity of the nation. Its historic presence in Poland presented a dilemma for him. To dismantle it rapidly would disorient adults whose lives had been structured around its authority. But to keep it as it had been in Poland up to that date would be to run the risk of church-state conflicts that could tear a nation apart. So retain the church and gradually defuse its power.

There are several other disciplines and impersonal regulations advocated by Rousseau, but I think the point is clear. An "individual" (male head of family) cannot be free unless he belongs to a nation governed by a common ethos; a nation cannot be free unless it is roughly egalitarian economically and its male citizens identify with it above all else as they participate in it. Such an improbable combination cannot be engendered unless a whole series of social disciplines and impersonal controls are introduced to support it.

The Government of Poland, in effect, provides a series of disciplines to negotiate the paradox of politics Rousseau had already identified in *The Social Contract*. The paradox was that before citizens could will and obey good laws they needed to have been imbued with civic virtue, but before they could be imbued with civic virtue they needed to have been governed by good laws and disciplines.[2] He had, in that utopian context, sought to resolve the paradox in principle through mediation by an almost divine legislator who could lift people beyond their historically imbued limitations. Every people has a history, and most of those histories point in specific ways against promotion of the highest human possibility. Poland was specific in its modes of deviation but typical in its fact of deviation.

The paradox of politics in principle is given a more deep and historical gloss with respect to Poland, which has a contingent history replete with multiple unfortunate happenstances; that territorial history contains many elements that push against the needed confluence of belonging, egalitarianism, freedom, participation, and nationhood. If the Legislator provides a fictive "as if" resolution of the paradox in Rousseau's ideal republic, *The Government of Poland* pursues a rocky route toward a less complete achievement as it struggles with and against the contingent installations of actual history to forge a nation. To be free is to belong to a nation, and to participate wisely in the nation to which you belong is to internalize a host of collective disciplines.[3]

The anxiety that infuses Rousseau's explorations of gender, sexuality, freedom, participation, belonging, and nationhood are abundantly on display in *The Government of Poland*.[4] The anxiety is that conscious and unconscious modes of resistance to the needed disciplines could undermine the things he most wants to pursue: civic virtue, belonging, and nationhood.

Rousseau's anxiety is exemplary, even for those who do not support the mode of national belonging he pursues. How so? Well, it is impossible to be free without internalizing some modes of discipline, belonging, and attachment. Belonging both enables and constrains freedom, then. It both supports and threatens it. That is one of the paradoxes to be engaged with respect to freedom, belonging, participation, citizenship, and equality. Indeed the paradox has become more acute today, when it also becomes incumbent to range beyond the modes of sociocentrism that convinced so many modern Western thinkers that they could limit attention largely to internal social processes or, in a more attenuated sense, that the natural forces most pertinent to social life move along gradual trajectories. Today the question becomes how to renegotiate persistent tensions between freedom and belonging during an era when fateful intersections between the social organization of life and planetary processes of climate, ocean currents, tectonic plates, glacier flows, and species evolution with powers of their own have again become so palpable. It is hard to see how a communitarian could come to terms with these conditions without making radical changes in the notions of community, belonging, and attachment that infuse these traditions.

Belonging to the Normal Self

It may seem to a few that pursuit of the nation is the chief problem, that to drop that pursuit is to resolve the issue. Well, pursuit of the nation—and of any singular identity—does pose a series of major problems today. But to dissolve those collective pursuits into a plurality of identifications still does not suffice. Some will say that individualist or negative images of freedom, as they are sometimes called, escape the living paradoxes Rousseau and other nationalists encounter. But individualism actually relocates the issues rather than eliminating them.

To avoid the dangers of pursuing nationhood Berlin, Richard Flathman, and Hayek deflate positive, collective freedom in order to protect the freedom of individuals. But when you scratch these theories it becomes clear that they too presuppose a context of belonging in which individual freedoms are set. Thus Flathman in his early work did emphasize the priority of negative freedom as the space to do what you want. But later he acknowledged the central role for disciplines that enable us both to be free individuals and to obey the reasonable dictates of the state.[5] A set of disciplines, Flathman came to see, actually set intrinsic conditions to individual freedom. To expand upon Flathman, you might say that you can't even do what you *want* unless you have internalized a set of disciplines and norms that allow you to set priorities among the mad rush of desires that would otherwise circulate through you. Indeed you can't *perceive* what you want until your eyes, ears, skin, and nose have been disciplined through prior activities to organize multiple portals of the sensorium into memory-saturated, intersensory perceptions. A "haptic image," for instance, is an image in which a memory of the texture of that which was felt before—say, the texture of the skin of an old person—now enters into the quality of the visual image itself. Without tactile experience folded into tacit memory the visual image would lose its texture. Discipline of the senses is thus an ineliminable part of freedom, even as many of its modes also constitute constraints on freedom.[6]

Let us pursue the problem of individualist belonging through one strain in the work of Berlin, the defender of freedom from collective restraints who might be assumed to be an outlier on the issue of belonging. There is much to admire in his classic essay "Two Concepts of Liberty." Berlin worries productively there about the authoritarian proclivities of those who think that the diverse human goods can fit readily into the unity of one society. He is a pluralist, though not, unfortunately, of the sort who plays up the productive *tension* between the politics of established diversity and the disruptive politics by which new identities, faiths, rights, and aspirations periodically surge into being to jostle established balances. His basic idea (at least in the essay under review) is that the essence of freedom, or liberty as he prefers to call it, is the provision of social space in which individuals can do what they want. Limits on this space are necessary, but there is not much to freedom unless that space is ample.

The republican critique of Berlin—with which I concur as far as it goes— is that he does not appreciate enough how the space of negative freedom rings hollow if citizens reside in an authoritarian regime whose rulers can take those very liberties away if they choose.[7] Moreover, even when such a risk is low—if it ever is—freedom is not at home with itself until participation in self-governance is operative. So now freedom involves both spaces of action and the right to participate in self-governance.

Note, though, that both Berlin's position and the republican critique of it remain contained largely within the assumption of *sociocentrism*. Sociocentrism, in individualist, nationalist, communist, neoliberal, and republican traditions, assumes that a political economy is either in charge of nature, or that the limits nature poses to it are set on long, slow time, or, in a more attenuated version, that if we lift the human footprint nature will settle down into patterns that are benign for us. Given any of these assumptions, questions of agency, explanation, and belonging in practice tend to devolve around attention to internal cultural practices. The debates between different types of sociocentrism are over which internal factors are the most important.

Let us turn, then, to Berlin on the question of belonging. Since he is critical of the pursuit of nationhood—as a pluralist should be who seeks to allow a diversity of values and constituencies to negotiate political settlements—it may seem that belonging does not achieve much priority within the pursuit of negative liberty. But it does, even as Berlin relocates the *site* on which it is set. Consider a few quotations from the essay in question.

> The essence of the notion of liberty, both in the "positive" and "negative" senses, is the holding off of something or someone—of others who trespass on my field or assert their authority over me, or of obsessions, fears, neuroses, irrational forces—intruders and despots of one kind or another.

> If I wish to preserve my liberty, it is not enough to say that it must not be violated unless someone or other . . . authorizes its violation, I must establish a society in which there must be some frontiers of freedom which nobody should be permitted to cross. . . . What these rules or commandments will have in common is that they are accepted widely and are grounded so deeply in the actual nature of men as they have developed through history, *as to be an essential part of what it means to be a normal human being.* Genuine belief in the inviolability of the individual entails some such absolute stand.[8]

"Obsessions," "irrational forces," "the actual nature of men," "trespass," "a society," "a normal human being." The regular individual belongs to the logic of social normality, and an embedded social sense of normality places and delimits the space of negative liberty. In the years after Berlin composed this essay on negative liberty, previously normalized notions of male prerogative, sexual normality, gender sickness, racial difference, and secular context have been precariously reconstituted through interconnected, painful political struggles. In underplaying the obdurate tension between established diversity and political struggles of becoming by which some established normalities become denormalized and replaced, Berlin also overplays the stability of the normal and the extent to which belonging to it sustains the character of negative freedom. Indeed in locating the positive freedom he resists largely within a socialist society or communist nation, he doubly underplays the creative role played by the politics of denormalization in modern life. That is, he underplays the importance to freedom of uncanny and rocky processes of creativity that periodically unsettle both some established standards of normality and the terms of national unity that have made this or that constituency suffer.

The Berlin essay, again, is unconsciously set in a matrix of sociocentrism, the normal self, and human exceptionalism. To be normal in the Berlin imaginary is to presuppose those background conditions. But those are the very assumptions that increase the injuries and perils of the late modern age as some world regions take the lead in polluting and warming the world and others are on the front lines to receive the resulting injuries.

There is a sense of belonging in Berlin, then, but its tacit quality both disables him from *dramatizing the importance of the issue to his day and ours and diverts his followers from rethinking the problem of belonging in the new world of today.* What sites and modes of attachment *are* appropriate to an era when planetary forces impinge with cataclysmic effect upon so many dimensions of life?

I do not blame Berlin too much for the faults and illusions his essay expresses, serious as they are. They were broadly installed—though in different ways—in Euro-American pursuits of both negative and positive freedom during the time in which he wrote.[9] They were so in part because of the cold war and in part because the parties to Western debates and struggles at that time were mostly blind to the world-historical trajectory of radical climate change to which they were contributing. I do say, however, that those earlier fault lines do make things more difficult today. We are haunted by the destructive legacies of belonging and normality these doctrines have bestowed upon us.

Belonging to the Market

Let us look, then, at a classic model of sociocentrism and belonging through the lens of another mid-twentieth-century thinker, one who also might at first glance be thought to shuffle these ideas to the side. Friedrich Hayek, a consummate devotee of free markets, emphasizes the freedom of the individual; he is an obdurate critic of any notion of freedom tied to a rubric of collective planning and action. Even some modes of liberalism attract his ire, as when he says, "It was only liberalism in the English sense that was generally opposed to centralization, to nationalism and to socialism, while the liberalism prevalent on the continent favored all three."[10]

Hayek supports true individualism over socialism, social democracy, communism, nationalism, fascism, and those continental forms of individualism that slide too close for comfort to several of these social forms. It appears that there is nothing for individualists to belong to and no need to belong once they join Ayn Rand and Rand Paul in transcending the driveling pursuit of belonging itself. Nonetheless, once you peer into Hayek's thought you soon find that the issue of belonging haunts it too. He pursues *a nation of regular individuals who belong to the matrix of the impersonal market.* Individualism, in his hands, moves closer to some notions it initially purports to oppose. Again, consider a few quotations:

> Quite as important for the functioning of an individualist society as these smaller groupings of men are the traditions and conventions which evolve in a free society and which, without being enforceable, establish flexible but normally observed rules that make the behavior of other people predictable in a high degree. The willingness to submit to such rules, not merely as long as one understands the reasons for them but so long as one has no definite reasons to the contrary, is an essential condition for the gradual evolution and improvement of rules of social intercourse; *and the readiness ordinarily to submit to the products of a social process which nobody has designed and the reasons for which nobody may understand is also an indispensable condition if it is to be possible to dispense with compulsion.*
>
> Man in a complex society can have no choice but between adjusting himself to what to him seem the blind forces of the social process and obeying the orders of a superior. So long as he only knows the hard disciplines of the market he may well think the direction by other intelligent human brains preferable.
>
> It was men's submission to the impersonal forces of the market that in the past has made possible the growth of a civilization without which this could not have happened: it is by thus submitting that we are every day helping to build something that is greater than any of us can fully comprehend. It does not matter whether men in the past did submit from beliefs of humility . . . ; the crucial point is that it is infinitely more difficult to comprehend the necessity of submitting to forces whose operation we cannot follow in detail than to do so out of the humble awe which religion, or even respect for the doctrines of economics did inspire.[11]

"A free society," "the willingness to submit to such rules," "an indispensable condition," "the hard disciplines of the market," "submit to the impersonal forces of the market," "[a rationality] greater than any of us can fully comprehend." To be free as individuals we must submit to the discipline of the market. To belong to the market we must act as if its freedoms, discipline, and uncertainties set indispensable conditions of individual freedom. Freedom, belonging, and impersonal market rationality are bound together in this problematic. *The pursuit of Hayekian freedom indeed is bound to the pursuit of a nation of regular individuals tethered to the disciplines of the market,* even as it recognizes a rather strong divide in which most prepare to be only entrepreneurs of themselves by competing for jobs and a livelihood while a smaller number of entrepreneurs forge, run, and finance the firms in which the others work. Hayek did not worry much about the need to regulate the internal structure of firms, even though he worried every day about regulating the internal structure of labor unions. Nor did he ever prove that the impersonal regulation of markets regularly produces impersonal rationality.[12]

Belonging to a nation; belonging to the normality of the self; belonging to the rationality of the impersonal market. Each mode of belonging competes with the others. But all give priority to the experience of belonging in relation to the exercise of freedom, as each defines freedom. In doing so each carries front and center the question of the relation of freedom to belonging.

The problem is that none of these formulae comes close to being sufficient today, partly because most play down too much the critical role of creativity in freedom, partly because all—though Berlin does qualify this—tend to postulate a single peak of belonging that falls below the plurality of sites needed today, partly because, except for Rousseau, none thinks closely enough about how belonging and freedom are intercoded, and partly because each either sets aside planetary and cosmic dimensions or situates them within a matrix of gradualism not alert enough to the autonomous powers of a variety of bumpy, nonhuman force fields imbricated with every mode of social life.

In the chapters that follow I will return periodically to the triad freedom, belonging, and the planetary, asking how to reconfigure the first two pursuits in relation to our fraught relations to the third. For to modify sociocentrism, as many are now doing, is also to disturb specific notions of freedom, human exceptionalism, and belonging to which it was attached. I will also explore how such reconfigurations could help to spawn a series of political responses to the crisis of climate change. I do not promise that these explorations and speculations will be sufficient to the problems and issues posed. I only insist that these are issues that cannot be avoided today.

Can neoliberalism break with the features expressed in the Hayekian version once planetary forces come sharply into view? A few possibilities suggest themselves. First, its proponents can participate in denialism, a feature most common in the United States, where neoliberalism and evangelicalism have formed a new constellation. Second, it can strive to protect itself by preserving corporate and consumption priorities and introducing high-tech strategies to, say, dim the sun. But those are extremely dangerous, as Naomi Klein has shown so effectively.[13] Third, local initiatives to take over power plants and re-configure them could be introduced, as has happened in Germany. Nice work. But that creates uneasy tensions in which the national policies of neoliberalism probably have to be modified more radically to keep the momentum going.

The most severe problems in the theories of freedom noted so far are, first, that they do not delve far enough into the issue of belonging they pose and, second, that they together express modes of sociocentrism and humanist exceptionalism that differentially plague several regions, classes, and species today.

Classical Communism and Sociocentrism

In symposia I have participated in and lectures I have given over the past few years, some have emphasized the idea of the capitalocene and the idea that communism is the answer to our ills has sometimes been broached. Don't talk about Soviet communism, these critics say; it was merely another version of state capitalism. So capitalism is the devil. Well, yes, extractive capitalism in several of its forms has a whole lot to answer for, as I have shown in other studies.[14] Both established capitalist practices and capitalist idealisms need revamping from the ground up.

But communist idealism, in its classic form, does not fare that well either. In the past, when I talked and wrote about the question of importing freedom into socialism, I would sometimes be told to stop worrying.[15] Either, it was said, communism as the one correct form of socialism would resolve the issue automatically if enacted, or freedom must be treated as a bourgeois idea not in need of transfiguration.

In the first case Marx was said to have outgrown his early infatuation with freedom; in the second inordinate trust was placed in an automatic solution to a problem that is actually vexing in every social mode of organization. Moreover, to withdraw from debates about freedom and to allow neoliberal ideology to monopolize the idea is to surrender to the foe before the battle has been joined.

Here I will respond briefly to such putative corrections by reference to an essay Marx wrote rather late in the day. "The Critique of the Gotha Pro-gramme," written in response to the 1875 debate within European socialist circles, displays the element of sociocentrism haunting Marx's thought as well as limits to the communal ideal of freedom he pursued within the orbit of those assumptions.

The first part of the essay is devoted to showing that equality could not be attained under the Gotha plan, given the failure of its proponents to come to terms with the labor theory of value. It is the last part that will receive our attention. The idea is that after a transitional dictatorship of the proletariat, in which the old society is stamped out, a new social form will emerge:

> In a higher phase of communist society, after the enslaving subordination of the individual to the division of labor, and therewith also the antithesis between mental and physical labor has vanished; after labor has become not only a means of life but life's prime want; after the productive forces have also increased with the all-round development of the individual, and *all the springs of co-operative wealth flow more abundantly*— only then can the narrow horizon of bourgeois right be crossed in its entirety and society inscribe on its banners: from each according to his ability, to each according to his needs!

> The capitalist mode of production, for example, rests on the fact that the material conditions of production are in the hands of non-workers in the form of property in capital and land, while the masses are only owners of the personal condition of production, of labor power. If the material conditions are so distributed, then the present day distribution of the means of consumption results automatically. If the material conditions of production are the cooperative property of the workers themselves, there likewise results a distribution of the means of consumption different from the present one.[16]

"A higher phase," "the springs of cooperative wealth flow more abundantly," "there likewise results a distribution of the means of consumption." These heady statements carry great attractive power. Anybody who has worked in a factory, a bowling alley, or a fast-food restaurant will recognize the attractions of overcoming workplace alienation and the urgent need to do so. Indeed upper-level workers employed by the electronic bookseller Amazon today find their labor subjected to intense surveillance and punitive control.[17] Alienation from the process and results of work remain powerful forces in late modern capitalism. The small minority who own the vast proportion of capital exercise massive power over the ends of the economy, the direction of politics within capitalist states, and intensification of the inequalities of race and class within and across states. Capitalism is ugly, exploitative, and dangerous today, most radically so in its extractive and neoliberal modes.

But does classical communist *idealism* itself speak sufficiently to modes of exploitation, alienation, and danger today? It does not, first, because its own notion of abundance is too closely tied to resolute projects of economic mastery over nature. It does not, second, because the worker cooperatives its supporters sometimes envision, while invaluable, do not alone guarantee that regional and other differences of resources between collectives will avoid generating new market-like inequalities within and between regions. It does not, third, because it fails to come to terms sufficiently with variable degrees of autonomy between a mode of production and the types of consumption adapted to it. It does not, fourth, because it does not speak sufficiently to the modes of governance needed, both within states and at a more global level, after states have withered. It does not, fifth and foremost, because it fails to register how a host of unruly planetary force fields with impressive powers of their own are imbricated with every actual and imaginable social and economic process.[18]

In other words, the idealism of "The Critique of the Gotha Programme" shares a couple of things with the capitalist idealism it exposes and seeks to replace. The critique of capital Marx offered there is better than the abstract alternative he poses to it. The goal is to belong to a communal order and to act freely within it, while many of its adversaries want people to belong to the nation, the normal individual, the impersonal market, or some combination thereof. Marx's theory of alienation remains highly relevant today, as does his account of primitive accumulation and what happens inside the factory gates. Those modes of exploitation operate behind many gates of many types today. They inform critiques of capitalist class exploitation and alienation. But they are insufficient to the contemporary condition.

In this respect, at least, Marx joins Rousseau, Berlin, and Hayek. All four are carriers of sociocentrism, though in different ways and to different degrees. They make it necessary to rethink the issues of freedom, belonging, and human exceptionalism in relation to a host of planetary processes. One fascinating thing is how some recent work in the Marxist tradition now joins with others in folding ecological concerns into their texts, modifying their notions of labor, class, capital, biology, nature, and communism as they do so.[19]

The Ambiguity of Futurity

But can freedom really be a viable pursuit today? Is it possible to complicate our sense of belonging once the insufficiencies of sociocentrism, cultural internalism, and human exceptionalism in their various expressions are exposed and countered? A growing number of voices insist, against the modes of futurist idealism and realism adumbrated so briefly above, that it is time to forget about futurity. The future sucks, and pursuit of it sucks us into its maelstrom. Drop freedom, belonging, and futurity.[20]

My sense is that such orientations both express things about the contemporary condition and deny how the authors of such responses are implicated in these very concerns. Yes, reproductive futurism—wherein a universal future is projected around the primacy of child bearing and raising—becomes oppressive if and when it squashes a variety of other ways to relate to the future. But it is not only in childbirth and child rearing that individuals and institutions express orientations to the future. Dispositions to the future are invested in everything we do; work, consumption, housing plans, child rearing, teaching, studying, reading, lovemaking, gardening, political campaigns, prayer, schoolwork, sports, exercise regimes, doctor visits, and retirement funds are inveterately invested in future anticipations marked by presumptions of trust in the future pursued. Even writing about how futurism is oppressive expresses a desire to rework that particular set of anticipations. To drop the element of futurity from these practices would be to prepare an exit from life itself.

Michel Tournier, in his novel *Friday*—presented as a rewrite of Daniel Defoe's *Robinson Crusoe*—gives us a sense of how life without futurity might feel. Robinson, an English Quaker sailing in 1759 on a sturdy vessel under a competent captain, felt pretty good about the future facing him, his ship, his faith, and his imperial regime. Then a sudden storm off the shore of Chile drove the boat against a reef. He wakes up alone with the hull of his boat stuck on a reef close to an island. Fighting off despair, and eventually looting the hull of that ship for food and supplies, he tries to fashion a small boat in which to escape. He calls it *The Escape*.

When that future-oriented task fails he finds himself haunted by vultures who fight constantly among themselves and also follow his every move with great interest. They sense that he will soon become meat. "But although he had of necessity grown used to their presence, he found it less easy to endure their repulsive habits. Their love commerce, like that of lubricious old men, offended his enforced chastity. Filled with outraged melancholy he watched the male, after a few grotesque skips, heavily tread on the female, sinking its hooked beak into her bare, blood-red neck while their rumps came together in obscene embrace."[21]

Then one morning, though he had no idea how long he had been on the island, as the days had faded into nights and the nights into days, his hoe broke. Total demoralization set in. He yielded to the temptation of the mire, plopping into a tepid swamp of slime: "By degrees the nightmare of squids, vampire bats, and vultures which obsessed his mind vanished into that mephitic mist filled with the drone of mosquitoes. Time and space dissolved, and a face appeared in the clouded sky. . . . Weakness pervaded Robinson, exquisitely sweet. A smile parted his lips, amid the rotting grass and water lily leaves. A small leech had attached itself to the corner of his mouth."[22]

Immersion in the slime intensifies the scrambling of past, present, and future that had been under way. His memory had already been shaky in the absence of others with whom to review events. Moreover any focus on the lived present, without tacit awareness of the other two moments to which it is obstinately attached, renders the present a blur—a vague and pulsating cacophony of partial, disconnected experiences. That is why punctual notions of time are so crude and abstract, as Tournier teaches readers who had been attached to the first study of Crusoe. "Now-time" is either imbricated with layered memory and anticipation, or it becomes "blur-time."

Forays into temporal distraction, experienced for short pulses of time, can indeed provide grist for rethinking punctual orientations to past and future—orientations inscribed in the present of a Quaker living in the British Empire that continue to play a major role in capitalist orientations to nature today.[23] They also provide a cipher of what happens if you try to give up commitment to the future completely. Robinson soon rises out of that slimy trance-like state, prepared to shed some of his previous habits and assumptions. He strives to build a new orientation to past and future, not yet knowing what such an arduous task will involve.

We too need to rethink embedded assumptions in Euro-American life about past, present, and future, even as we fend off the despair that can accompany the need to do so. Such a rethinking needs to reach into recomposition of the institutions we inhabit. Don't worry too much about the composition of the "we" yet; we will get to that issue soon enough.

The Anthropocene and the Planetary

In singling out Rousseau, Hayek, Berlin, and Marx I do not mean to suggest that differential propensities to sociocentrism and human exceptionalism are confined to them. We can identify a host of recent figures in the humanities and human sciences who head in similar directions. These propensities are discernible in the work of Euro-American theorists such as Hannah Arendt, Walter Benn Michaels, George Kateb, Jürgen Habermas, John Rawls, and innumerable others.[24] Even Foucault did not escape them sufficiently.

Sociocentrists and exceptionalists often worry about taking nature and science too seriously. They worry, properly so, about practices of reductionism in the natural and social sciences that, when accepted and applied to culture, squeeze out space for human agency, dignity, freedom, and political enactment. But they too often respond to these dangers by turning away from alternative work in anthropology, philosophy, neuroscience, geology, and complexity theory that, first, refashions the character of human agency without taking a reductionist route; second, identifies modes of agency within and beyond the human estate that help to constitute and limit human agency; and, third, as a corollary, identifies large, nonhuman, partially self-organizing processes that periodically enter into fortunate or fateful conjunctions with capitalism, socialism, democracy, and freedom. The internalists also repress the temptation to pour an aesthetic element into nonhuman processes, though Darwin himself had done so in 1871 when he modified an early version of his theory and talked about the role of intraspecies attractions in bird evolution. Exceptionalists ignore such forces to monopolize agency, dignity, meaning, and artistry for the human estate alone. They thus carve out precarious space for human agency even as the positions they stake out increasingly place it under threat. We *must* be the only artists and poets on the earth, they insist, allowing occasional exceptions for this or that dog or cat. A variety of other humanists now challenge these priorities—the late work of Derrida and Cavell comes to mind—but I do wonder whether they have adequately overcome the temptation to gradualism that still haunts so many humanist orientations to large-scale, nonhuman processes. I will explore that issue later.

The time of the Anthropocene (as it is sometimes called) reveals dramatically the insufficiencies of human exceptionalism, sociocentrism, and cultural internalism, three assumptions that will periodically come up for review in later chapters. But why invoke the Anthropocene as a corrective in this context? What, more closely, does *it* mean? Is it a good concept with which to help frame the contemporary condition? Does the very name suggest that climate, ocean currents, species evolution, glaciations, drought, and soil processes changed slowly before agriculture, industrialism, technology, or capitalism bounced onto the scene? Does it therefore continue to inflate the powers of humanity while now treating them as perverse rather than rational? Does it, moreover, tend to postulate a generic humanity as the cause of a generic peril, when it should distribute causalities among regions and countries more radically, with older northern capitalist regions generating most of the adverse effects and others absorbing a disproportionate share of the burden? Does it let capitalism off the hook?

It *is* imperative today to focus on how Euro-American capitalist states and imperial orders have manufactured a world climate and ecocrisis that injures and displaces populations in vulnerable regions, as it also hits poor, racialized constituencies in the inner cities of capitalist states sooner and harder than it does the captains of industry. As we shall see, transnational fossil fuel corporations and crony states have displaced and decimated Amerindians, Nigerian minorities, peasants in Bangladesh, Indonesian locals, Bedouins on the Arabian peninsula, Pacific island peoples, and others yet. And these predatory practices now blow back through fracking operations to more privileged zones in the home states themselves.[25]

In a fascinating essay in *Nature*, Simon Lewis and Mark A. Maslin review a series of proposed "golden spikes" to grasp the beginning of the Anthropocene.[26] They see from the start that the term is not designed first and foremost to explain closely *how* it happened—the numerous forces from agriculture, capitalism, Christianity, and colonialism that launched and sustained it. It is designed to mark its dating so that complex explanations of how it occurred and who has suffered the most can then be perfected. They propose "the Orbis hypothesis" as a golden spike. Between 1492 and 1610 the European holocaust against the Americas was enacted, fueled by colonialism, annihilation, slavery, monopolization of land, and disease.[27] The population of perhaps 54 to 61 million in the Americas declined to 6 million by 1650. A holocaust, fueled by multiple European forces. In light of this holocaust and the resulting blip downward in the carbon index, the authors are tempted to place the golden spike in human-induced climate change around 1610. But they concur that there are other candidates. One can discern several possibilities, such as the period after 1600, when the decimation of Amerindians lowered carbon emissions; 1800, when a steady growth in human-induced CO_2 emissions occurred; 1900, when industrial, extractive capitalism was well under way and the carbon index reached a level (296 ppm) that burst through the self-maintaining tolerances of the Holocene; and the 1950s, when capitalist and communist societies produced "the Great Acceleration." The Great Acceleration has since accelerated even more, with older capitalist states producing the greatest accumulation of atmospheric and ocean gases, several zones outside those centers suffering the worst consequences, and recent capitalist states such as India, China, Russia, and Brazil joining the rapid acceleration club. Given this temporal situation, my sense is that it is best to speak of *numerous inflection points*, seeking to date cumulative advances as you pay attention to the dominant social, spiritual, and economic forces in play at each stage.

I thus remain ambivalent about using the term, though I think it is useful for some purposes. It is first and foremost a geological term set in relation to the trends and periodic volatilities of other geological periods. So from the start it resists the assumption of gradualism in nature historically adopted by many second-order sociocentrists in the social sciences, those who acknowledge capitalism as a geological force but fail to come to terms with the bumpy geotemporalities that preceded human influences and must inform study of planetary forces today. To respect the bumpy history of climate, ocean currents, glacier flows, bacterial crossings, and species evolution *before* the advent of the Anthropocene is to explore how triggering events in this new era can and do join forces with self-induced and intersecting amplifiers of multiple sorts in several nonhuman processes. When that combination is engaged you can see how the results that emerge often greatly exceed the triggers that start them off, whether those triggers come from, say, extensive fossil fuel use, a huge asteroid hitting the planet, or a change in the ocean conveyor system.

The proponents of the concept Anthropocene in geology and climatology and oceanography are not always good at explaining just which regions, cultural priorities, and economic practices have contributed to it. That is up to us, however, in relation to their studies of the forcings, dampeners, and amplifiers of planetary forces that they are increasingly good at identifying and charting.

So the Anthropocene charts a geological era of rapid climate change set in relation to past geological eras. In the past processes in this or that nonhuman zone could remain relatively quiescent for a long time and then change rapidly on their own without significant interventions from human agriculture, capitalism, communism, technology, Christianity, or industrialism. Several mass extinction events prior to the Holocene, for instance, had nothing to do with human activity. To explore the Anthropocene is thus also to connect a variety of self-organizing processes that preceded it, periodically tipping over a short period of time, to the new triggers of capitalist and communist projects of mastery of the earth. Use of the concept may also help to place activists in the humanities into closer conversations with geologists, biologists, oceanographers, anthropologists, and paleontologists. That in itself is nothing to sneeze at when humanists and scientists need to participate together with others to fend off the worst effects of climate change.

To name the Anthropocene, then, is not to name a new era of human mastery nor to name perverse human interventions into forces that are otherwise gradual and self-maintaining. It is to challenge human exceptionalism by coming to terms with bumpy processes of planetary self-organization that interact with each other and with human cultures. It is also, on my usage, to name perils emanating initially from Euro-American regimes that now imperil other regions that did not initiate these processes. It is, moreover, to dramatize this condition in ways that encourage more constituencies in several regions and walks of life to respond politically to it. And it is to invite those in the humanities to forge intellectual and political alliances with geologists, glaciologists, climatologists, and paleontologists who link this era to several other bumpy periods that preceded it. The preciousness of classical humanism must be challenged by what I call *entangled humanism*.

We belong to a large, bumpy variety of temporal processes that exceed us, even as powerful, fossilized constituencies in some older capitalist states—led by the oil interests and the Republican Party in the United States—refuse to acknowledge the dangerous planetary processes with which we are imbricated and resist modes of positive organization to respond to them. So I focus on planetary forces and various cultural modes of imbrication with them, occasionally using the word *Anthropocene* to do so. But I also oppose any sense of generic human responsibility for the contemporary planetary condition, a sense that has sometimes been associated with that term. Generic responsibility must be replaced by regionally distributed responsibilities and vulnerabilities. Finally I resist any notion implying that a host of planetary processes were slow, gradual, or providential before capitalist states became entangled with them. My aspiration here is to face the planetary while connecting that face to regional, racial, and urban issues with which it is imbricated.

An Invitational, Diversified "We"

What orientations to the future are most promising during an era when the planetary dimension of being has again become so visible and intrusive? To what pluralities, human and nonhuman, might we "belong"—even if we decide that the term *belonging* must be suspended in favor of a pursuit of plural sites of attachment?

As I pursue these questions I hope it becomes clear that this study poses provisional responses without purporting to clear the issues up altogether. Consummate answers are suspect today.

That said, it might be wise to focus on forging a militant set of constituencies oriented to interim responses to pressing issues of the day. If and as each minority gains a measure of success, you can look up again to see where to turn next. Why? In part because it is wise to be dubious about the power and credibility of old capitalist and communist idealisms during an era of rapid, human-induced climate change. But also because to challenge sociocentrism is to render problematic the projection of *any* smooth horizon into the future. The planet is too large and multifarious for that. One of the attractions of sociocentrism over the past few centuries was that it supported a series of conflicting, smooth ideals, even as the opposed parties were in fact rushing blindly together into the Anthropocene.

At various points in this study, I adopt a "we" voice. As will become clear, that voice seeks to hook into a pluralized and invitational "us." The idea is to become part of an active cross-regional pluralist assemblage composed of multiple minorities in different parts of the world rather than to place any constituency at the center or top of a singular unity. No single class, nation, faith, gender, state, order, region, party, racialized constituency, or age group can form the authoritative center of the militant "we" needed today. For example, indigenous peoples already form indispensable elements within it, advancing many promising ideas about human relations to the past, pursuing indispensable modes of activism, pressing oil corporations and northern states to acknowledge the horrors they have introduced as settler states pursued a fictive future on each new "frontier," calling for reparations, and pressing others to pursue more sustainable practices. Such movements and practices can teach others a lot about how to internalize a positive sense of material austerity.[28]

But even they may not have all the answers today. Their rich and diverse traditions arose in a world with a small total population, and the world now stumbling under the fragile hegemony of extractive capitalism holds 7 billion and counting. The world is in a pickle; no preset orientation is perhaps entirely sufficient to it.

Each element in the aspirational assemblage projected here expresses several loyalties and identifications as well as those assembled by this invitational "we." Each constituency works on itself as it calls out to the others, so that none remains exactly as it was before it became attached to this assemblage in the making. Old notions of pluralism as a coalition of diverse interests are thus insufficient to it. We seek an evolving, complex, cross-regional "we" that propels diverse constituencies into larger assemblages, even as each constituency retains a host of differences. It will assemble, if it does, to respond to a planetary condition asymmetrically distributed in its effects and dangers, as participants also pay attention to other local, regional, class, racial, state, and religious questions. Many of these forces, as we shall see, are already imbricated with the effects of the Anthropocene. The new assemblage, if it grows, will build upon a host of environmental movements currently in play, some of which already pursue new connections across regions and constituencies. If such interconnected populist movements do crystallize, could they eventually foment general strikes in numerous countries and regions at the same time? Such strikes would impose demands upon multiple institutions from the inside and outside at the same time; the sources of injury, energy, and hope they draw upon would emanate from several sites.

Yes, such a plural, invitational "we" may fail to generate the energy and momentum needed in time. It is thus an improbable necessity rather than speaking to a highly probable constellation. Assembled from diverse sites during a period of temporal urgency, facing diverse effects upon different regions and classes, the potential, pluralized "we" in question resides in a world and time of tragic possibility.

CHAPTER 2 SPECIES EVOLUTION AND CULTURAL CREATIVITY

The male Rupcola Crocea is one of the most beautiful birds in the world, being of splendid orange with some of the feathers curiously truncated and plumose. The female is brown-green, shaded with red and has a much smaller crest. Sir R. Schombusk has described their courtship; he found one of their meeting places where 10 males and 2 females were present. The space was from four to five feet in diameter, and appeared to him to have been cleared of every blade of grass and smoothed as if by human hands. A male was "capering to the apparent delight of several others. Now spreading its wings, throwing up its head, or spreading its tale like a fan; now strutting about with a hopping gait until tired, when it gabbled some kind of note and was relieved by another."

The males successively take the field, dancing and singing, it seems, competing to impress the females through song and dance. The females, it seems, appraise the performances according to their judgments of taste. As with the Amherst pheasant who seeks "to please the females during courtship who not only raise their splendid frills, but twist them, as if I have seen myself, obliquely towards the female, on which ever side she be standing, obviously in order that a large surface be displayed toward her."

—Darwin, *The Descent of Man*

With these examples and myriad others the Darwin of 1871 corrects the theory of natural selection and survival of the fittest he had advanced in 1859. He is no longer exactly a "Darwinist." He displays a readiness to interpret the relational meaning and purposes of bird behavior, and he sinks an aesthetic element deep into the evolutionary process by observing how birds seek to attract one another and respond differentially to those attempts. The aesthetic element in the matings skews the evolutionary process in ways that exceed the determinations of natural selection and survival.[1]

Darwin, the naturalist, admits that he is unable to say how the transmission process actually works after aesthetic taste is consummated and mating occurs. His theory is also replete with disturbing Victorian images of race, gender, and hierarchies of civilization. They slide effortlessly into his readings of evolution. The anthropocentrism they support, in which all priority is given to the human estate in relation to other species, is also sorely in need of repair. And Darwin's "gradualism," by which he insists that all species transitions occur on long slow time, creates a related problem that will be discussed in chapter 6.

One way to respond to such limits is to replace Darwin with the genocentrism found in much of evolutionary theory from at least 1970 to today. That approach faces two problems, however. First, as we shall see further, it is even less able than the later Darwin to render intelligible some complex results of the evolutionary process, such as consciousness, reflexivity, responsibility, and freedom. Second, its early proponents were themselves influenced by a highly contestable model of human culture that infiltrated the renderings of mutation, gene replication, natural selection, and survival of the fittest. Thus

> Ronald Fisher, working in the early twentieth century, was the founding father of neo-Darwinism. Fisher was a mathematical genius and systematically devised many of the techniques . . . in every science today. Fisher was also an outspoken racist and passionate advocate of eugenics. He feared that it was the least fit members of society who were outbreeding the aristocrats and threatening to dilute the mental resources that make human civilization possible. To this day, neo-Darwinists tend to be free market libertarians. . . . The period from 1970 to 1985, when the selfish gene was being enthroned . . . was just coincidentally the same era in which the unrestrained competition of free market capitalism was hailed as the one true economic system.[2]

This example suggests that there are always internal connections between a theory of evolution and the panoply of cultural concepts expressed in it. Put another way, even if you seek to insulate an image of species evolution from cultural processes, some set of cultural concepts will infiltrate the account given. The influences work the other way too, with whatever view of evolution you explicitly or tacitly accept sliding up into your cultural theory—even if that means you draw a sharp distinction between culture and biology to protect the former from the ravages of genocentrism. The issue is not whether there is interplay between these domains but how it is pursued, what cautions are introduced and what adventures are rendered possible.

One could also reject evolutionary theory, as creationists do, or ignore it, as some cultural theorists seek to do, or postulate a rupture in the evolutionary process that underpins the uniqueness of the human estate. But the creationist approach ignores a vast geological and fossil record that, in effect, also requires its defenders to reject out of hand much of modern science. The attempt to ignore evolutionary theory is apt to fail as well, as you find yourself tacitly committed to a theory you do not examine. The rupture alternative, in turn, can be consistently pursued, since it is possible to have faith in a designing God who gives special priority to human beings and whose hand mysteriously guides the evolutionary process. While I do not accept the theme of intelligent design, I do appreciate one of its achievements: it has maintained pressure on the genocentric model, pointing to gaps in the fossil record and problems in the genocentric mode of explanation, thereby helping to pave the way for other critiques. There is a feature of that approach, however, that gives people like me considerable pause. Besides our inability to be infused by the faith infusing this doctrine it combines a theocentered image of evolution with a highly anthropocentric image of the cosmos. There are, by the way, some conceptions of divinity that do not postulate a highly anthropocentric God; they are compatible with a relatively unguided evolutionary process. Henri Bergson and William James leap to mind here, and the traditions of Hinduism and Buddhism do as well.

Today perhaps a model of species evolution is needed that appreciates the complexity of these processes while emphasizing numerous entanglements of human beings with a vast array of beings and force fields that qualify its sense of uniqueness, its sense of being at the top of things, and its modern sense of world mastery. We are distinctive but not unique; many of our prized capacities are also operative to some degree in other species, and the most vaunted capacities are entangled with multiple other beings and forces that allow them to be. Even our vaunted capacity to come to terms with our mortality seems to be shared to at least *some* degree by crows and elephants. Perhaps whales and dogs too. And if you broaden the species provincialism of the human estate a bit, there are achievements in other species that put to shame their corollaries or substitutes in us. Pollinating insects detect light patterns indiscernible to us; dogs have a much richer sense of smell; honeybees apparently navigate by polarized light; whales have larger, complex brains and engage in complex modes of communication not yet explored closely by us; rattlesnakes track prey by infrared light; some birds deploy complex navigational systems; bats deploy sonar; dolphin hearing reaches 160 kilohertz, while ours is confined to a puny 20.[3]

The example of neo-Darwinism suggests it is unwise to advance a theory that seeks to bypass altogether culturally infused concepts of life and society. Doing so, you are apt to become a blind carrier of a specific cultural perspective. It is instead incumbent upon us to think critically about how such concepts function as we fold them into the inquiry. We may today be carriers of images of humanity and civilization that will seem as problematic to future generations as both the Victorian and neo-Darwinian images do to many of us today. Such awareness builds a tentativeness and exploratory outlook into whatever theory you currently accept.

How to proceed? My sense is that a theory of species evolution that passes the crucible of inherent credibility will be one that renders intelligible human capacities of consciousness, meaning, responsibility, significance, freedom, and self-conscious violence that have emerged from that process. It will do so without reducing these outcomes to mere epiphenomena that do not play an active role in life, culture, action, and evolution itself. This leaves considerable room for exploration, since there are several such accounts, ranging from neo-Spinozism to some versions of Buddhism to immanent naturalism. Because cultural concepts and assumptions inevitably enter into each such account it is perhaps wise to pursue a dynamic movement back and forth between phenomenological explorations of human experience, the findings of neuroscience, and evolutionary accounts of how the most complex capacities arose. None of these explorations sets a clean base from which the others proceed; each invites exchanges with the others when a new turn is taken in it. Maurice Merleau-Ponty in his early work seemed to demand that evolutionary theory must square with the findings of phenomenology. A one-way street. But in his later work he pursues a reciprocal movement between the cultivation of experience, the findings of geological evidence, and body-brain experiments.[4] The idea is to pursue a reflective equilibrium (as Whitehead would call it) in which movement in either zone provides presumptive evidence that the other must *somehow* take into account. The quest for such a reflective equilibrium is apt never to be finished. But it does mean that the findings of cultural theory and experience are relevant to those of evolutionary theory and allied fields.

I will now clarify themes advanced to this point by addressing a recent account that first embraces them and then takes a turn that I find to be implausible.

Mind, Cosmos, and Purpose

Thomas Nagel in *Mind and Cosmos* seeks to explain why physicalism is an unpromising theory of evolution. This is a bold and austere book, with perhaps each of its tendencies working a bit against the other. By "genocentrism" and "materialism" he means a program of evolutionary explanation that concentrates on genetic mutation, blind replication of those mutations, and competitive processes of natural selection that determine which mutations prevail and which disappear. Such an account, he contends, is difficult if not impossible to square with some of the most complex outcomes of evolution.

Our experiences of thinking, consciousness, responsibility, and judgment, Nagel says, do not square with such an evolutionary account of them. (He does not attend much to their expressions in other animals.) Thinking is tied to the experiences of meaning and significance with which it is entangled. Judgment is tied to following norms rather than being determined blindly by prior processes. Responsibility implies that you could have acted differently than you did. Self-reflexivity means that you can reconsider some first-order desires in the light of new reflection upon their assumptions and effects on you and others. We experience ourselves as able to act purposively and self-reflexively. It is extremely difficult, if not impossible, either to erase that experience or to render it compatible with the blind determinations of neo-Darwinism. Many revisions in neo-Darwinism have tried to square this circle, but Nagel contends that all have failed. As he says, "We take ourselves to have the capacity to form true beliefs about the world around us, about the timeless domains of logic and mathematics, and about the right thing to do." This is the "natural, internal stance of human life."[5] The "internal stance" can be placed into productive conversation with this or that external stance—where you study human processes from a third-person, experimental perspective. But the internal perspective can neither be eliminated altogether nor rendered compatible with a neo-Darwinian agenda. He doubts that softened versions work either.

The debates here are endless. But I will cut through them, now at least, by saying that I concur with Nagel on these points, even though I think his own program of "objective reasons" for conduct is too strongly stated. I concur too with his idea that critique is not sufficient. You need a positive program that can become a viable candidate to replace those to which you object.

Nagel discusses briefly the "intentionalist" perspective (often known as intelligent design), in which a God intentionally designed the long-term evolutionary process. But the program he supports is one in which the "materialist" laws of genocentrism are replaced by a natural teleology that places the achievements of consciousness, judgment, responsibility, and so on at the top of the evolutionary process. He uses the word *materialism* to cover only those research programs that seek to reduce higher processes to more simple, nonideational ones, evincing no awareness in doing so of the versions of "new materialism" and "immanent naturalism" that avoid those very modes of reductionism. This is perhaps due the narrow range of references in his book, limited to a few analytic philosophers and mentioning only once the biologists and philosophers I will consult.

For purposes of clarity I call the program he opposes *physicalist*. Thus he replaces the aspiration to "physicalist laws" with one to forge "teleological laws." He knows that teleological theories are traditionally theo-teleological, pointing to a divine hand that sets the end point and contributes to the means by which it is promoted. But he resists this option, partly because he is not infused with such a faith and perhaps partly because such a God is too easily invoked as a stop-gap response whenever a problem in evolutionary explanation is encountered. He seeks a unified theory. Here are a few of his statements about natural teleology:

> An expanded, but still unified, form of explanation will be needed. I suspect it will have to include teleological elements.

> But I have been persuaded that the idea of teleological law is coherent, and quite different from the idea of explanation by the intentions of a purposive being who produces the means to his ends by choice. In spite of the exclusion of teleology from contemporary science, it shouldn't be ruled out a priori. Formally, the possibility of principles of change over time tending toward certain types of outcome is coherent, in a world in which the nonteleological laws are not fully

deterministic. But it is essential, if teleology is to form part of a revised natural order, that its laws should be genuinely universal.

For these reasons, a holistic or emergent answer to the constitutive question comes to seem increasingly more likely than the reductive one as we move up from physical organisms, to consciousness, to reason.[6]

A deconstructionist could have a field day with several formulations by Nagel. The sentences in question are marked by strong assertions at the end, with qualifiers such as "I believe" at the beginning. (Compare "We *hold* these truths to be *self-evident*.") Such a combination underlines the intensity of Nagel's commitment to these ideas, but it also may draw attention away from bifurcation points at which other alternatives could be explored.

While concurring in his critique of genocentrism I have a few reservations about the positive program Nagel pursues. First, I find Nietzsche's objection to a strong teleological perspective rather plausible. If the earth has been around for 4.5 billion years (with life of some sort for 3.8 billion years) and there is a strong teleological bent to life, why has the final or highest state not been reached yet? And how does a finalist version come to terms with the persistence of periodic violence of numerous sorts? Does this suggest, perhaps, that *teleo-searching processes* are endemic to life rather than that there is a strong teleological bent to things? Also, what would happen if and when the end is attained? Would the dynamism and vitality seep out of life? The first counterargument adduced here exerts limited power, but it does suggest a need to make important distinctions of degree—comparing teleological theories attached to finalism to those that fold teleodynamic processes into the image of an open universe marked by what I later call *bumpy temporalities*.

Second, Nagel proceeds by what can be called argument by elimination: you list the possible options and then criticize each until only one candidate remains. But such a mode of argument depends a lot on putting all viable possibilities onto the initial list. I contend, as already implied, that he has skipped a credible alternative, one that also appraises evolutionary theories according to their abilities to makes sense of complex results of evolution.

Third, Nagel's position is in one sense closer to the one he opposes than he acknowledges. His opponents seek genocentric *laws*, and he seeks teleological *laws*. They are sometimes inspired by the idea that humans can be masters of the earth; he may be inspired by the idea that the world is, in the last instance, predisposed to us and our implicit destiny. Hence the criterion of "reassurance" he invokes. The physicalist and teleological perspectives certainly contend with each other. But they also complement each other from the perspective advanced here. Advocates of each think the world is rather highly predisposed to the human estate: it is either predisposed to our drive to mastery or to our implicit destiny. I think both views exaggerate. The complexity of things, viewed from the perspective of a human estate densely entangled with other agents and processes, is more fragile and dangerous than that.

The best critique, however, as Nagel agrees, is to offer a positive alternative. So I add a candidate to Nagel's list of genocentrism, divine intentionalism, and natural teleology. The alternative projects differential degrees of agency into multiple, heterogeneous, interacting systems, and it identifies periodic moments of creativity within and between evolving organisms. It does not altogether deny teleology; rather it insinuates differing degrees of creativity into *teleodynamic* processes.

Immanent, Creative Evolution

When you place philosophers of an open cosmos of becoming set on heterogeneous and interacting tiers of temporality into conversation with recent biological work in symbiogenesis and dynamic evolution, a promising alternative emerges. This alternative, rooted partly in evidence and partly in speculation, situates differential degrees of conditioned creativity and agency deep into the biosphere. It compromises genocentrism profoundly; it includes purposive elements within larger processes; and it rejects a *finalist* reading of teleology. It also folds the aesthetic element Darwin identified in bird and other species relationships deeply into dynamic processes. The interplay of attractions and searching processes may sink into the process by which two simple organisms combine through symbiogenesis to create unwittingly a new composite. Moreover since the focus is on *heterogeneous* systems that often interact, this perspective is compatible with the impact of external forces upon the "internal" dynamic of evolution, such as the asteroid identified by Luis Alvarez and Stephen Jay Gould that wiped out dinosaurs, periods of rapid climate change, the movement of tectonic plates, radical shifts in the ocean conveyor system, massive bursts of volcanic dust, and long-term drought. Even if simple purposive elements sink deeply into the evolutionary process, the differential effects of other force fields upon it cast doubt on a strong doctrine of teleology. Thus the glacial movement of tectonic plates that propels continents, allows mountain ranges to grow, and makes earthquakes erupt is entangled with the long history of life on earth. Tectonic movement may be lubricated by deposits of limestone, and those deposits reflect the prior history of microbes from which limestone is formed in part.[7] The more you extend the possible reach of *heterogeneous* intersections—the wasp and the orchid, asteroid hits and punctuations in species evolution, tectonic plate movements and microbe deposits, cyanobacterial release of oxygen eons ago and the first glimmerings of oxygenated life, crossings between Neanderthals and *Homo sapiens*—the less plausible a philosophy either of natural teleology or of consummate explanation seems. I doubt if either approach would now seem plausible to dinosaurs, for instance.

It seems to me that real creativity arises in part because the world is marked by heterogeneous connections of numerous sorts. The idea here, at any rate, is to curtail both the themes of *cultural internalism* and *cultural incommensurability* by amplifying those of *heterogeneous connections* between entities and processes of manifold sorts. When you do that you begin to break both unified narratives and to interrupt closed explanatory theories; you begin to experiment at those fugitive junctures where narrative becomes punctuated and explanation proves to be insufficient. You may even begin to appreciate signs of elbow room in the universe by which creative innovations occur for good or ill. That is, you now begin to adjust the *default intuitions* through which explanation, narration, and experimentation have been organized in several traditions.

A general theory of evolution would focus on such external-internal intersections. I focus for now, however, on more restrictive processes that nonetheless break radically with genocentric reductionism. I pursue some of the external processes in later chapters.

I begin with *symbiogenesis*, pressed upon evolutionary theory by the study of slimes and molds launched by Lynn Margulis, dismissively rejected by the "zoological" consensus of neo-Darwinism for a few decades, and now widely thought to play a significant role in evolution. Two different species enter into a symbiotic relation if they form a composite in which each needs the other. The relation morphs into one of *symbiogenesis* if the two genomes interpenetrate to form a composite organism. "These mergers, long term biological fusions beginning as symbiosis, are the engine of species evolution." The idea is that an accumulation of mutations can make a difference within a species, but the accumulation is too slow and discrete to foster species change. One now widely supported example of symbiogenesis is the process by which DNA from one bacterium entered another, at some point triggering a creative response in the receiving bacterium that generated the first nucleated cell, forging the unintended basis of future evolution. A more complex process is one in which lichens emerge from the creative conjunction of algae and fungi. Lichens are a composite of the two and still show the effects of this conjugation: "If certain lichens are placed in the dark the photosynthetic member . . . cannot live. . . . If lichens are placed under water for a long time the fungus drowns but the algae will just grow and grow."[8] So lichens are composites grounded in symbiogenesis. Other apparently well-supported examples include those in which slugs enter into a symbiotic relation with algae in a way that alters the capacities of the new composite, and when cow-bacteria symbiogenesis engenders a special stomach in the cow, a rumen, able to break down the cellulose of the grass the cow eats. Without symbiogenesis, no cows.

These are examples that do not involve sexual exchange and do involve genome transfers large enough to make a significant difference to evolutionary change. Are such processes actively involved in the evolution of other mammals, including humans? Margulis and Dorion Sagan speculate that this is probably the case; they place some bets on composites formed between viruses or bacteria and mammal tissue. For the cells that compose us now are inhabited by mitochondria, probable descendants of independent cyanobacteria that were once metabolically distinct.

One recently studied mode of evolution, located between the slowness of intraspecies mutation and the rapidity of symbiogenesis, is "interspecies breeding." The very process of course throws a conundrum into the settled idea of a species. There is considerable evidence that *Homo sapiens* and Neanderthals interbred sporadically around 100,000 years ago, leaving the former, for instance, with a skin protein that makes the skin more supple and resilient. A more recently discovered "species," the Denisovans, may have also interbred with some *Homo sapiens* on the steppes of Tibet, leaving behind genes that enable Tibetans to work at high altitudes with low oxygen intake. These findings remain a bit controversial at this writing, but they have helped one researcher to reinforce his earlier conclusion that evolution is more like a rhizomatic than an arboreal process.[9]

I have inserted the words *creative response* into the discussion, though I believe that Margulis and Sagan would not object to that insertion. It still needs to be redeemed, however, as I will try to do. The redemption proceeds from two sides: drawing upon philosophical speculation about a world of becoming and pointing to microprocesses that can plausibly be taken to exemplify such processes. For evolutionary creativity means micro-teleo-searching processes that ensue when interacting organisms are disrupted, sometimes issuing in a new result that exceeds the micro-intentions of both. Such an approach, if sustained, helps to make human creative capacities more intelligible as an evolutionary outcome, but it also presses us to qualify both strong, hubristic notions of human autonomy and finalist notions of agency. Neither strong agency, nor the simple realization of implicit tendencies, nor reductive determination but processes that fall into a zone of current indeterminacy between these alternatives.

If the things said so far are to be sustained, a more global take on evolution is needed. Biologists and philosophers of biology such as Susan Oyama, Stuart Kauffman, Terrence Deacon, and Evan Thompson provide experimental and speculative resources from which such work can be pursued.[10] They distinguish a pure notion of genocentrism from a strong "developmental" notion of evolution. Not all genocentrists fit the pure contrast model, but the further they depart from its purity, the more they may be pulled toward either a Nagel view or the one projected here.

Oyama and Thompson may provide starting points. If genocentrists say that organisms are the effects of gene assemblages, the developmental theorists insist that genes are elements within larger organisms and environments that do a lot of the work themselves. If genocentrists say that shared genes are the active agents in an organism, developmental theorists say "that the activity of the organism, *including self-stimulation*, is often a crucial aspect . . . and so are influences from other organisms."[11] If genocentrists insist that genes alone pass on phenotypes, developmental theories say that a variety of heterogeneous resources is required and, moreover, that the passage of gene "information" involves dynamic modes that greatly exceed mere "replication."

One piece of evidence advanced to support these modifications of genocentrism is the gene PAX6, which is associated with vision in both insects and vertebrates. When the gene from a mouse is inserted into a fruit fly, a fruit fly eye emerges at the point of insertion, not either a mouse eye or a mere mess. This suggests that the fruit fly must do a large amount of unconscious work to "translate" the mouse gene into a result compatible with its organic structure.[12] Does the intersection between the inserted gene and the emergent fruit fly also insinuate a redundancy into the site from which further evolution may emerge if another insertion occurs? At any rate it does suggest that fruit flies and mammal embryos do considerable work on the gene clusters they receive. The new gene clusters pose problems for them to try to resolve.

Margulis and Sagan lean on recent work in the physics of thermodynamics to suggest that there are creative developments in species evolution. But Deacon, while invoking both thermodynamism and "morphodynamism" as essential processes, also contends that evolution involves teleodynamic processes that both depend on the former and exceed their powers. This is the addition that brings thinkers like Whitehead, James, Deleuze, and Nietzsche into a close relation to current developmental theories. We engage in a teleodynamic search when we, say, enter into an open-ended conversation around a problem and end up with a new result that was not merely *implicit* in the starting point.[13] Deacon contends that simple micro versions of such processes occur at strategic points in the evolutionary process, when, for instance, a process of symbiogenesis is launched between two organisms or the noise of a mutation is creatively translated by an embryo into a new result. His introduction of teleodynamic process is compatible with available evidence and adds a speculative dimension to it. But speculation is not unique to him at these points. Proponents of the other theories do so too, with respect to how new conjunctions are formed and whether human agency could be an outcome of evolution as they conceive it. The speculative result in the cases of Deacon, Thompson, and Oyama fits neither a model of simple replication nor of strong teleology.

When this thesis is put into (teleodynamic) conversation with philosophies of becoming in a partially open universe, micro creative processes become inserted into evolution itself. That is why the title of Deacon's book, *Incomplete Nature*, makes so much sense. Nature is incomplete in that every mode of self-organization involves external connections and internal constraints that enable it to be this and not that. Without some constraints—that is, modes of limit and incompletion—human beings could not be selves projecting, however imperfectly, into the future. On my reading, nature is also incomplete in ways that periodically allow perturbations from elsewhere to trigger creative processes within or between entities that exceed the sufficiency of any closed explanation. Some of these processes are not merely unpredictable because the experimenters have incomplete information (though that happens); they are unpredictable because microprocesses of real creativity sometimes throw new results into the furniture of the universe. Such processes are conditioned, teleodynamic modes of *incipience* replete with pluripotentialities on the way, more than teleological processes by which the *implicit* becomes explicit as it progressively expresses the natural bent of the world. For instance, when starving amoebas seek to devour each other, there is a micro-intentional element in the striving of each. The result of the intersection, however, is sometimes that two haploid amoebae become one diploid, in which two sets of chromosomes are mixed together. This asexual evolutionary composite may involve simple micro-intentions at the initiating stage, but the result exceeds those micro-intentions.[14]

These are thus conditioned modes of creativity that proceed from interacting, striving organisms operating within certain constraints. It is not creation ex nihilo, *since every creative process is constrained and enabled by its preconditions of initiation.* The intersections are teleodynamic in the sense that they are irreducible either to simple processes of mutation, information, and replication or to a fundamental bent of the world already there. Put yet another way, there is a bent to things at the initiation of each transition, but that bent may shift to some degree as the result of teleodynamism. It is wise to disconnect creativity from the consummate agency of either a God or humans in order to appreciate how it arises out of heterogeneous connections between entities that sometimes display micro-intentionality. Those who invoke a God without giving It consummate agency can readily enter into relations of spiritual affinity with those of us who pursue heterogeneous connections without invoking a divinity. Those who invoke a consummate God while emphasizing its call upon them to respect diverse human entanglements can do so too, as we will see when we engage Pope Francis later.

At this point some readers are apt to say, "Is this not the very science of evolution that has been captured by neoliberalism, with its demand to tie together evolutionary processes, financial speculation, entrepreneurial creativity, private property, and the commodity form?" This is the theme Melinda Cooper advances in her powerful book *Life as Surplus.* She ties recent revolutions in evolutionary experiments, stem cell research, crop experimentation, and pharmaceuticals to a version of American neoliberalism organized around worker exploitation, debt imperialism and commodification. She contends that the new biology is "aligned" with neoliberalism, often saying "it is no coincidence" or "no accident" that the two have been brought together, sometimes even saying that they are "inseparable." As neoliberalism moves from an earlier model of shifting equilibria to later models marked by radical disequilibrium, catastrophe, and recovery, she finds that it increasingly fits images advanced by the new biology. We never really find out whether she thinks the new biology is itself false, or whether it is true but captured by neoliberalism. Indeed where she uses the language of alignment, Deleuze and Guattari, two theorists who appreciate complexity theories and radically oppose neoliberalism, would use the language of capture.

Cooper names some of the biologists and complexity theorists discussed in this chapter as figures bound to neoliberalism. Some may be; Kauffman and James Lovelock are apt candidates. But others, including Margulis, seem much more ambivalent to me. Others yet, including Sagan, Isabelle Stengers, and Ilya Prigogine, pursue those theoretical and experimental lines while actively resisting capture by neoliberalism. And many others, such as Bruno Latour, whose work I discuss later, have become active critics of how neoliberalism intensifies the climate crisis. The same goes for Wally Broeker in oceanography and Michael Benton in geology, both discussed in later chapters. Or take Sagan, the son of Margulis, in his recent work: "Are we godlets in the making? Maybe. But right now it don't look so good. Our chattering monkey minds and taste for technical sweets are not in accord with Team Gaia, the long-evolved, long lasting gradient reducing virtuosities pioneered by ecosystems, including versions of the same forest ecosystems that fostered our own 'recent' evolution."[15]

My conclusion is that the new complexity theory is not in itself definitive on this matter. Some practitioners, perhaps implicitly tied to a cosmology of temporal progress through periodic catastrophes, may incline in the direction Cooper delineates. Others, perhaps moved by a sense of tragic possibility in a world of multiple temporal intersections that are not necessarily predisposed to the welfare of the human estate, are among the most effective critics of neoliberalism. Think, for instance, of how Soviet Realism captured film for a time in the Soviet Union. That was an ugly combination, but it did not mean that other imbrications between film and the wider cultural life could not be invaluable. Neoliberal capture of the new biosciences is partly grounded in a neoliberal insistence upon human entitlement joined to a world hierarchy of regions, races, and classes. That combination helps to vindicate its exploitation of marginal populations, as well as of animals, microbes, forests, and plants. Those complexity theorists who oppose human exceptionalism and appreciate the complexity of heterogeneous connections may be essential sources to draw upon in resisting and surpassing neoliberalism.

In a chapter of *This Changes Everything*, Naomi Klein reviews how a series of complexity theorists in oceanography and climate have responded militantly to neoliberal plans to dim the sun to reduce climate warming without changing the economic processes that trigger warming. For example, she quotes Sallie Chisolm, a renowned expert on marine microbes: "Proponents of research on geoengineering simply keep ignoring the fact that the biosphere is a player (not just a responder) in whatever we do, and its trajectory cannot be predicted. It is a living, breathing, collection of organisms (mostly microorganisms) that are evolving every second—a 'self-organizing, complex, adaptive system' (the strict terms). These types of systems have emergent properties that simply cannot be predicted. We all know this! Yet proponents of geoengineering research keep leaving this out of the discussion."[16]

It would indeed be tragic if ecotheories on the Left elided the actual and potential value of creativity in life and politics because such themes have been hijacked by neoliberal financial imperialism. It is wiser to explore the theories and resist the capture, since we need to fold creative thinking and action into modes of resistance and pursuit of alternatives. I very much admire Cooper's delineation of debt imperialism and its strategies to capture complexity theories, but I resist, as will become increasingly clear, repudiation of those sciences themselves.

Social Process and Cultural Creativity

The insight triggering such an amateurish foray into evolution by a mere political theorist is that any plausible theory of species change must strive to render more intelligible how capacities of consciousness, meaning, creativity, responsibility, and judgment *could* emerge from evolution. Such a theory will not "explain" their emergence entirely, for the insertion of a creative element into conditioned processes means that explanation is often inherently incomplete, in both biology and the human sciences. I know such a finding makes some in both domains shudder. Moreover such an account must be compatible with the reality of complex variations across cultures in the modalities of agency, freedom, responsibility, and the like. The perspectives reviewed above seem to me to be on the road to rendering complex human capacities more intelligible. If so, that counts as one piece of evidence in their favor. Indeed such findings extend the idea of culture well beyond the human estate. The corollary, however is that attention to such an account of evolution may also help us to think about distinctive human capacities somewhat differently than we have heretofore. At least it may lend plausibility to some views that have heretofore struggled to receive a close hearing. My focus here is on freedom, creativity, and consciousness.

Neither a negative nor a positive image of human freedom is strongly supported by such a picture. Negative freedom, in one of its neoliberal versions, treats the desires and "preferences" of people as already given and not susceptible to further analysis. Individuals are free to the extent they can act upon those desires within the constraints and rationality of the impersonal market, even if advertising technologies and cultural binds have contributed to those desires.

Positive freedom challenges two exaggerations in this picture: that desires must be taken as they are "given" in the exploration of freedom and that the impersonal regulation of markets is reliably rational. The attention in positive theories of freedom to processes of self-reflexivity, by which we reconsider established desires in the light of newly disclosed knowledge of their effects, provides an invaluable corrective. But a positive image of freedom is most at home with itself in a teleological theory that points to modes of self-realization that, in tandem with a larger community and cooperating cosmos, corresponds increasingly to the natural bent of things. In one of its modes it fits the sort of theo-teleological image developed earlier by Charles Taylor and now qualified by him.[17] In another naturalistic mode it may mesh with the relation between mind and cosmos articulated by Nagel.

My suggestion is that the account of evolution sketched above can illuminate things about the creative element in human freedom that do not fit neatly into either the positive or the negative image. I start with a couple of formulations by Nietzsche, whose critical engagements with Darwin in *Will to Power* anticipated several themes explored above. In particular he appreciates the creative element in freedom, extends the element of striving deeply into the biosphere, suggests important revisions in familiar accounts of human agency, autonomy, and consciousness, and interrogates theories that postulate a strong predilection of the world to either human mastery or dialectical modes of self-realization.[18]

Nietzsche understands the self to be a complex social structure consisting of a multitude of interacting drives replete with significant variations of completeness, complexity, and speed. Each drive is entangled both with others within the self and with a larger variety of human and nonhuman processes. For example, the drive to maximize entrepreneurial freedom is essentially bound to larger processes such as markets, media-supported ideologies of how markets work, and intersections between capitalist expansion and climate change. Counterdemands to seek freedom through reform of corporate-state combines, in turn, are tied to the institutional complexes in which they arise, to the possibilities available to craft social movements, and to the panoply of historical strategies available for adoption or revision. Nietzsche is thus a philosopher of multiple entanglements. He is an "individualist" only to those who remain stuck in a two-slot system in which you must be either an individualist or a holist, an advocate of negative freedom or of positive freedom. People stuck in these binaries ignore the richness of protean connectionism.

But no need to take my word for it. Let's consider the relation of multiple drives to consciousness and freedom in *Daybreak*. Nietzsche says, "However far a man may go in self-knowledge, nothing however can be more incomplete than his image of the totality of drives which constitute his being. He can scarcely name even the cruder ones; their number and strength, their ebb and flood, their play and counterplay among one another, and above all the laws of nutriment remain unknown to him." He goes on to say that "the so-called ego is thenceforth a fellow worker in the construction of our character and our destiny."[19]

To Nietzsche every self is replete with multiple, heterogeneous, culturally inflected drives, periodically intensifying, blocking, overwhelming, or infecting one another. The "unity" of a self is actually a series of interfolded and conflicting pathways, with some paths being more deeply situated and widely entangled with others. To change an entrenched drive is thus to shift significantly the current organization of the self, including the relation of that drive to a series of others. Drives form unions and conjunctions below the threshold of consciousness, influencing behavior. Semblances of some of these unions reach consciousness, but that semblance is more abstract than the nest from which it is drawn; many drives are inferred from their effects rather than being knowable by introspection. We knowers are largely unknown to ourselves . . . because of the complexity of the heterogeneous, purposive drives that help to compose us. So far, so obvious.

But what is a drive? The word *drive* can function as a noun or a verb, as is true of the word *arrest*: you are under arrest; you are being arrested. The noun even contains a trace of the verb within it, as when you were running just before being placed "under arrest." That's not fun. The predicate in "The rose is blossoming" can be construed either as a snapshot of a bloom already there or as the process of blooming. The predicate in fact includes both dimensions. The situation is similar with drives: "You have a drive; it drives you." A drive expresses movement, impulsion, pressure, even sometimes implacability. Think of smoking, illicit sex in an alluring setting, compulsive gossip, the silent insinuation of resentment into high moral principles, a new thought, a burst of laughter, a stutter as you find your speech stuck at a protean bifurcation point. Note too that such a perspective does not demand a strong theory of which drives must prevail for the species as such in every society. Nietzsche offers a *philosophy* of how emergent drives function in relation to each other, consciousness, and the world more than a fixed *theory* of what shape they must take everywhere. The latter kind of theory tends to be *too* explanatory, failing to appreciate enough the elements of variation and creativity within the play of drive complexes and the new unions emerging from them. Once you see how "will to power" conveys a plastic process of forward movement in human life and nonhuman processes more than a fixed theory of what shape that movement must take, this becomes clear. Since specific drive complexes are neither universal nor always set in stone once they are forged, it is easier to make sense of the generous spirituality of enmity Nietzsche seeks to promote between lived perspectives. For relational drive complexes already there can be worked upon *tactically* to an uncertain degree. Back to that point soon.

Drives, as the examples above suggest, express more than impulsion too. Drives are not *blind forces* merely pushing forward, as a glacier grinds along. A drive, triggered by an event that it encounters, *is a simple affect-imbued mode of relational perception, striving, and interpretation on the way.* A drive's power of perception may be very simple, something like that of a tick when it senses heat and butyric acid but little else. As when something in you notes a flicker in the face of a stranger that draws you tacitly to the memory of your deceased mother. You stare a moment too long without explicitly intending to do so. A drive's intentionality may be extremely simple too, similar to that of a tick that intends to make contact with warmth but does not intend to infect that warm body with Lyme disease. In that case the effect exceeds the intention.

A nest of drives may be cloudy as well, as when intense erotic pressures drive you forward but are unsettled or vague about what gender or part of the body at which to aim. Or when we dimly pursue a political project together but are uncertain as to what strategy to adopt. In such cases the cloudiness may be real for a time, not merely an epistemological limitation that screens actors and observers from an object that is clear and intact in itself. Drives are *teleodynamic* in their internal relations, their entanglements with larger social processes, and their variable degrees of sensitivity to nonhuman processes. Artists often work on the cloudy relations between drive structures and our relations with the world.

Am I working on Nietzsche as much as interpreting him? Well, I think that what I am saying is roughly compatible with his view. But after a certain point the issue does not matter that much to me. The idea is to draw sustenance from a thinker, to work on him or her, and then to see whether the emergent result is coherent and illuminates experience enough to be defended. The point is that *if* you grasp Nietzsche's drives in this way, you will see more sharply why tactics of the self could be so important to Nietzsche, why they carry some potential to be successful, and why self-reflexivity, while pertinent, shines a dimmer light on the nest of drives than self-reflexive theories of freedom of self and collective realization tend to acknowledge. You may also begin to discern how a series of movements back and forth between tactics of the self, the micropolitics of social movements, macropolitics, and cross-state citizen movements are crucial to critical politics today, as Nietzschean-imbued thinkers on the Left such as Foucault, Elizabeth Grosz, Deleuze, Massumi, and I have tried so hard to show.

Heterogeneous drives infiltrate, augment, and wrestle with one another. That is why they are not well understood dialectically. They periodically combine or coalesce, sometimes creating a new result out of teleodynamic exchanges. The new effect is neither the result of an *aggregation* of blind causes nor an explicit outcome of that which was *implicit*. To reduce it to the latter would be to subtract the "dynamism" from the "teleo" in drive entanglements and micro-explorations. The relational, teleodynamic capacities of drives provide an element in the real creativity of human life, while this feature also poses sharp qualifications to highly centered visions of autonomous human agency.

Again both Nietzsche and Whitehead think that the power to regulate the nest of drives directly by self-conscious reflection upon them is limited, partly because consciousness shines a dim spotlight on the twists and coils that help to compose our relational tendencies and partly because a drive's stubbornness may sometimes exceed the power to alter it by such direct means. They both also resist articulation of a universal *theory* of drives on the grounds that to demand such a theory is, first, to act tacitly as if culturally specific drive structures are universal and, second, to pretend to explain more closely processes on the way that may well have elements in them of real creativity sprinkled here and there. So these two thinkers both advance *philosophies* of drive processes and creativity and resist tightly demarcated *theories* of drives, such as theories that posit a set of universal drives that must find expression in all times and societies or those that pretend drive processes are in principle subject to full explanation. In a world with elements of creativity, explanation is in principle often incomplete.

I believe that Foucault, Grosz, Massumi, and Deleuze join Nietzsche and Whitehead in each of these respects, and so do the theorists of evolution I have highlighted.[20] The trio of Nietzsche, Foucault, and Deleuze pursue tactics or arts of the self where others may seek the sufficiency of a consummate explanation, a deep interpretation, or a system of judgment. The guiding principles here: Don't explicate too much; cultivate care; experiment politically.

Ethics and Tactics of the Self

This is where tactics of the self and media micropolitics come in. I will bracket attention to the latter now to focus on the former and turn to intersections between micro- and macropolitics in later chapters. A tactic of the self, on this reading, is an experimental strategy to touch and work on entangled microperceptual or micro-intentional tendencies flowing beneath direct conscious awareness and regulation. That is the most powerful way the ego operates as a "fellow worker." The accompanying problem, however, is that such tactics are often experimental. You do not know for sure what will bubble up when you become a guinea pig of your own complex, layered self, nor when you compose a new social movement replete with local protests, TV presentations, erotic entertainment, Internet publicity, musical inspiration, experimental shifts in production and consumption habits, and cross-country actions.

Consider a few examples of tactics of the self applied to a nest of micro-intentional processes and exchanges. You might engage in meditation, allowing this or that portal to forge new affiliations with other drives. You might prime your dream life before going to sleep, crystallizing, say, a stubborn intellectual problem in which you have found yourself heading in two incompatible directions, hoping that, after the dream work is done, a new idea, concept, political strategy, or intellectual theme will bubble up at daybreak for further appraisal and consideration by movements in which you participate. You might engage in neurotherapy, whereby a therapist encourages you to move this neuro sign up on the wall and that one to the right, to see what changes in mood and thinking emerge. You might listen to inspiring music with a huge crowd at a protest, allowing the drive landscape within to be jostled by the intimate relation to others. You might attend a compelling film with others, allowing multimodal intersections of music, image, rhythm, plot, and words, say, to work on specific resistances in you and the constituencies with which you are entangled. Consider *Brokeback Mountain*, for instance. Consider what emotions unfold as you gradually realize that the two cavorting young men on the mountain are caught in the gaze of high-powered binoculars. You might listen to the soundscapes of John Luther Adams to see whether sensitivity to the sounds of insects, birds, wind, streams, and fire now becomes more refined. Untrained perceptions, as both Nietzsche and Buddhists try to teach us, are lazy and coarse; the intentions and judgments flowing from them are apt to be so as well.

Each of these tactics can be tethered to an ethic of cultivation whereby you experiment with tactics to accentuate gratitude for the excess of life over being and attachment to that strange element of creativity that periodically courses through and around us. As Nietzsche says, attending to the call to *tend* to heterogeneous drives artistically, "Out of damp and gloomy days, out of solitude, out of loveless words directed at us, conclusions grow up in us like fungus: one morning they are there, we know not how, and they gaze upon us, morose and grey. Woe to the thinker who is not the gardener but only the soil of the plants that grow in him."[21]

An ethic of cultivation is not derived from a transcendental argument, nor does it involve obedience to a set of divine commands. It taps into contingent strains of attachment and presumptive generosity that are already there, seeking to amplify them and to adjust them to situations that sometimes change significantly. I will not exemplify micropolitics here, since that will be explored in a later chapter in a long discussion of role experiments. But a noble goal of both arts of the self and micropolitics, you might say, is to become somewhat other than ourselves, as we engage blockages in and between us, doing so to robustly affirm a world of multidimensional pluralism and to become attentive to the fragility of late-capitalist exchanges with several non-human force fields.

Nonetheless the question often pressed by neo-Kantians, Straussians, deliberationists, rational choice theorists, and finalists (who disagree among themselves) is "*What* or *Who* provides the seed or authority for such attempts?" (Are those who most intensely press such questions themselves sometimes poised on the edge of passive nihilism, in that *they* cannot be ethical unless an eternal source or transcendental argument provides them with a set of commands?) The response to the question is two-pronged. A world that includes moments of real creativity does not mesh well with the quest to find sufficient, eternal banisters of moral authority and judgment. We must thus *qualify* the latter expectation, even though we too draw upon embedded assumptions during periods of relative quiescence. We also resist the blackmail of moralists who insist we meet demands flowing from the linear philosophy of time in which *they* are tacitly enclosed. Of course we seek selective modes of alliance with them, if and when possible, but it would be unethical to succumb to such blackmail since we do not accept the ontology of time in which their demands are set. This is one of the ways we coalesce with those biologists who discern a creative element in species evolution.

To proponents of a world in which distributed creativity is periodically in play within and beyond the human estate judgment often requires close attention to dense situations, some elements of which may be new. On this reading, ethicopolitics can sometimes require creative thinking to *be* ethical. Such situational considerations can be informed by the presumptive receptiveness of an affirmative spirituality. But they are not determined entirely by it nor by the universality of a systematic ethical theory. A judgment, during a period of accelerated tempo, is thus a creative response to the past tied to a projection of future possibility that may become real or may need to be adjusted after experimental action based upon that projection.

The living seed that encourages cultivation of a positive spirituality is thus the strain of existential gratitude already festering within and between us, if we are lucky, for the fecundity of life. That is why an element of *luck* finds a place within an ethic of cultivation joined to a logic of immanence, periodic creativity, and situational judgment. *If* such a seed is there it can often be amplified tactically and brought to situational judgments and political actions when a new event jostles this or that chunk in the received banisters of judgment. If it is not there, or if its collective amplification is overwhelmed by events, we may face a tragic situation. The latter possibility follows from the theme that ethicopolitical life is a thing of this world.

However, in a second move we present ours as a *contestable source* of ethical life, in the best instance to be placed in respectful competition and potential political collaboration with carriers of other ethicopolitical sources, as they too hopefully acknowledge the deep contestability of the sources they embrace and as they too become open to an ethic of presumptive generosity with others. This is part of the process by which a critical pluralist assemblage might be built today, one oriented, for instance, to respond critically to the effects of the Anthropocene. Indeed I will try to make the case in chapter 5 that a cross-regional politics of swarming already under way could become condensed into cross-regional general strikes in which citizens in several places put pressure on multiple states, corporations, international organizations, churches, universities, and investment groups to radically reconstitute the extractive cultures upon which they are currently based. An ethos of cultivation anchored in positive care for this world, then, invites the formation of positive assemblages; it also acknowledges that situations can arise when radical modes of opposition to prevailing practices become imperative.

This process will be nudged along by people who join together in fury against the contemporary condition and yet do not resent the world too much because of the deep contestability of this or that heartfelt creed or faith coursing through them. That is the second prong. Deep pluralism is essential to the formation of a critical, pluralist assemblage.[22] Sure, we carriers of an ethos of cultivation in a world of becoming can't help but suspect that noble versions of other ethical perspectives draw tacitly upon the very earthy sources we celebrate. There is an incipient seed of self-conceit within us too, though we strive to modulate that strain by working tactically on it.

Modes of creativity that simmer within and between us, an ethic of cultivation in a world of periodic creativity, indispensable intersections of tactics of the self, micropolitics, and macropolitics, and identification with an entangled human estate periodically facing a series of negative boomerang effects emanating from the hegemony of neoliberalism and the nonhuman force fields imbricated with it—all these work back and forth on each other in the image projected here. Those who share such an image are eager to help forge a militant pluralist assemblage to respond creatively to the fragility of things. Its participants may even joyfully contest final sources with one another, as they seek and pursue affinities of spirituality. For a formal religious or secular *creed* (think of neo-Kantianism, Christianity, Hinduism, Nietzscheanism, etc.) bears an attenuated relation to the *ethos* or *spirituality* infused into it, partly because of that unruly nest of drives that exceed the contours of its formality. Such attenuations sometimes pave the way for formation of a positive, more militant pluralist assemblage in a world that is increasingly minoritized along multiple dimensions. The unruliness of drive structures allows us to work on each other from time to time, not merely by argument but also by activating modes of attraction across creedal differences.

As you come to terms with the complexity, layered character, and opacities in motion that constitute a self as a rich, entangled assemblage, you may also be on the way to a more refined grasp of how the politics of manifold pluralism works on a complex social field. To explore the multiplicity of drives is to break the theory of individualism set in the simplicity of a centered self whose exchanges with itself and others are organized around a will, a contract, or a preset schedule of wants. It does not fit well with a philosophy of holism or finalism either. A drive within the social structure of the self may be triggered by relations with others within the self and by the ingression of outside forces, intentional and otherwise. An ethos of multidimensional pluralism can sometimes be encouraged by such heterogeneous modes of communication, conveyed in the exchange of gestures, postures, words, voices, images, rhythms, and the resonances between them. For drives find communicative expression in facial expressions, bodily postures, rhythms, and unconscious gestures as well as in words and arguments. Better, it is the interplay between these modalities that does the work. Of course such an array can coalesce in destructive and dangerous ways too, particularly when a cultural ethos of existential gratitude is overwhelmed by the forces of cosmic resentment. Hence Foucault on the micro-macro politics of neoliberalism, Deleuze on the micropolitics of fascism, and my exploration of the dangerous and creative consolidation of an evangelical-neoliberal resonance machine in the United States.[23]

Chance and Creativity

We may now be in a position to interpret an otherwise dark saying by Nietzsche. By this point he has already repudiated both holistic (or finalist) and mechanistic cosmologies. Now, however, he hesitates to situate his own alternative entirely in the language of chance. Chance, you might say, is the only available qualifier to invoke against those who conceive the world in mechanistic terms *if you yourself lack an interactive image of creative process.* While countering both organic and mechanistic images of species evolution and human action, Nietzsche says that we need "to recognize the active force, the creative force in the chance event—chance itself is only the clash of creative impulses."[24]

Chance as the unexpected effect of a "clash of creative impulses." If you embrace the idea that drives within the encultured body, in layered cultural entanglements, and in several intersecting nonhuman fields express intensive perspectives pitched at differential levels of complexity, then a clash between exploratory impulses or perspectives on the way can periodically issue in a new formation. That new formation is thus entirely reducible neither to what was implicitly there nor to blind causality. It is in part a creative event on the way, *expressing* a conditioned teleodynamic that allows some modes of *incipience* replete with pluripotentiality to be consolidated in this or that way. The creative outcome depends on the interplay between those modes of incipience and the situation encountered. So the creative element in human agency is closer to something we participate in than to something we intend from the start or control through autonomous agency. It depends on clashes between creative impulses that insinuate an element of chance into the emergent result rather than to chance as entirely responsible for that which deviates from efficient causality.

Human freedom is thus precariously tied to an aesthetic of conditioned creativity; the teleodynamic element of creativity touches simmering drives within a complex self; multilayered cultural relations include noisy transmissions of numerous tendencies within and across entangled selves; the element of creativity can be tethered to destructive or constructive moments in ways that may pose the question of how to cultivate tragic wisdom; the cultivation of gratitude for our strange, modest participation in modes of creativity that also exceed us may help to amplify our attachment to this world; and the further cultivation of that attachment may increase our appreciation of the complexity of freedom and the presumptive embrace of it for others. And since "individuation" occurs through these transmissions, neither a philosophy of holism nor that of market individualism fits the entangled world in which we participate.

The conjunctions among these multifarious forces are replete with uncertain turns and twists, as the words *may* and *can* suggest. And they suggest that both consummate theories of cultural explanation and systematic ethical theories regularly overreach themselves. Nonetheless as we negotiate these disjunctive conjunctions, as we explore differential affinities of capacity between us and several nonhuman processes, we might find that our attachment to this world also ripens. We do not seek to belong to an organic world but to heighten our *attachment* to a world replete with differential degrees of incompleteness, danger, and creative possibility. To appreciate human entanglements with a variety of nonhuman forces, some of which themselves participate in teleodynamic activity, may help to ennoble the larger ethos in which we participate. Of course there is no guarantee that the needed ennoblement will unfold in time or that it will be linked to state and global modes of politics sufficient to the time. There are few guarantees in an entangled world in which a differential element of creativity folds into the conjunctions between heterogeneous processes on the way and in which an ethos of positive engagement informs the thinking of many. In such a world we are both partial products and constrained participants.

This effort has been governed by the idea that theories of species evolution, cultural process, and political creativity need each other, even if many practitioners on each side of the often fraught cultural divide between biology and cultural studies want to avoid close engagement. But perhaps the imminent demise of genocentrism is now loosening up the great refusal on both sides of that line. Because culture is in part an outgrowth of species evolution and evolution is permeated by heterogeneous connections, we can draw insights from each mode of study to illuminate limits and possibilities for the other. My attempt to pursue such a discussion mobilizes the theme of periodic and conditioned creativity: creativity, when it arises, helps to bring something new into being; it grows out of intersecting, heterogeneous searches without being intentional in a grand sense; and it retains a reserve of mystery or uncanniness. Indeed the term *creativity* (rather than *creation*) is a strange locution, introduced, I think, by Whitehead—after the thought bubbled up as if from nowhere—to allow that strangeness to play out in multiple venues.[25] It contests both those who invest total creativity in an omnipotent God and those who subtract it entirely from the world. It teaches us that we cannot master the world even though we can act creatively in it when a change in its course challenges a set of assumptions we have heretofore made.

There are other ways to explore the interdependence between biological and cultural theory, as Nagel's thoughtful attempt shows. The least effective way to proceed, however, is when biologists either insulate themselves from the pressures exerted by the problems and achievements of cultural life or sign up for neoliberalism, and when political and cultural theorists do the same with respect to biology and the bumpy processes of evolution. The latter types often proceed by pointing critiques only at those versions of genocentrism that are the least compatible with human freedom, creativity, and meaning. Or they treat as necessary a set of alliances between some new biologists and neoliberalism. Each mode of reduction—biological and cultural— unconsciously holds up a mirror to the other.

It must also be said, however, that while Nietzsche's intuitions about drives, freedom, and creativity are suggestive, it may be possible to put more meat on those bones without subtracting the very processes of creativity I am trying to pinpoint. It is particularly important to pay attention to drives and collective modes of action. I devote the next chapter to making a bit more headway on that issue.

CHAPTER 3 CREATIVITY AND THE SCARS OF BEING

In *The Use of Pleasure*, the second volume of *History of Sexuality*, Foucault confesses (at least part of) the motivation behind his decision to study how the early Greeks fashioned themselves as subjects of erotic pleasure:

> It was curiosity—the only kind of curiosity, in any case, that is worth acting upon with that degree of obstinacy: not the curiosity that seeks to assimilate what it is proper for one to know, but that which enables one to get free of oneself. After all, what would be the value of the passion for knowledge if it resulted only in a certain amount of knowledgeableness and not . . . in the knower's straying afield of himself? There are times in life when the question of knowing if one can think differently than one thinks, and perceive differently than one sees, is absolutely necessary if one is to go on looking and reflecting at all.[1]

Again the desire is to learn "to what extent the effort to think one's own history can free thought from what it silently thinks, and so enable it to think differently."[2]

The statement, often quoted, is haunting. To me it expresses dissatisfaction with extant conceptions of freedom while nonetheless placing freedom at the center of things. It closely links freedom to thinking, to perception, and indeed to getting free of oneself. It places freedom at the center without promising to provide a definition that fits neatly into preset conceptions of desire, agency, intention, and purpose.

Foucault cannot be happy with the Anglo-American tradition of negative freedom, which, as we have already glimpsed, focuses on the ability to do what you want; it thus tends either to ignore how wants are formed or to bury that issue in the questionable assumption of impersonal market processes that regulate the attainment of desires. Foucault explores how modes of discipline, governmentality, and biopolitics infiltrate individuals, private corporations, civil society, and impersonal market processes, channeling desires and actions.

He cannot be that happy with the tradition of positive freedom either. It is usually set in the context of a communal, national, collective, or divinely inspired organic image of the good life. Individuals and communities are free to the extent that their desires—once they have been wound through complex loops of self-reflexivity and institutional reform that deepen and realize their implicit form—take the shape of goals and ends that fulfill us in the long run.

Foucault troubles both of these conceptions. Sure, he would include the ability to act upon desires as *part* of freedom. He also prizes the self-reflexivity that advocates of positive freedom celebrate. But, like Nietzsche, he supplements reflexivity with indispensable "techniques of the self" by means of which you act experimentally upon extant tendencies of agency, desire, belief, and action that reside below consciousness or beyond regulation through recourse to a reflexive arc of reflexive engagement with initial desires. Thus: "I desire to smoke, but as I reflect upon that desire from the second order perspective of my deepest life goals, I now seek to supercede that desire. And yet the reflexive arc alone does not enable me to quit." Foucault goes beyond the reflexive arc because it does not sink deeply enough into the cultural constitution of a self or institution.

Tactics of the self (and micropolitics on constituency and institutional scales) work on encultured habits and molecular tendencies to action below direct conscious control installed in the soft tissues of life. Such tactics are not governed by a singular goal of intrinsic realization. Foucault thinks that these techniques both exceed the reflexive arc and periodically result in surprising turns that are both essential to the idea of freedom and unamenable to being fit into a conception of an intrinsic, final human end.

The negative and positive images of freedom, then, are both flat, even flat-footed, as Thomas Dumm has shown in his admirable chapter in *Michel Foucault and the Politics of Freedom* with respect to Isaiah Berlin, heterotopias, and the macro-politics of discipline. Both images not only presuppose problematical ideals of society; they depreciate the place of real creativity in practices of freedom, and they thus draw our attention away from the uncanny ways creativity emerges as a force. In chapter 2 we began to think about the uncanniness of human creativity through the work of Nietzsche on drives. Now we will pursue the question further with help from Herbert Marcuse, Whitehead, and Deleuze.

Are we *agents* of creativity? Or does creativity qualify the ideas of agency as either mastery or intentional autonomy? What role does *intentionality* play in it? If intentionality precedes creativity, does that precedence in fact not deflate creativity, merely relocating the site (now inside the formation of intentionality) where the mystery of creativity is lodged? Does the inclusion of creativity in freedom, then, subtract agency from freedom? How could that be? If coming to terms with creativity requires us to qualify traditional images of agency, what does it do to extant notions of causality? What is the relation, if any, between creativity in the human estate and variable degrees of creativity in several nonhuman processes?

Would it be better, after such questions have been posed, to return real *creation* to God or to dissolve it into notions of scientific explanation that purport to eliminate it? Or perhaps creativity is a process in which we participate in uncanny ways even though we do not preside over it. At least, when we preside over something, the creative element has already been squeezed out.

Attention to the complexity of creativity complicates familiar images of desire, will, agency, intentionality, collectivity, and freedom.

Creativity and Agency

Whitehead introduced, I believe, the awkward locution *creativity* into late modern philosophical thought. He probably thought that the more simple locution *creation* was too agent-centered in both its theological and humanistic uses. *Creativity* is an "ultimate term" in Whitehead's philosophy, meaning, I take it, that you can show when it occurs and point roughly to how it happens, but you can neither do without the conception nor delineate the processes involved entirely. Creativity is an uncanny process within which we are embedded rather than the effect of an agent; it is tinged by an aura of mystery.[3] It happens within constraints. The constraints are explained in large part by the fact that at any moment in chronotime the universe is composed of "actual entities" of innumerable types that help to set preconditions for new events. An actual entity is any formation that has some tendency toward self-consistency, such as a rock, a cell, a liver, a tornado, a system of ocean currents, a continent, an organism, a civilization, a mist, or a human being. Remembering that the human organism is itself composed of many interacting bodies of heterogeneous sorts—including viruses and bacteria infused into our organs, brain nodules inherited from reptiles, and social modes of communication pitched at multiple levels—we can say that the creative process is lodged in reverberations within and between entities, including the energized excesses that overflow them.

It is through the periodic acceleration of "vibrations" within and between entities that novel formations emerge. As Whitehead says, "Newton would have been surprised at the modern quantum theory and at the dissolution of quanta into vibrations."[4] When elements from one entity press toward another there is the issue of whether, and if so in what way, it "ingresses" into it. And then there is the "concrescence" by which the entering element is reorganized to fit within the entity and the entity is modified to adjust to the entering element.

Two or more elements in tension; vibrations between them; creative formation of the new through concrescence. Theorists of thermodynamic systems in disequilibrium such as Ilya Prigogine have taken preliminary steps to show how such a mode of self-organization could work. But more is needed to come to terms with some complex processes. Drawing sustenance from Terrence Deacon, the biologist and neuroscientist who embraces complexity theory, we can now think about vibrations that periodically display a "teleodynamic" character. They do not, as we have already seen with respect to the relations between an embryo and a mutation, express a *telos* embodying a final purpose; they point to teleo*dynamic* processes irreducible to finalism. "Teleodynamic activity," Deacon says, "is what we must engage in when trying to make sense of unclear explanation. . . . And it characterizes what is difficult about creative thought processes."[5]

A paramecium blocked from climbing the glucose gradient at which it aims backs up and adjusts its route. A dung beetle pushing dung toward a destination makes more complex maneuvers to reach its end when it is blocked. A sunflower points toward the light and heat from the sun, even if the seeking does not extend so far as to form the concept *sun*. So these behaviors are purposive, teleological, but the searching process involves means to an end, not creative adjustment of the end.

Sometimes, however, not only the means but the end is altered. An individual or collectivity may initially pursue a cloudy end and find it becoming condensed into something more solid as it proceeds.

The element of creativity is thus linked to a teleological component. It involves movement back and forth between at least two actants, say, a genetic mutation and a searching response that translates part of it into a signal received, or an inner, searching dialogue between drives in the same self upon receipt of a shock, or, on another plateau, a fecund conversation between two people in which the result that emerges was not implicit in the beginning, or, on yet another, a late-night political meeting in a stressful situation from which the idea of holding the first teach-in emerges. (I participated in that teach-in. Nobody planned it until it emerged from stressful give-and-take after the governor of Michigan had placed students and faculty at the University of Michigan under threat.)

Such creative searches occur in a cosmos assumed to be open to an uncertain degree. So you have teleo-searching processes without ontological finalism. Moreover the searching processes that contribute to *human* creativity are not themselves reducible to the conscious, intentional activities of molar human agents. Instead they first flow into conscious agency from below, reflecting the upshot of searching activities in play below the dim searchlight consciousness that shines on its internal conditions of being. These processes already possess micropurposive quality as they reinforce or struggle with each other. Then consciousness plays a modest role as the results are both altered and filtered into it. The communications involved are apt to be bumpy, since each layer operates at different levels and speeds from the others with which it is in communication. And horizontal modes of communication are always in play too.

Creativity makes human freedom both real and risky; it also renders conscious agency and intentionality more uncanny than they would otherwise be. Nietzsche grasped some of this complexity, as we have already seen. We now need to pursue it further.

Civilization, Instincts, and Scars

In an attempt to release modern capitalism from modes of collective instinctual repression that confine freedom, creativity, and presumptive generosity—and that thus spawn support for the oppression of marginalized peoples and places—Marcuse in *Eros and Civilization* reworks Freud's theory of necessary instinctual repression. It might be helpful to review his effort in light of the discussion of creativity I have launched.

Contending that Freud's use of the terms *civilization, drives,* and *repression* are too generic, blind, and deterministic—though the element of blindness is not always constant in the theory—Marcuse introduces the idea of "surplus repression" to give greater specificity to collective practices of repression. He does so to explore how to overcome excessive modes of repression in modern capitalism. The collective self-repression and repression of others set into motion by surplus repression are destructive and dangerous; once the circle of repression begins to rotate, many constituencies plagued by it are tempted to help impose it on others in turn. It now becomes difficult to identify political sources of energy with which to break the circle. As Marcuse says, the attempt to break it often encounters resistance from many who experience the effort as an attack on their very freedom. The attempts are experienced as attacks on what they urgently want to do, become, or believe, even if there are ambivalences circulating in them. And of course we must bear in mind that the critic may be mistaken too.

Surplus repression is that part of cultural repression that is needed to protect a hegemonic order minus the part it would take to sustain a more vibrant, inclusive civilization. It is thus doomed to be both a needed category of exploration and experimentation and one that is deeply contestable. For the measure of its operation in the present rests upon contestable assessments of possibilities that have not been enacted. The surplus is projected forward as a claim; successful political experiments help to vindicate it retroactively. Drives to vindicate same-sex relations in a culture that demonizes them are, on such a reading, apt to be tainted with some degree of self-doubt by those pursuing such relations until the fund of surplus repression has been lifted.

I am sympathetic to Marcuse's critique of surplus repression and his demand for a reshaping of cultural relations, even though I also think that the view of "nature in itself" he advances tacitly plays down too much the periodic unruliness of a variety of nonhuman force fields with which we are entangled, internally and externally. As will become progressively clear, I am a supporter of entangled humanism in which the entanglements include both layered human cultural processes that enter into bumpy relations and nonhuman processes that exhibit periodic unruliness. Here, however, my focus is on his reading of socially imbued instincts, the very forces that stand somewhere between the human and the nonhuman in conceptions of human exceptionalism. I will not ask whether his representation of Freud is adequate; I focus on his radical reform of Freudian theory as he grasps it.[6]

Surplus repression is that degree of instinctual repression required by the extant order but not by civilization as such to thrive; it supports modes of social domination and scapegoating linked to income inequality, gender hierarchy, toil, imperialism, needless wars, racism, scapegoating, surplus guilt, and self-laceration by constituencies low on this or that hierarchy. As such it speaks to radical theories of positive freedom, even though it does not postulate one end state as the implicit end toward which freedom tends.

It is difficult, however, to transcend surplus repression because it is entangled with modes of repression that are essential to the good life and also because different ideas of it are tethered to contestable images of future possibility. Such debates run deep, for every interpretation of an order contains within it tacit assumptions about other positive alternatives that are possible. Hence the debate between Freud and Marcuse rests in part on their differences as to which alternatives are worthy of consideration. That question acquires new urgency during the era of the Anthropocene, when a whole series of classical ideals is called into question and new thinking seems to be required. I will set that issue mostly to the side right now, though, and speak to it in the last two chapters. The question I pursue now is this: Assuming you know what aspects of cultural repression are surplus, what other instinctive energies and purposes could be drawn upon to help overcome it?

Freud, on Marcuse's reading, justifies too much repression on the grounds that it is essential to *civilization as such*; today several law-and-order perspectives radically trump Freud on that score.

It may be, however, that the debate between these two is muddied to the extent that Marcuse fails to discuss closely *how* "instincts" themselves come into being. He does not think that all "secondary" instincts come into play through the "primary" instincts of Eros and Thanatos. Indeed he credits Freud with toying with the idea that there is a proto-instinctive life in operation below those two primary instincts.

Marcuse says, embracing Fenichel on this point, that the late Freud "made a decisive step in this direction by assuming a 'displaceable energy, which is in itself neutral, but is able to join forces either with an erotic or with a destructive impulse.'"[7] To emphasize this point, as Marcuse does, *is to locate considerable cultural plasticity in the consolidation of instincts*, depending upon the way the reality principle is defined for different constituencies within a social order. On the other hand, Marcuse does not say that much about just how nonrepressive instincts do or could emerge in order to help with the productive work needed. The question is critical to a philosophy of political activism as it negotiates the divide between those theories of radical exploitation that give oppressed constituencies few tools to draw on and identifications of positive modes of internalization that can be drawn on within those structures to challenge the order without threatening to repeat its dogmatism and authoritarianism in a new way. Interpretations that identify few or no spaces of positivity within regimes of repression threaten to be morally satisfying as schemes of accusation but ineffective as sites of positive political enactment.

To hone in on this question, let me ask again: What is an "instinct"? Bearing in mind the preliminary account of drives in the previous chapter—and the way the terms *instincts, drives, impulses,* and *dispositions* are interwoven—it is pertinent to set out several possibilities. One could claim that an instinct is biologically wired, socially encoded, or plastic, or some combination thereof; one could say that, once formed, it is either blind or purposive; one could say that it is formed primarily through repression, or through confrontation with a reality principle, or by other means as well; one could emphasize the entanglements of instincts with each other so that intersections and compromises between them play unconscious roles of importance in what emerges into action and consciousness, or one could emphasize the steadfastness of dominant instincts; one could say that instincts are closely bound to direct social processes of communication, or that the instinctual dimension lacks sociality once it has become ensconced; one could say that the most basic reality principles are generic to civilization as such, or that such principles vary significantly across civilizations.

As I read him, Marcuse emphasizes that instincts are socially encoded, purposive, and entangled in multilevel modes of social communication. They are also interactive with each other and with conscious ego demands. Above all, under current conditions, they are organized by necessary and surplus *repression* more than by any other means. They are potentially open to reorganization by radical social movements and the release of surplus repression. Late in the book he qualifies this last claim somewhat when he explores the necessity of engaging the realities of time and mortality.

How are purposive instincts formed? Marcuse's focus, again, is on modes of repression through which purposive tendencies are driven underground far enough to escape consciousness but close enough to make a difference to action. They then work destructively upon both conduct and consciousness from these entrenchments. Yes. But another mode of instinctual infusion and organization works alongside both necessary and surplus repression. Marcuse does not deny that, but he does not explore the issue either.

In his groundbreaking study of mirror neurons Giacomo Rizzolatti concentrates on how everyday practices of self-performance and subliminal reception of the actions of others *encode purposive tendencies into selves and social relations.* They enter into our moods, perceptions, culture, and relational skills as we observe and act with others.[8] If you are a tennis player, for instance, with developed tennis skills, you tend to simulate the actions of accomplished players when watching them play. You may even notice that sometimes your body anticipates and moves with the action. If you go out to play a game after watching—and simulating—a brilliant match you may even find that your performance now rises to a new level. That will be more noticeable, perhaps, if your opponent has not watched the same match.

Rizzolatti's work can fruitfully be read in relation to poetic attempts by Nietzsche, Walt Whitman, and Jane Bennett to activate embodied responses to nonhuman and human agencies that usually fall below the threshold of awareness. They seek to encode such receptive sensibilities more firmly into biocultural life. Bennett, for instance, reviews how the postures Whitman both studies and invokes through his poetry infiltrate moods, actions, and judgments. The postures are mediators between reception and mood.[9]

How, though, do these modes of collective incorporation work? Here is what Rizzolatti says: "The sight of acts performed by others produces an immediate activation of the motor areas deputed to the organization and execution of those acts . . . ; through this activation it is possible to decipher the meaning of the 'motor events' observed, to understand them in terms of goal centered movements. This understanding is completely devoid of any reflexive, conceptual or linguistic mediation, as it is based on the vocabulary of acts and the motor knowledge on which our capacity to act depends."[10] So this aspect of the instinctual life is culturally encoded into instinctive propensities; that encoding is not necessarily the result of either necessary or surplus repression. Does Rizzolatti underplay the role of layered memories, social relations, and conceptual elements involved in these modes of unconscious incorporation? Perhaps he does. At least I find convincing the modifications introduced by Victoria Pitts-Taylor when she emphasizes the roles of brain plasticity, layered memory, situated social life, and multilevels of social communication in the relations between mirror neuron activity and social sensibilities.[11]

It is helpful to see how encoding sometimes occurs below language, that is, how bodily responsiveness, distinctions, moods, and tendencies to judgment can emerge from our behavior and the observations of others that do not invoke the mediation of a syntactically rich language. Indeed if the former processes were never in play at all it would be difficult to understand how infants could acquire through social transactions the initial capacities from which the miracle of language unfolds. It would also be difficult to appreciate the rich complexity of nonhuman, animal behavior. But once the process is set into play it gets complicated by a series of other socially and conceptually mediated, affective memories and purposes.

Whether there are mirror neurons in human beings, and how they work to incorporate social experience into the collective instinctive life, is still being debated in neuroscience, though research based on them seems to be gathering a lot of steam. But the reason cultural thinkers as diverse as Spinoza, Whitman, Nietzsche, Proust, Merleau-Ponty, Deleuze, Whitehead, Malafouris, Massumi, and Bennett were primed to anticipate *some* such powers even before this research in neuroscience emerged is that the poetic experience of human receptivity to culture and nature they have tested in live experiments leads them to project some such mode of reception and self-organization. It is wise, then, to project some such socially mediated capacities into the sensorium, even if it turns out that the current theory of mirror neurons only imperfectly captures it. Rizzolatti helps us to grasp how such receptive, absorptive, and performative capacities work. If his exact formulations underplay the efficacy of poetic experience, they are flexible and open enough to work on.

Many of the collective processes under consideration now are unconscious and instinctive. Yet they are not organized by repression. What, then, prohibits them from being conscious? Perhaps several things are in play. First, they form the pivots of cultural perception, mood, thought, judgment, and action when the limited capacities of consciousness are focused elsewhere, attentive to that which depends in part upon these instincts. As when I, immersed in the depth experience of a beach setting that fades off into the sea, become entranced when a group of dolphins swims by. Here I do not attend to the contributions my internalized capacities make to the experience of depth. I focus instead on the depth experience of dolphins swimming in the sea. Second, some brain and bodily subsystems that receive and work on such infusions are themselves too simple, cloudy, or crude to be lifted into the refined zones of cognition without additional work being done on them. I immediately sense a strange shape on the ground in the woods. I jump or freeze before an explicit image becomes conscious. The amygdala system that initially responds to the vague image moves too fast to be sorted out within consciousness. The response that precedes conscious awareness is nonetheless not purely innate either. It has been encoded by past experience into that simple, fast-moving system. When aspects of the experience do become conscious they do not now emerge exactly as they were upon initial, cloudy contact. The disturbing shape is now more slowly translated into a snake that scares me or a stick that makes me embarrassed to have jumped. Third, the speed with which the initial processes work primes our moods and affective responses as these both operate below consciousness and are selectively lifted into slower, more refined modes of consciousness. As Rizzolatti says, our perceptions and tendencies of action would be "pale and colorless" and "destitute of emotional warmth" unless they were imbued with such a nest of culturally infused bodily tendencies, even if these very infusions flow into consciousness without themselves being clean objects of awareness. A more collective instance is in play when white working class males who already feel that they have been excluded from both the priorities of neoliberal capitalism and those of pluralizing social movements respond viscerally together to the body language, thinly veiled threats, and aggressions of Donald Trump at a campaign rally.

Such layered body-brain processes provide the platforms upon which fear and anxiety emerge; they also provide a "neural substrate" for possibilities of "empathic sharing."[12]

When we add these supplements to the Marcuse story we can speak of tacit instincts that are neither simply wired innately, nor formed by modes of necessary repression, nor the result of surplus repression. Among these non-repressive instincts are some that expand operational skills and some that may infuse joy, sympathy, and presumptive generosity into relational propensities. There are also those that tend to insulate us—perhaps innocently at first—from the unnecessary suffering of others. Which are which is the object of intense political debate.

With this story of how some culturally infused, purposive instincts are neither wired into innate human biology nor the effect of repression, we can now introduce a few axioms of practical wisdom into Marcuse's quest to overcome surplus repression. They may be already at work, at least tacitly, in his theory. First, it is important periodically to augment already formed modes of perception and judgment by broadening the inflow of experience, particularly into zones where marginalized populations reside. It is also important, during the Anthropocene, to augment perception of nonhuman beings in situations where the action dictates of daily life draw attention away.

Second, it is ethically and politically important to work by tactical means to increase the element of presumptive, instinctive generosity with which we enter into social engagements.

Third, to sustain or invigorate positive political energies it may be important to cultivate zones of joyful encounter amid the suffering we feel directly or encounter in others. At least Spinoza, Nietzsche, Deleuze, and James

Baldwin thought that such a pursuit was critical. Baldwin, who faced severe racism and accepted a tragic image of human possibility over a providential view, affirms the need to cultivate love of life as you organize oppositional movements. He says, "Most people guard and keep; they suppose that it is they themselves that they are guarding and keeping, whereas what they are actually guarding and keeping is their system of reality.... One can give nothing whatever without giving oneself—that is to say, risking oneself." Or again, "It is the responsibility of free men to trust and celebrate what is constant—birth, struggle and death are constant, and so is love though we may not always think so.... I speak of change not on the surface but in the depths—change in the sense of renewal."[13]

All three of these maxims are also crucial to cultivation of the "gift-giving virtue" in *Thus Spoke Zarathustra* and to pursuit of a "spiritualization of enmity" in *Twilight of Idols*.[14]

A fourth axiom, already at work in Marcuse's text, may now be stated more forcefully. In doing political work to challenge and overcome surplus repression in a culture it is important to draw simultaneously upon positive, culturally organized instincts already woven into daily life, if your daily experiences are fortunate enough to contain such elements. As we participate in a social movement we draw creatively on some parts of the instinctual life to counter and recast other aspects; we seek to intensify our sensitivity to the joys others feel and the modes of suffering they undergo. This is where the *arts of the self* in Nietzsche, discussed in chapter 2, touch the *collective politics* of freedom from domination pursued by Marcuse.

Some will say at this point that the pursuit of joy and presumptive generosity is not available to those facing the most severe oppression, that righteous anger is important at these points and that productive political activism can proceed without an element of existential joy within it. Yes, righteous anger and fury are essential to obstructive political engagements during the era of the Anthropocene, as we have already glimpsed and will soon pursue further in discussing the urgent need for cross-regional general strikes. But I doubt that dissident struggles are apt to avoid replicating some of the evils they resist unless such positive existential dimensions are folded into the movements as well. Think of leftists, for instance, whose accusatory attacks within the Left divide the movement as they catapult the accusers to prominence. Such activities insinuate an accusatory ethos and mode of dogmatism into the assemblage promoted. The key point to remember is that neoliberal economies solicit and collect *ressentiment* in order to displace it upon vulnerable constituencies. Challenges to them must strive to break that logic.[15] Not every constituency is in a position to fold an element of joy into dissident politics. That is why it is particularly important to do so if you are in such a position.

The productive task is to build upon zones of positive experience when it is possible to do so with close attention to the suffering of oppressed constituencies. *If* you participate in a relatively privileged social position—or even in one in which strains of joy punctuate the modes of subordination or oppression you experience—it now becomes a task to fold positive instincts into thought and action as you address issues of systemic injustice and suffering.

That task, as is already becoming clear, is complicated and fraught with ambiguities. For even horizontal processing is double-edged. Today, in countries like the United States, income inequality, gated communities, elite private schools and colleges, closed fraternities, racial profiling, isolated prisons and prison towns, enclosed resorts, first-class flights, segregated school districts, differentiated airport security lines, and innumerable other modes of separation promote horizontal processing that fosters innocence and denial about the consequences of class, race, and gender hierarchies. You might call this the innocence of confined sweetness. It can promote ugly effects.

These can be read as conscious and unconscious political strategies to confine and cordon off presumptive generosity and expansive social connections. Such horizontal, nonrepressive processing can thus spawn cultures of oppressive innocence and blind neglect.

Given such a double coding of the passive syntheses of social incorporation it is clear how processes of benign neglect become encoded into studied innocence. Here the task is to expose how the structures work without destroying the presumptive seeds of generosity within which the innocence is set. A delicate task. Perhaps these are occasions when the accusatory mode should be dampened (though not eliminated) so that an invitational mode of incitement can play a large role.

Foucault of course opposed "the repressive hypothesis" in the domain of sexuality by talking about the positive cultural organization of specific modes of sexuality.[16] Some of those modes subjugated people without repressing a biologically determined set of instincts already there. If we add the cultural organization of instinctive dispositions supported by Rizzolatti to Marcuse's armory of concepts we may in fact draw Marcuse and Foucault closer together. A fruitful line of inquiry may be to use Marcuse to augment Foucault and Foucault to augment Marcuse, drawing Rizzolatti into discussion with both.

The Scars of the Past

The question of how to draw on positive, horizontally formed instincts to surmount both surplus repression and the passive nihilism that haunts many during the Anthropocene will be pursued in the final two chapters, as we explore the politics of role experimentation and swarming. I need now to open up a preliminary line of inquiry.

In *Process and Reality* Whitehead speaks briefly of the "scars" left behind when one action is adopted out of two or more live potentialities. He is not talking about traumas that later become installed in the recesses of memory, periodically flooding into life without necessarily being recalled explicitly. A rape, a beating, a humiliation, the premature death of a loved one, a holocaust—these are not at the focal point of Whitehead's attention, though they surely deserved his attention. They are more fixed and traumatic than the scars on which he focuses.

He is addressing somewhat lighter moments in the past when a stream brimming with pluripotentiality flowed toward action, often proceeding too fast to cross the threshold of consciousness. A tacit selection is made from the micro-agencies at work. The open plurality that preceded the selection now simmers in the background of being, available to enter into future vibrations when a new situation arises.

A "scar," on his account, is a partially formed tendency that was not consolidated because another fork had in fact been forged and taken. *The fork not taken now subsists as a partially crystallized instinct or collective set of arrested, thought-imbued energies.* It may ripen in a new situation as it enters into new vibrations with that situation. Such scars *subsist* in life: they are too cloudy and underdetermined to exist. These patterns of subsistence teach us, Whitehead says, how "the actual cannot be reduced to mere matter of fact in divorce from the potential."[17]

Such a potential, not fully formed, simmers within a nest of purposive instincts of an individual or the multiple tendencies of a constituency. Whitehead in fact is suggesting that many instincts are inhabited by pluripotentialities on the way that have not made it into actuality because some others had been consolidated. How? Well, "a feeling bears on itself the scars of its birth; it retains the impress of what might have been but is not. It is for this reason that what an actual entity has [in the past] avoided as a datum for feeling may yet be an important part of its equipment."[18]

So loose instinctual residues from a past that never was periodically exert pressure on life. The scar left behind, however, bristles with uncertain potential. It may be activated under new circumstances, forging an uncanny relation with the new situation from which a new bout of creativity arises.

The intrarelational character of such an uncanny process is suggested by Proust. Marcel is speaking of his fraught relationship to Albertine, the young girl (or perhaps boy?) to whom he had been intensely attached. He invokes differential memories between him and Albertine and proceeds to more opaque scars that continue to do their work:

> I had often seen Albertine reproduce with perfect accuracy some remark which I made to her at one of our first meetings and which I had entirely forgotten. Of some other incident, lodged forever in my head like a pebble flung with force, she had no recollection. . . . For between us and other people there exists a barrier of contingencies, just as in my hours of reading in the garden at Combray I had realized that in all perception there exists a barrier as a result of which there is never absolute contact between reality and our intelligence.[19]

Sometimes the pebble takes the shape of an incipient process on the way from a past that never was. That incipience enters into reverberations with other elements. Occasionally something new is consolidated out of the co-searching process. A new idea, feeling, tactic, perception, desire, plan, or inspiration may bubble into being as if from nowhere.

Creativity thus forms an uncanny element of human relations. Creativity is a critical *element* because freedom would be flat or dead if it did not radiate with the potential to become something new; the process is *uncanny* because creativity is neither the simple result of a preformed intention nor the realization of a preordained principle waiting to be elaborated. Either of those conditions would kill creativity.

Perhaps we can now turn to Deleuze to explore further how the uncanny processes of creativity work and, more, to better appreciate how the nexus between creativity, freedom, and presumptive generosity is crucial to critical theory and collective action. Whitehead introduced such themes without really exploring the need to yoke them to dissident political action.

The Powers of the False

If creativity plays a critical role in human freedom, for both good and ill, it is pertinent to explore further its relation to agency and intentionality. One promising way is to engage Deleuze on the "powers of the false," importing what I take to be the congenial notions of teleodynamic activity and scars of the past into his thinking.[20]

The false is not, for Deleuze, simply an untrue proposition. It is the outside that pummels or presses into the inside. It seems to operate on more than one level of instigation. Let us call a *problematic* a loose complex of affect-imbued ideas in which each leans on the others and some enter to a degree into others. A cultural problematic is too loose to be a logical system; it houses too many inter-involved elements to be a mere heap or aggregate. Let's say that now the carriers of a problematic encounter a dramatic event that throws them into crisis.

Such a thing happened, for instance, during the Lisbon earthquake in 1755, as thousands were killed on All Saints Day in the triple whammy of a huge quake, a tsunami, and a citywide fire caused by the timbers in church roofs falling on candles lit to celebrate the occasion. Several well established and interrelated existential problematics were jolted. The event did not contradict each, for there were numerous ways to save each. Instead it jolted each out of its collective slumber. Let us note just a few shining lights, bearing in mind that each stood for a larger constellation of affect imbued judgments. John Wesley, the English Protestant, responded to the event by *intensifying* the Protesstant critique of the essential immorality of Lisbon and Catholicism. Both the city and the Church deserved the divine punishment they received, he said. Some Jesuit priests insisted that the punishment foretold the end of the world, which would arrive on the same day the following year. Lord Pombal, apparently attracted to a strand of the Enlightenment, responded by building the first earthquake-resistant housing in Europe and by torturing and hanging the leading Jesuit who warned of the Second Coming. Voltaire responded by writing a heartfelt poem denying the desert of the afflicted and then—after seeing that the poem was soon brushed off by many—by writing a biting satire entitled *Candide*, a story that satirizes the Enlightenment theme of "the best of all possible worlds" and several widespread Christian visions of divine voluntarism and punitiveness. I imagine that Pombal's vision of the Enlightenment would also have excited his ire.

Each of these guys (as well as the constituencies with whom they were in contact), were very probably haunted initially by a struggle among contending drives or collectively imbued instincts, some of which pointed to a punitive response and others in a more generous or beneficent direction. The very *intensity* of each eventual mode of response, once the internal struggles had been resolved, intimates this. It was, for instance, conceivable that a simmering sense of empathy for the victims could have risen in Wesley until he felt an overwhelming urge to interrogate previous doubts about the desert of divine punishment that were lurking in his sensorium below the reach of his official theology. That moment of possible incipience, however, was in fact resolved in another direction, leaving new scars behind. He saved his creed by intensifying accusations against the city and the Church after the destructive event that had shocked him and his devotion to his creed.

Still a new adventure of theological experimentation might have been triggered by these intersections between the event, his history, and multiple drives incited by it. Or it is possible that scars subsisting from that resolution and another new situation might support a new direction in the future. This is indeed how Bartolomé de las Casas had responded to roughly comparable events at an earlier time, eventually calling (unsuccessfully) upon Spain and the Catholic Church to reconsider the imperious conversion drive with which they and he had begun when they encountered, annihilated, and enslaved the "pagans" of the New World. Scars, disruptive events, creative interventions.

The Wesley turn not taken carries us to a subtle feature of "the false." If a collective drive or individual instinct is a section of the past contracted into a tendency toward potential action in the present, the false is the site of an incipience in the nest of drives that simmered in the past but never became consolidated. It has become a scar. *The false, on this register, is an incipient mode of affect-imbued thought that once festered as a cloudy, intense incipience on the way but was not actualized in action.* It is the cloudy fork that was not taken. It is thus an element in the past that never was, too pluripotential to be implicit and too intense to be erased. It is a potential turn not consolidated in clarity, action, or identity in the past because another mode of incipience did become consolidated.

The past that never was may fester again in an individual or constituency under new circumstances that express sufficient affinity to the previous fork to be activated again. A creative conjunction is now formed between "the false" and the new situation. The protraction of the collective present thus periodically draws creative sustenance from reverberations between a new event, an incipience that never was, and the consolidation of new actions or judgments in the present.

We have now stepped onto the edge of the continent charted by Deleuze in *Cinema II*. I am not saying that the incipience not pursued is the only thing that Deleuze means by "the powers of the false." But it does form one of its dimensions. So when he explores the flashback in film, he is particularly interested in the type that *pulls us back to a previous bifurcation point that could have turned in more than one direction*. We are drawn back to a moment when a subliminal searching process was in motion and one turn was taken. The potential not taken simmers as a scar from the past; it can be summoned at a later date to enter into conjunction with a new situation. This is the moment at which "the powers of the false" ruminate below collective attention.

A dynamic searching process is thus set into motion. Out of it something new may emerge, for good or ill. The crystalline image in film draws us toward such an uncanny process. In the "organic image" thought and action are bound together in a time that is linear and a space that is homogeneous. As when John Wayne knows what must be done and quickly screws up the courage to do it. Or Brigitte Bardot ties herself fanatically to a heroic male figure only to meet eventually the violent death waiting for her all along. Death was in the cards because she temporarily stepped out of the normative role assigned to her gender to save the male through heroic action. Because the action was needed and the norm had to be reinstated she must now meet the death already waiting for her. Two variations of the organic image lodged in the collective experience of audiences: John and Brigitte. Growing up I preferred the latter story type to the former, even though I then could never quite make out the necessity of those death scenes. Deleuze scrambles both versions of the organic image in his reading of the crystalline image: "The crystalline image is completely different: the actual is cut off from its motor linkages . . . and the virtual for its part, detaches itself from its actualizations, starts to be valid for itself. The two modes of existence are now combined in a circuit where the real and the imaginary, the actual and the virtual, chase after each other, exchange their roles and become indiscernible."[21]

Such a break in an organic image can occur in film when a sound image and a visual image enter into a relation of dissonance, as, to take a simple example, when the image of rising mushroom clouds in the last scene of *Dr. Strangelove* is conjoined to the lighthearted music with which the film ends. We now become suspended in the middle of an "irrational cut," a cut or dissonance between visual image and sound that disconnects us from action-oriented perception and judgment. Judgment now becomes suspended and thinking becomes exploratory. You may now—if you sink into the moment rather than angrily or derisively reacting to the experience of dissonance engendered by it—become something like a seer for a time.[22] You do not take charge of an action-oriented upshot already normatively inscribed in you. Rather you allow the shock to encourage subliminal communication between multiple drives that have now become activated and shaken by the event. Some drives, thrown into turmoil by the shock, are experienced as collective habits inadequate to themselves; others are activated as pluripotentialities that had previously been blunted.

A searching process is launched during the period of suspension; an incipient moment blocked from actualization in the past now enters into uncanny communication with a new situation. Perhaps, if not today, then after a strange night of dreaming, a new concept, tactic, desire, judgment, feeling, or pursuit will bubble up as if from nowhere. *The dream now functions as an instrument of reorganization more than an object of endless interpretation: it primes and foments creative activity.* In one case you may find yourself concluding that a new kind of satire is needed to awaken a populace to the way the shock of the Lisbon quake rattles a series of collective judgments, as Voltaire found himself doing after that heartfelt poem had failed to dislodge the series of preset, collective, and accusatory judgments brought to the shock of Lisbon. The powers of the false help to foment creative thought and action on some occasions, occasions in which thinking is neither entirely determined by antecedent events (the fork not taken never was) nor remains on the same track as before.

The false thus sets a condition of possibility for political participation in real creativity. The *powers* of the false set into play the possibility of challenging a moral image of eternal judgment with an image of situational judgments appropriate to a world composed of multiple interacting tiers of time. The period of the Anthropocene may make such an image of the false even more important to place into competition with other images than heretofore.

Belonging and Belief in a Punctuated World

The fraught relation between the powers of the false and the possibility of periodic creativity does not sit well with a phenomenological vision in which collective belonging to the world becomes more automatic as we delve more deeply into the layering of worldly experience. By "belonging" I mean the feeling of comfort that comes with the sense of layered fit between self and world and between collectivity and world. Such a mode of belonging fits best with an organic image of things.

That is why Deleuze appreciates Kierkegaard, the knight of faith in divinity that can never consolidate itself into a steady doctrine, almost as much as he does Nietzsche, the nontheist who affirms an ungoverned cosmos and *prizes* dangerous dissonances that unsettle belonging, open doors to creativity, and challenge us to intensify attachment to this world. The uncanny processes of creativity *interrupt* the presumption of organic belonging. If we live during a time when neoliberal capitalism impinges more radically than heretofore upon more nonhuman processes with powers of metamorphosis, such as climate, bacteria and viral flows, glacier circuits, ocean currents, soil processes of self-renewal, and bee patterns of survival and pollination, we also live during a time that threatens to break the fantasy of belonging to the world automatically. The implacable demand for such a mode of belonging conjoined to historical awareness that it is now lacking constitutes one source of those secular and religious fundamentalisms that now surge in and around us. As happened to Wesley at another time, an existential demand is shaken by events. One response is to reassert it with new intensity and punitive thrust. That is apt to unleash a destructive search for scapegoats.

Another response is to work on ourselves to value creativity and to appreciate dynamic processes of metamorphosis beyond the human estate with which we are entangled. You do so while also acknowledging that creativity cannot be fit into a vision of organic belonging. Nor do creativity and *sufficient* explanation, nor do creativity and unpunctuated narratives, nor do creativity and mastering a plastic world. Modesty about our place in the cosmos now includes awareness of how nonhuman force fields with powers of their own simultaneously impinge upon us and become infused into us. Those mitochondria in our cells were once independent microbes that became part of us. They now help to constitute us. Modesty about our place and appreciation of the conditions and contours of creativity go together in such an image.

When Deleuze talks about "restoring belief in this world" he is, I think, struggling to overcome both the drive to belong to a world assumed to be intrinsically equipped with a "system of judgment" and the counterfantasy of consummate mastery over the world. Both at once. Both fantasies are transduced into *belief in* a world replete with powers of metamorphosis and uncanny shocks that periodically jolt us from stupor. It is a bumpy world in process, with the pace of metamorphosis sometimes slow in this zone and fast in that one. The zones periodically intersect, creating new events. Some new events can be dangerous; some set conditions of possibility for human creativity. Both possibilities, often enough, arrive together. If in the crystalline image "the link between man and world is broken," then perhaps the quest for automatic connection "can only be replaced by *belief.*"[23] Belief here means both reflective belief anchored in refined thought about the character of this world and infusions that sink more deeply into the visceral (or "molecular") register of life.

When Deleuze criticizes "the system of judgment" in *Cinema II* he is *not* opposing every act of judgment. He is instead contending that a preset collective *system* of judgment is too crude and universal in character to foment the sensitivity and creative powers needed to respond to new situations with care and experimental courage in a world marked by multiple fields of temporality. Infuse elements of openness and hesitation into the comfort and crudity of the systematic, he contends, doing so not to become evil but to become more subtle and exploratory when shifting and surprising conditions arise.

The interruptions between thinking and narrative that Deleuze charts may help to explain why many attached to organic narrative are prepared to minimize the element of creativity in human freedom. Some reserve that capacity to a single God who is its sole agent; others appreciate human creativity but cordon it narrowly within a domain of "art" rather well insulated from the cultural issues of identity, ethics, inequality, diversity, and the politics of the Anthropocene; others love creativity but restrict its legitimate site to entrepreneurs acting within the putative rationality of an impersonal market; and of course yet others project a universe in which everything "in principle" is susceptible either to deterministic explanation or to a dialectic in which the implicit becomes more explicit. These are collective *systems* of judgment.

If, however, you embrace the bumpy relations between creativity, narrative dissonance, and uncanny processing it is wise to challenge the organic sense of belonging with another image. You now struggle to become linked to the joys and dangers of a dissonant world through the *artifice* of belief. That need becomes all the more acute when you can no longer readily treat nature as "the environment" upon which to act, nor as an organic whole to which we belong, nor as a deposit of resources predisposed to economic mastery.

The task now is to overcome existential resentment of the experiences of dissonance, partly because dissonance sets a condition of possibility for the modest element of creativity in which we participate. The task is to overcome hubristic modes of explanation, crude doctrines of human sovereignty, naïve philosophies of belonging, and settled *systems* of ethical judgment. For the dissonances of experience belie the reliability of all four of them.

Belief in this world does not mean that you *embrace* every event that occurs; you must resist some and fight fervently against others. It means that you strive to become *worthy of events* by affirming a world that is not predisposed to be our oyster. This, to me, is a juncture at which Deleuze, Whitehead, and Foucault meet, amid significant differences between them. Marcuse and Baldwin may meet them there too.

If you prize the gift and risk of creativity, if you conclude that this element is worth affirming despite the risks it brings, if you think freedom is flat or dead until an element of creativity breathes life into it, if you admit that we are often overmatched by nonhuman force fields, then you may seek to overcome the existential resentment often expressed today as concern over the "lack" of automatic belonging to nature, God, culture, or history. You may even become wary of the idea of definitive argument as a consummate power of human being. A speculative element now enters thinking; an affirmative element enters belief about the temporal conditions of human existence; and an experimental element infiltrates collective political activism. All three.

Incompleteness, the insufficiency of argument and explanation, and time out of joint now lose their standing as mere lacks or deficits. They become ambiguous conditions of risk and possibility. To affirm *belief* in this world is thus to come to terms *positively* with a world in which gaps, breaks, dissonances, events, dangers, and messy intersections unfold. Such an orientation is well suited to the advent of the Anthropocene, if you suspect that none of the historical options people have struggled over heretofore is entirely up to the task before us.

To respect the uncanny element of creativity is perhaps also to accept that you will not understand entirely how creativity works. To purport to understand the element of creativity completely is to show that you do not grasp the uncanny element in it.

Our capacities of periodic creativity carry dangers with them, particularly when attached to vengeful or narrow spiritualities. A new derivatives system, a new cluster bomb, the rapid spread of a new disease, a new climate pattern wreaking much of its slow violence outside the centers of extractive capitalism, or a new vengeful social movement: all can be creative. There are no existential guarantees here linking creativity and attachment to the world. Many in the academy sense this. Some who do, again, may seek to *quarantine* the creative process, reserving it to art alone, or to the will of God, or to impersonal markets, or to financial entrepreneurs. But creativity is difficult to quarantine. Moreover it must become widely distributed during the era of the Anthropocene. It is better to embrace it cautiously.

I have wandered a bit to place in conjunction several issues relevant to the interinvolved questions of freedom, creativity, danger, and collective belief in this world. Reflecting upon the abundance of life over subjectivity, the nest of drives and teleodynamism, pluripotential incipience, an ethos of cultivation, the scars of the past, the limits of explanation, belonging and narrative, the gift and dangers of creativity, cultural drives to quarantine creativity, the importance of tactics of the self and micropolitics, the powers of the false, the element of dissonance within thinking and being, the place of the event, and a shift toward forging belief in this world: to my mind all these dimensions need to be explored together as we try to rethink freedom, danger, and possibility.

Having previously noted some connections across difference among Foucault, Marcuse, and Whitehead, I close with a few quotes from Deleuze in *Cinema II*. They may indicate how the problematic pursued here makes contact with his enterprise too:

> Narration, whether explicitly or not, always refers to a system of judgment. Falsifying narrative frees itself from this system.

> Falsifying narration, by contrast (to progressive or continuous or dialectical narration), frees itself from this system; it shatters the system of judgment, because the powers of the false (not error or doubt) affects the investigator and the witness as much as the person presumed guilty.

> But the good is outpouring life, the kind that knows how to transform itself, to metamorphose itself, according to the forces it encounters.

> The power of the false is delicate, allowing itself to be recaptured by frogs and scorpions.

> Everything changes if in the perspective of becoming. What we can criticize in the forgers, as well as the truthful man, is their exaggerated trust for form: they have neither the sense nor the power of metamorphosis: they reveal an impoverishment of *élan vital*.[24]

One way to read—or to work upon—the connection between Marcuse and Deleuze is to say that the release of surplus repression pursued by the former to allow new diversities to proliferate flows into the pursuit of reciprocal relations of presumptive generosity by the latter to enable positive relations among minorities in a world without a majoritarian center. Together they allow us to glimpse the possibilities of a new pluralism as well, as will become more clear in chapters 4 and 6, the pursuit of relations of positive entanglements with other species heretofore disabled by the demands of humanist exceptionalism.

I do, then, draw sustenance from Deleuze on the powers of the false, creativity, belief in this world, and goodness as presumptive generosity. But I also contend that the cultural consolidation of rights, responsibilities, obligations, identities, justice, and the like are crucial *second-order formations*. As such they can be subjected to change in the light of new situations and sensitivities, as when, say, a new right of religious freedom, doctor-assisted suicide, or same-sex marriage emerges from multifaceted struggles and revisions from an old system of judgment. Or when, during the late stages of the Anthropocene, regional struggles secure new rights to relief from rising seas, extreme weather events, loss of habitat, and other slow violences wreaked by extractive capitalism upon urban areas within its centers and numerous regions outside them.

Some *solidifications* are indispensable, so that people can expect to be treated in this way rather than that, to be held responsible for that set of acts, to be exempt from specific accusations, and to pursue dictates of justice widely understood. But such stabilizations are typically more crude than the politics of situational sensitivity, so they must also be punctuated periodically by dissonance, responsiveness, and struggle. To embrace the ethical ambiguity of stabilization, destabilization, and restabilization *is* to believe in a world of becoming without a lot of eternal banisters. It is to fold presumptive generosity into the mix. I christen such a combination *reflective attachment* in the next chapter, after I have dug more deeply into nonhuman systems of self-organization.

This is not a species of relativism; it values sensitivity, existential gratitude, and presumptive generosity generically; it also seeks to surmount existential resentment and punitiveness wherever it finds them. It is, then, a double-edged mode of valuation appropriate to a world periodically punctuated by surprise and the uncanny powers of the false.[25]

One source of denialism with respect to the relation between capitalism and climate change is the sense that to acknowledge it as a powerful reality would be to accept radical shifts in established identities, faiths, corporate power, modes of consumption, rights, regional asymmetries, and class hierarchies. It would. That sense indeed constitutes a powerful source of denialism. These strategies of denial, concentrated in the United States more than anywhere else in the world, invite comparison to how several states and religious institutions responded to the shock of the Lisbon earthquake in 1755, struggling to save a system of beliefs and judgments jeopardized by the event through intensifications of belief.

I hope that this chapter lays a seedbed for chapter 5, when we consider specifically how role experiments, a politics of swarming, and cross-country general strikes enable us to respond to the urgent dangers and political delays marking the Anthropocene. Before we can pursue that task, however, we need to confront more closely a series of bumpy processes that both preceded the Anthropocene and now flow into it.

In the early 1950s a young geologist named Marie Tharp began to suspect that the ridge running along the floor of the Atlantic Ocean had a notch cutting right through its middle. Her advisor and mentor called the idea "girl talk" at first; later, with a reasonable minimum of mansplaining, he endorsed it. Tharp and Bruce Heezen eventually collaborated to push the theme of continental drift, a bad name for an important process that had also been pursued by others. The name is a misnomer because it turns out that rather than the continents drifting, the plates beneath the oceans are moving outward. They push against the continents, then, from the middle of that *rift* in the Mid-Atlantic Ridge, a ridge that had become clearly delineated by geologists only after World War I. The two collaborating scientists now saw that the whole Atlantic Ocean "must be pulling apart along the rift."[1] That would mean ocean basins as well as the continents are in motion. But how?

By at least the mid-1960s the revolutionary theory of plate tectonics was well established, though it is important to recall how late in the day it became widely accepted. It helped to make sense of the notch in the ridge, the movement of continents, and the apparent process of ocean expansions. "The plate tectonics hypothesis squared all these circles simultaneously by continuously producing ocean crust at the ridges, and then sliding it back into the mantle at the ocean trenches."[2]

These ocean plates in motion, slabs of crust about 100 kilometers thick, gradually separated the single continent of Pangaea into the series of continents we know today, separated by major oceans. There is some evidence that microbes help to grease the movement of these plates. But it is not only that the discovery of plate tectonics and continental drift has a rather recent history; the plates themselves have a history too. They were apparently organized about 3.2 billion years ago out of earlier silos through which some of the red-hot magma of the early period forced its way to the surface of the world. Though they move slowly—several centimeters a year—they do so in fits and starts. The processes of subduction—by which the expanding plates on the ocean floor expand out to grind against continental shelves that are lighter in density—move slowly, but they periodically generate earthquakes and volcanoes. The mountains of today were mostly formed by subduction processes. Bumpy temporalities. Well before the Anthropocene, or even the Holocene.[3]

We have seen huge earthquakes wreak havoc in Japan, Chile, and Haiti over the past couple of decades, erupting suddenly. One with the potential to be larger than any of these is in Cascadia, a subduction zone close to the states of Oregon and Washington where a plate of ocean crust and the continent rub slowly against each other. The friction and elasticity of the continental plate will give way at some point, probably creating the largest quake in the history of the United States, followed by a huge tsunami.[4] A large bump in the temporal flow.

Before the rise of the Anthropocene, climate, methane emissions, ocean currents, species evolution, seasonal shifts, glacier flows, and drought and flood patterns also went through long periods of reasonable stability punctuated by short bursts of significant change. There was, for instance, the Eemian interglacial period which began 130,000 years ago due to a shift in the wobble of the earth and lasted for 15000 years. The sea rose 20 to 30 feet because of ice melt from Greenland and Antarctica; it buried much of Florida and the warming climate brought hippos into the Rhine Valley. Closer to home, there was a sudden warming trend 14,500 years ago that caused sea levels to rise 65 feet over a 400-year period. That was followed by a very cold Younger Dryas period 12,800 years ago. The climate then shifted back to warm 11,500 years ago, during a transitional period that some speculate was as short as "three years."[5] The Holocene, the 10,000-year warming period up to the Anthropocene, got off to a stuttering start. It enabled agriculture and animal domestication, the former starting spontaneously in several regions of the world and the latter limited by the regional availability of animals that could be domesticated to, say, pull a plow.[6] After the Holocene was well under way there was an abrupt interruption by a cold period 8,200 years ago. It returned to a warm period in Europe and Africa 5,500 years ago as rapid aridification of the plush valleys in the Sahara and Mideast burst forth, perhaps spurring the biblical myth of the Garden of Eden, with its story of desertification as divine punishment of posterity for sinning by the first human inhabitants.

Between 800 and 1300 CE the Medieval Warming Period occurred. Its sources are still in doubt, though an unusual reduction in volcanic activity, increased solar activity, and possible intensification of the Gulf Stream are sometimes cited. According to Brian Fagan in *The Great Warming*, it had benign effects on harvests in Europe, at least until the Great Plague to which it made an indirect contribution. The severe droughts it created on the Eurasian steppes, combined with the use of horses in battle, the creative invention of the stirrup, and the strategic brilliance of Genghis Khan, enabled the nomadic conquest of much of Europe. Only the death of one of the khan's sons in Germany seemed to stop that advance. Its effects on human life in the far north of Canada may have been rather benign, as far-ranging Norse and Inuit traders profited from more open seas to exchange iron and ivory. The current territory of California was trapped in major droughts during this warming period that severely weakened Amerindian populations. The Mayan civilization, with its huge cities and complex organization of aqueducts flowing into mammoth caverns of water, was dissipated into dispersed localities during the Medieval Warming Period, perhaps due to the long droughts. But the people of Chimu in Peru, under even worse drought conditions, survived as a civilization because of a different mode of life: they "drew on centuries of experience with irrigation, social conservation, and water management. Their pragmatic strategies for survival were remarkably effective."[7] Others more recently have suggested that this warming period was more concentrated in Europe than in other areas of the world.

Between 1350 and 1850 a new "little Ice Age" descended on Europe. It was highly erratic and peaked in the 1690s. Did a reduction of solar activity, a new flurry of volcanoes, and the reduction of CO_2 emissions occasioned by the American Holocaust contribute to it? Its forcings and amplifiers are still under exploration, though a slowing of the Gulf Stream may have been involved. It was a highly erratic period concentrated mostly in Europe and the North Atlantic, with relatively normal winters oscillating with those of extreme cold. It seems that the northernmost Norse outposts were starved out during this period. The temperature declines did not sink to the extreme levels of the Younger Dryas period. One very cold winter, however, followed by a cold, dry summer in 1788, resulted in a grain crisis that spawned bread riots in France. The creativity of the French Revolution was supported by several conditions of possibility, and the erratic character of the little Ice Age was among them.[8]

Today there is some evidence that the planetary ocean conveyer system, in play for centuries, is slowing down again, and the West Antarctic glacier is collapsing irreversibly.[9]

The planet itself consists of a series of interacting, partially self-organizing systems that often intersect. They may remain stable for a while and then go through rapid changes. So be wary of accounts in the human sciences on the Right, Center, or Left that revolve around themes of sociocentrism. These might take the form of a social constructivism that focuses only on how different human cultures "constitute" nature, or a history driven by internal, structural forces, or cultural progress of mastery over nature, or a history of capitalism driven by internal contradictory pressures, or a view that reduces agency to (human) linguistic processes alone and ignores variable degrees of nonhuman agency, or a providential image of nature in the last instance, or even a recent view that capitalism generates the Anthropocene but that climate and other nonhuman processes did not go through volatile changes on their own before that. Some advocates emphasize cultural diversity and make invaluable contributions to our understanding of regional and racial exploitations. But if they treat nature as a steady context or environment, or a set of indefinitely available resources, or composed of stable patterns with only gradual change, or a set of organic balances in itself, or a standing reserve, they misread key aspects of the Anthropocene and numerous critical moments in planetary history before it.

I am not saying that humans did not make significant changes to their environment until, say, 1610. They did. There is now ample evidence that civilizations in Europe, Asia, Africa, and the Americas burned and razed forests for agricultural and other uses thousands of years ago, for instance.[10] The point rather is that the relative proportion of human influence on planetary processes, when there were only tens of millions of people on the planet, were significantly smaller, and planetary forcings and amplifiers periodically played a very large role. They continue to make major differences today.

When in 1783 the skies in Europe darkened for two years and weather systems were transformed, many, unaware of the huge volcanic eruption in Iceland, concluded that the world was coming to an end. Apparently Edvard Munch's *The Scream* was painted after he was shocked by the eerie glow that dominated the sky during a later Icelandic eruption. Munch said, "I was walking along the road with two friends—then the sun set—all at once the sky became bloody red. . . . I felt a great unending scream piercing through nature."[11] It took Ben Franklin, that crusty old naturalist and devotee of Parisian women, to figure out what had happened as he made a reluctant trip back to the States in 1783. His exploration challenged later drives to cultural internalism in literary theory and sociocentrism in the human sciences.

Panexperientialism and Emergentism

Elsewhere I have focused on the contributions neoliberal capitalism makes to the Anthropocene.[12] Another question is how to characterize the dynamism of the Anthropocene, the contributions nonhuman processes make to it, and the implications of its conjunctions with capitalism for our conceptions of human and nonhuman agency. To grapple with these questions may deepen our grasp of the dynamic relations among contemporary capitalism, climate, and a broader range of nonhuman processes. If you contest both deep ecology—which emphasizes the gradual self-maintaining character of nonhuman processes if and where the human footprint is light—and those versions of capitalism, scientism, and communism that treat nature as a deposit of resources for ready use, two overlapping and contending orientations come to mind. While both emphasize the periodic volatility of nonhuman systems, one treats the line between life and nonlife as fundamental and the other construes that line of demarcation as set in a larger series of differences of degree.

As we have seen, Terrence Deacon, in his thoughtful revisions of genocentric theories of species evolution, finds teleodynamic processes involved when species change is under way.[13] Lynn Margulis came to similar conclusions in her explorations of symbiogenesis. Species change incorporates microsearching processes at strategic periods when, say, symbiogenesis is under way or an embryo responds with microcreativity to interspecies breeding. The latter involves, as we saw earlier, micro-searching processes on the part of perturbed embryos that subside when a new plateau is reached or the embryo dies. This is not, on the Whiteheadian reading I seek to explore and revise, teleofinalism of the sort reasserted by Thomas Nagel.[14] It is *teleodynamism*.

But Deacon and Margulis are hesitant to push whispers of teleodynamism deeply into *inorganic* nature during phase transitions, for example into tectonic plate movements, ocean current transitions, climate pattern shifts, or water self-purifying processes. Such a hesitancy, which tempts me too, encourages Deacon to postulate chance "coupling processes" between nonliving forces to explain how life *could* have emerged from nonlife. He calls the transition from nonlife to life "emergence" and the living changes that occur after that "evolution." So he postulates a key bumpy transition, with intermediary molecular structures in between. He thinks that coupling processes that enabled the emergence of life can be projected plausibly into the long prehistory of life.

Other thinkers, such as Alicia Juarrero, Galen Strawson, and Steven Shaviro, identify a more extensive continuum here. Strawson offers reasons to doubt any philosophy of radical emergence, discussing how the commonly reviewed emergence of liquid from a mass of sliding molecules that are not wet individually fails to provide the needed analogy. It is the aggregation of molecules sliding over each other that does that job, not a shift in their collective character, as suggested by the thesis of radical emergence.[15] Similarly in reviewing the autocatalytic processes by which a nonbiological system evolves into a biological system Juarrero says, "A precursor of teleology is detectable in the way such structures of process operate. Whether embodied in physical, chemical, biological, psychological or social processes, homologous, irreversible dynamics appear to be at work in constructing nature's levels of organization. . . . A naturalized account of purposiveness such as I am attempting must identify other biotic and abiotic processes that are rudimentary, primitive–'proto' goal directed."[16]

Juarrero thus identifies proto-searching processes in some "nonliving" systems. Whitehead's process philosophy, replete with interfolded modes of ingression, prehension, concrescence, potentiality, and creativity, expresses a radical version of this view. He criticizes mind/body dualism more relentlessly than most of his predecessors and descendants. Indeed he doubts that the elements for a resolution of that problem will be in place until philosophers, scientists, and theologians supplement the "external" reading of nonhuman processes as blind matter with a perspective that locates differential degrees of feeling and internality in them. His speculative philosophy contends *that differential degrees of feeling, experience, and liveliness subsist well beyond humanity and other modes of organic life.* This thesis comes out dramatically in the following quotations from *Modes of Thought*:

> Process for its intelligibility involves the notion of a creative activity belonging to the very essence of each occasion. It is the process of eliciting into being factors in the universe which antecedently to that process exist only in the mode of unrealized potentialities. The process of self-creation is the transformation of the potential into the actual, and the fact of such transformation includes the immediacy of self-enjoyment.
>
> The points I would like to emphasize are, first, that this sharp division between mentality and nature has no ground in our fundamental

observation. Secondly, I conclude that we should conceive mental operations as among the factors which make up the constitution of nature. Thirdly, we should reject the notion of idle wheels in the process of nature. Every factor which emerges makes a difference. . . . Fourthly, that we now have the task of defining natural facts so as to understand how mental occurrences are operative in conditioning the operative course of nature.[17]

Whitehead's theme is reminiscent of an ancient, radical "perspectivism" that Eduardo Viveiros de Castro finds in Amerindian peoples who perceive variants of personhood and intentionality in nonhuman beings and forces:

"Multinaturalism" could be used to designate one of the most distinctive traits of Amerindian thought, which emerges upon its juxtaposition with modern, multicultural cosmologies: where the latter rest upon the mutual implication between the unicity of nature and the multiplicity of cultures . . . the Amerindian conception presupposes, on the contrary, a unity of mind and a diversity of bodies. All animals and cosmic constituents are intensively and virtually persons, because all of them, no matter which, can reveal themselves to transform into persons.

Personhood and perspectiveness—the capacity to occupy a point of view—is a question of degree, context and position. . . . Certain nonhumans actualize this potential more fully than others.

Thus if a subject is an insufficiently analyzed object in the modern naturalist world, the Amerindian epistemological convention allows the inverse principle, which is that an object is an insufficiently interpreted subject.[18]

The resonances between this account of Amerindian cosmology and the thought of Whitehead are intense, even though the Amerindians came to their understandings through close, lived experiences with nonhuman actors and Whitehead was jostled toward it by the event of quantum mechanics. Viveiros de Castro appreciates such comparisons, since he spends much of his book comparing Amerindian cosmologies to the work of Deleuze, a thinker both indebted to Whitehead and intrigued by non-Western, nomadic cosmologies.

Viveiros de Castro focuses on multispecies perspectives and the creative, often violent conjunctions they spawn. He says, "Two different species that are each necessarily human in their own eyes can never be simultaneously so in the eyes of others."[19] This is so, I suppose, because each needs some of the others for food and materials and because the very light on the world a perspective offers tends to make that of others opaque. Blood, Viveiros de Castro loves to repeat, is beer to the cougar. It is not that easy to occupy deeply another's perspective, though some aspects of it are already coded into relational experience. However, a shaman can go much further, and apparently we are all potentially shamans to some degree. That is, with the right kind of attentiveness and work, we can enhance our awareness of the relational intentionalities of different species.

The work of Viveiros de Castro invites comparison with a few postcolonial ecothinkers consulted in the final two chapters of this book. It also touches that of writers who move back and forth between multispecies perspectivism in Ghana and the thought of Nietzsche.[20] Such cross-cultural forays have faced criticism within anthropology for advancing a too radical focus on ontological anthropology. Critics say that such an approach too often ignores imperial intrusions into Amazonian life, that it reifies and purifies Amazonian ontologies, and that it downplays needed critiques of capitalism. Reading an article on this topic by Lucas Bressire and David Bone I was tempted to reply, "Yes, ontological purism can never suffice, but do you not yourselves fold an onto-cosmology into your studies of asymmetries between global corporations and localist life as you explore such violences? Could that basic perspective be rendered more reflexive in and through your fieldwork, even as you refuse to confine yourself to ontological questions?" The answer I was eventually given in the text comes remarkably close to embracing a perspective I have pursued in recent books and continue to do in this one: "This world is one of unstable and rotational temporalities, of epistemic and material ruptures, of categories and things unravelling and being reassembled. It is a world composed of potentialities but also contingencies, of becoming but also violence, wherein immanence is never innocent of itself."[21] So it is ontological purism the authors eventually resist, not its *inclusion* in the give-and-take of critical inquiries. I agree with that version of their theme. Advocates of perspectivism, however deeply it is projected into the world, need to connect the theme to specific engagements with, say, freedom, perspectivism in non-Western traditions, the fragility of things, planetary forces, the role of neoliberal capitalism, the asymmetrical regional effects of the Anthropocene, the recent relations between postcolonial studies and environmentalism, and interim strategies of political action.

Certainly much more could and should be explored about possible connections and differences between the "minor" tradition of Euro-American thought in which Nietzsche, Whitehead, and Deleuze participate and rich modes in play in several regions outside capitalist centers. Critical movements back and forth could open the door for further comparisons between the traditions of perspectivism and panexperientialism, as more of us face up to the powers of the Anthropocene. I will open that door a bit wider now to those comparisons by pursuing a strand of this discussion within a minor tradition of Western philosophy, the tradition that resists dominant nature/culture and nonlife/life divisions. I explore this literature with respect to the question of inorganic, partially self-organizing systems pertinent to the Anthropocene. The idea is to explore the vexed and controversial question of whether inorganic processes express degrees of feeling, striving, or experience and to think about processes highly pertinent to life during the Anthropocene. One of Viveiros de Castro's quotes above suggests that some Amazonian peoples extend experience to (what we usually call) the inorganic, but to my knowledge he does not pick up that issue again. Whitehead's panexperientialism does invoke such capacities. I myself am touched by uncertainty about the issue and a hesitant propensity to break with Whitehead on this score.

Standard Objections to Panexperientialism

Let us review briefly a few objections to panexperientialism, mostly coming from traditions inspired by human exceptionalism. The most common criticisms are that it attributes agency to things like rocks, that it acts as if simple things can have reasons for action, and that it is an assumption not needed to explain the behavior of either micro- or macroprocesses. The first two express misunderstandings of the philosophy. Thus David Ray Griffin, a follower of Whitehead, distinguishes between "aggregative individuals" and "compound individuals." Aggregative individuals, like rocks, are laden with quantum processes with the potential for micro-experience, but they do not have macrocapacities of intentionality, agency, creativity, and the like. Here you find micro-experientialism but not macro-panexperientialism. The quantum micro-indeterminacies are canceled out by the laws of large numbers.

The second type, compound individuals, have evolved so that their responses exceed the external pressures applied to them. Some examples do not conform neatly to the usual distinction between life and nonlife. Those who make this delineation are also apt to refuse the label *panpsychism* in favor of *panexperientialism* because the first term carries with it the suggestion of formed selves and modes of consciousness reaching deep into the world, and the second term projects traces of feeling, experience, and nonconscious searching capacities deeply into the world. These are not just set in micropro-cesses but, to varying degrees, in macroprocesses without strong centered selves. Self-organization, as a process wherein "self" means the absence of complete external determination rather than a centered, conscious self, is the idea here. Species evolution, ocean currents, and climate processes are candi-dates for these attributions.[22] What about plate tectonics?

The third critique of panexperientialism may carry us closer to the nub of the matter. Do we need to postulate at least traces of feeling and periodic searching capacity into all processes, so that during periods of criticality the result of reverberations exceeds the scope of deterministic explanation? The advantages attributed to panexperientialism are, first, that it draws us closer to solving the mind-body problem because it does not initially attribute total blindness and determinism to material processes and then struggle to explain how the body could interact with the mind. It thus does not have to deny freedom of the mind, or engage in implausible tricks to defend it, or treat the mind-body relation as a paradoxical mystery not open in principle to further clarification. It treats the mysteries that remain as potentially resolvable, or at least reducible.

Second, the thesis, if true, also offers promise of overcoming another dual-ism: the issue of how human beings with capacities of freedom, conscious-ness, and responsibility could have emerged from "blind processes" with no traces of such experience. Third, if a plausible case is made on its behalf it might reconfigure the modern disjunction between the traditions of the hard explanation of natural processes and the soft hermeneutics of cultural pro-cesses. It might, for instance, project critical periods of heightened agitation into both human and nonhuman processes.

I am not saying that I entirely buy the Whiteheadian reading. But it at-tracts me as a lure to test and work on, perhaps modifying it in order to save it. For example, one might agree with Whitehead that there are no "inert" facts since every entity carries processual tendencies, but one might hesitate to move from that finding to the conclusion that every entity embodies some degree of internality or feeling. Sure, tectonic plates convey resistance, and resistance is one element of agency. But it does not seem sufficient to ascribe agency to tectonic plates. More is needed. It is pertinent to observe that some quantum theorists concur that their methods enable them to offer only ex-ternal, probabilistic explanations of quantum phenomena, and a few project micro-experientialism into them during periods of perturbation. So perhaps that is the next place to turn.

Quantum and Experiential Processes

Perhaps what is needed is a *double process* by which scientists reflect on their analyses of nonhuman processes by asking themselves to what extent they can render intelligible human capacities of intentionality, freedom, meaning, and creativity joined to one in which practitioners of the human sciences explore how new work in biology, neuroscience, species evolution, quantum mechanics, and climate change affect their traditional renderings of human processes. To exemplify how one such attempt at just such a double process was put into play a few decades ago, consider the movement back and forth pursued by Arthur Eddington during the advent of quantum theory. (I argue the need to extend this into a three-way process of exchange in chapter 6.)

Eddington, an English astrophysicist writing in the 1920s, was one of a few astrophysicists who understood Einstein's theory soon after its publication. He was also a pacifist and a Quaker who resisted being drafted into World War I. Mechanistic physics, he said, is incapable of rendering intelligible our actual experience of human thinking, judgment, and creativity. Even the quantum theory of his day—more simplified than that of today—reports only "pointer readings"; it then tries to fit these patterns together through algorithms. Those readings, however, are consistent with an *internal take* on the phenomena in which you project traces of feeling and liveliness into elemental particles. In this way you move closer to a conception of the nonorganic activity as "not foreign to our view that the world-stuff behind the pointer readings is of a nature continuous with the mind."[23]

Eddington claims no entailment of panexperientialism, merely an enhancement of its plausibility. Here is how he defends the thesis further:

> But now we realize that science has nothing to say about the intrinsic character of the atom. Why not then attach to it something of a spiritual nature of which a prominent characteristic is *thought*. It seems rather silly to attach it to something of a so called "concrete" nature and then to wonder where the thought comes from. We have dismissed all preconception as to the background of our pointer readings. . . . But in one case—namely for the pointer readings of my own brain—I have an insight which is not limited to the evidence of the pointer readings. That insight shows that they are attached to a background of consciousness.[24]

Eddington was sympathetic to the inhibitions that stopped fellow quantum theorists from making this leap. The first inhibition is that it threatens to place science closer to popular religion, and many fear that such a proximity could overwhelm science in cultural life. There is ample reason, we see today, to take note of that fear. But is that reason grounded in experiment and plausible experiential insight, or does it reflect contingencies of the science-religion culture wars? Is it at least possible that some participants in both "cultures" could be informed and chastened by closer exchanges with the other?

The Kantian problematic, with its version of human exceptionalism and postulates of a pliable nature subject to the dictates of human understanding, still informs much of cultural theory. It also inhibits the to-and-fro movement envisaged by Eddington, even though Kant himself started to crack that perspective late in the day with his presentation of organisms capable of self-organization. But outside of that revision—one that cannot make a practical difference to the understanding, in his view—the Kantian story projects the idea that our "apodictic" experience of human thinking itself shows that scientists, to become consistent with their cultural performances, "must" postulate a strong view of the human agent and of nature as consisting of nonagentic objects of understanding.

Nonetheless, a weakened version of the Kantian test may still prove promising. The vicissitudes of experience are too porous and replete with cultural specificity to sanction a strong view of performative contradiction here. For instance, cultural readings of experience during the era of Enchantment or the Prose of the World invested the hand of God in each and every plant and thing. And Kant himself later insisted that we must postulate a noumenal self to make sense of human agency during the era of Newtonian science. And, as noted, he also opened the door a crack, late in the day, to a possible exploration of self-organizing processes in all modes of organic life.[25] Perhaps, then, it is wise to say that the fungible element of experience does make it implausible to support agency as either epiphenomenal or completely determined by modes of efficient causality. Beyond those alternatives there is room to keep thinking about the character of human agency. Can movement back and forth between the temporal vicissitudes of experience, the sciences of complexity, anthropological study, and philosophical speculation sustain conceptions of nonliving activity that are compatible with a viable image of human subjectivity?

A closely related inhibition for scientists, as Eddington saw, came from the claim that the external science of pointer readings provides a reliable method for checking itself through replication, while the insights of human experience can often be expressed in radically different ways. But long histories of dispute within the sciences suggest that these differences between the two domains are overstated. Even the reliability of tests available in each domain do not diverge as radically as suggested, since observations and test procedures in the natural sciences are theoretically imbued. Moreover several versions of contemporary neuroscience now *require* working back and forth between external experiments and experiential reports. Let alone eye and hearing exams.

A third inhibition, one emphasized by Eddington, is that the findings of scientific research sometimes change fast, so that scientists hesitate to extrapolate from a new plateau to larger issues while that plateau is being pursued. The third hesitation is significant. When Eddington wrote, for instance, the Newtonian world of causality had broken up rapidly and the inability to detect both the position and the velocity of quantum activity was under intense discussion. But the phenomenon of nonlocality had not yet been uncovered, and dark matter and dark energy were not on the agenda of discussion. My meager understanding of the latter two is that they were introduced as theoretical assumptions to save the classical theory of gravity after it was found that some movements of the galaxy were at odds with that theory. Does this mean that we should drop the issue under investigation here? No. For the question of how and whether assumptions in cultural life and cultural theory square with those in the natural sciences remains after these new theoretical assumptions have been introduced. The speed of changes in the natural sciences does not count against this exploration unless and until the gaps between the two modes of understanding are resolved.

Perhaps, however, the periodic speed of such changes does make it understandable that cultural theorists are sometimes wary of those who confidently transfer the implications of the latest scientific theory immediately to the dictates of cultural life. Sometimes it *is* wise to wait out the latest turn in science, on the grounds that its implications for cultural life are too much at odds with deeply rooted modes of experience. For instance, as we saw in an earlier chapter, the confident upshots for cultural life not so long ago projected by genocentric biologists are now giving way rapidly to dynamic theories of evolution that carry different implications for the understanding of human intentions and agency.

The main difficulty in Eddington's theory of quantum experience, it seems, is that he concentrates agency in nonhuman *microprocesses*. He did not explore how a variety of inorganic macroprocesses might or might not express variable degrees of agency themselves. To succeed, panexperientialism needs to find expression in both macro- and microprocesses and in both organic and inorganic processes. So let's examine a macro case that speaks both to the Anthropocene and to this issue.

The Ocean Conveyor System

The oceans were added to the earth a billion or so years after the planet was formed. They have histories. Moreover "it turns out that switching an ocean current on or off, or rerouting it, is geologically commonplace."[26]

The self-organized ocean conveyor system in operation today flows from the Gulf of Mexico to the north, where it diverges into two northern flows. Benjamin Franklin seems to have seen how the significant difference in temperature between surface and bottom waters suggested an underwater current. He christened the part of the system he studied "the Gulf Stream."

How does the ocean conveyor system work? A key transition occurs in the Arctic as a wind draws pure water into the atmosphere, leaving heavier, salty, cold water behind. The formation of ice carapaces in the region also leaves more salt behind in the water. The colder, saltier water then sinks to the ocean floor. "These descending masses of cold, salty water are today the powerhouses of the Earth's oceanic circulatory system."[27] The current then drives south on the ocean floor. When the currents again reach the Gulf area, after having been warmed in the South and brought to the surface because the water is now lighter, the northward flow warms the land to east and west in Europe and North America. A main current bumps into Greenland, where the water, now made heavier by gradual cooling and an increased saltiness due to losses through evaporation, again *drives downward*, reaching the sea bottom to start its slow return trip on the ocean floor to the south. This downward thrust of oxygenated water and the southern flow on the ocean bottom make life possible at lower ocean levels. The ocean conveyor is slow, extremely large, and powerful, carrying an amount of water several hundred times the volume of the Amazon River. Similar processes are at work in the Kuroshio current flowing into the Pacific.

The planetary circulation system collects massive amounts of carbon, as new waves of warm water heading north absorb atmospheric carbon at a faster rate than either cold water or reflective ice does.[28]

Wally Broeker and others have shown that the conveyor system closed down rapidly during the Younger Dryas era, 12,800 years ago. Within one generation or less the temperature dropped an average of 28 degrees in the Greenland and Arctic regions. The closure, according to one contested theory, was due to a rapid period of deglaciation that preceded it, when cold freshwater from the midwestern section of North America poured in huge amounts into the Greenland area, where the downward drive had previously occurred. The lighter, desalinized water, forming in the winter as a crust of ice over the ocean, now sank at a much slower rate, until the self-organizing momentum of the conveyor system was overwhelmed and it ground to a halt. The word *overwhelmed* is revealing here, since it suggests a trajectory with *self-momentum* that could absorb and resist counterpressures up to a point. It later took new, powerful triggers before the self-amplifying process of northern surface flow and ocean basin flow south became active again. The latter process was correlated with a warming period in the North Atlantic.

Broeker and others claim that the conveyor belt is now weakening again. The melting of the Greenland glaciers releases masses of cold, salt-free water into the northern Atlantic, and the current fails to push downward at the previous rate. This view was contested by other glaciologists and oceanographers until very recently, when new evidence was found of colder surface waters, called "the blob," in the Greenland area. Michael Mann, a leading climatologist and former skeptic that the ocean conveyor would slow or stop rapidly again, has now changed his thinking: "I was formerly skeptical about the notion that the 'ocean conveyor' circulation patterns could weaken abruptly in response to global warming. Yet this now appears to be underway."[29] If it were to close down, most contend that a rapid, extreme cooling period would settle into Europe and northeastern America, though climate warming would probably continue elsewhere. As the sun heated the now stagnating oceans without a conveyor in play, rapid reheating, increased acidification, and a drastic loss of deep water life would occur. Very recently researchers identified a previously unknown current they call the North Icelandic Jet.[30] It apparently remains uncertain just how it does and could affect processes already under review. Stay tuned.

Here is a somewhat less worried view about the North Atlantic situation advanced by Jan Zalasiewicz and Mark Williams before this most recent evidence:

> Could the system be brought to a halt again, to plunge northern Europe into another deep freeze, even as the rest of the world warms? Well, there are no more great masses of ice on the North American continent, but there is still a great ice cap on Greenland, and rivers flowing into the Arctic from Siberia. Lately, the Arctic ocean has begun to freshen

slightly as rivers have tended to flow more strongly and Greenland ice has begun to melt at its edges. For the time being this is not enough to disrupt global current patterns. It is a system to watch very closely, though, in coming decades.[31]

That perspective, again, was advanced before the most recent evidence reviewed above. And of course "watching very closely" does not suffice in this case. If and when a tipping point arrives and the conveyor system shuts down, it will be too late to do anything about it. What is needed, to be discussed in chapter 5, is radical ecological action now to reduce the flow of CO_2 into the atmosphere and oceans in order to discourage such a tipping point from occurring.

The ocean conveyor system is replete with processes of self-organization, circular intensifiers, dampeners, tipping points, and periods of rapid phase transition. Classical concepts of regularity and efficient causality are thus insufficient to it. Consider, for instance, how the actual rate of Arctic ice melting has consistently moved faster than computer models project. These models have, among other things, ignored the role of large waves in their calculus. As the melting ice enlarges the space of open seas during the Arctic summer, the combination of more open water and more intense winds produces larger waves than heretofore experienced. As Mark Harris, a geologist, has discovered, the larger waves hasten the rate of ice breakup on the shores, and the expansion of open water and wind enlarges the waves yet further. These feedback loops can in turn escalate into ever faster spirals.[32]

Or take how the rapid rivers that formed on the surface of melting Greenland glaciers speed the processes of melting faster than computer models expected. The flow along the top speeds up the melting and increases the absorption of heat from the sun; then the water dives down to the bottom through holes and gaps, creating a slippery surface between ice and ground that again speeds up the flow. The point is that once a series of such interacting processes is set into motion they tend to speed up each other, creating a cascade effect. Once a glacier melt starts, its own dynamisms speed up the melt, so that the eventual result greatly exceeds the triggering event. These rivers and spirals, pockmarking the glaciers, have to be studied in the ground, the ice, and the water to see what is happening. Then they can be fed as new data into the models.

So these planetary processes fit a model of self-organization replete with forcings and amplifiers that generate periodic tipping points. But do they also harbor simple modes of "vector feeling," aim, and satisfaction, as Whitehead and others might suggest? The question applies not to the organisms that inhabit them and make real differences but to the basic components of the systems themselves. If there are vector feelings, do they make any difference to the macroflow during periods of phase transition? Whitehead's claim, remember, is that creativity is always conditioned creativity, operating within shifting thresholds of constraint and possibility. But for creativity to be in play there must be some degree of vector feeling at critical junctures. And these feelings would make *some* difference to which emerging possibility was actualized during this or that tipping point. At the very least they would make a difference in the timing of a tipping point. A few scientists purport to find something like memory in water molecules, with the type of memory varying depending upon the recent history of the water flow. But this controversial theory is still denied by most who have tried to verify it through experimentation.

To state the issues so baldly is to reveal the extent to which the culturally trained instincts many of us have adopted are disrupted by an obdurate philosophy of *pan*experientialism. I count myself a troubled member of this group, attracted to the way panexperientialism promises to resolve the mind-body problem—no mean feat—and yet suspecting that internality and teleodynamism are *emergent* at some bumpy juncture. Perhaps Griffin would call the macroprocesses reviewed above "aggregative," to relieve the need to say that they contain experience. But if so, that would show that the reach of panexperientialism is neither as great as sometimes suggested nor as pertinent to the study of some of the planetary processes most important to our time.

Experience does reach much deeper into being and becoming than human exceptionalists have acknowledged. An experiment to amplify the vibrations of yeast when vodka is poured on it so that we can now *hear* the new intensities is highly suggestive. It suggests that the denial of internality to nonanimals embedded in much of Western philosophy and cultural sensibility reflects a limit in our unaided powers of perception more than a trait of the thing perceived. It also suggests that modes of internality and feeling in yeast shift with changes in its experience, shifting from expressions of quiescence to efforts to ward off discomfort—even though the yeast does not have a cortical system.[33] And the evidence that plants secrete poisons when they sense the vibrations of beetles that have not yet touched them is also highly suggestive. Moreover several nonhuman organisms display complex collective and purposive behavior, as crocodiles do when they signal each other below the level of human audibility and shorebirds do when they respond to the attack by a peregrine falcon by "suddenly taking flight and in a swirling mass designed to confuse" the falcon.[34] Only those who have had the subject/object division pounded into them as a *necessary* dogma of philosophy, science, or religion (or all three) would subtract the intuitive attribution of thought, purpose, and collectivity to the beings in these last examples.

Such findings do suggest that differential degrees of internality, striving and feeling sink very deeply into organic processes. It was only our crude perceptual powers that inhibited the awareness of such variations of feeling in the past. But, again, what about ocean currents? Or tectonic plates?

At this point it might be helpful to underline a tacit difference within philosophies of panexperientialism. Some versions focus more on micro-entities that harbor whispers of feeling, internality, and so on; Griffin, Strawson, and Eddington tend in this direction. Other versions call attention to periods of quiescence punctuated by moments of criticality at which interacting processes roll back and forth, engendering something new; Whitehead and Deleuze exemplify this tendency. Thus Whitehead says that the "parts" of an entity are so related that "their mutual aspects, each in the other, are peculiarly effective in modifying the pattern of either. This arises from the intimate relation of whole to part. Thus the body [entity] is a portion of the environment for the part, and the part is a portion of the environment for the body. This sensitiveness is so arranged that the part adjusts itself to preserve the stability of . . . the body." During periods of transition "the modification of the total pattern would transmit itself by means of a series of modifications of the descending parts, so that finally the modification of the cell changes its aspect in the molecule."[35] And, as he soon says, such transitions apply to nonliving processes studied by physicists as well as to species studied by biologists, though the degree of elemental "deformation" in each varies.

Given these considerations, is it now wise to drop the term *panexperientialism* in favor of a notion of *differential modes of temporal transition, each with its own degree of liveliness and real uncertainty*? The memory of an iron bar that has been bent is very different from that of a dog who has been beaten or a human who has suffered a trauma, even if there are some elements of affinity between them. The modes of liveliness at moments of criticality also differ across entities, so that the criticality of an ocean current, the avoidance behavior of yeast, the teleodynamism of a disturbed embryo, and the creative invention of new concepts by human beings take part in the same world. But emergence from one mode to another may involve a process of what I am calling bumpy temporality. Equally important, again, *within each mode of activity* there are times when volatility is heightened during criticality and periods closer to equilibrium, when activity is more condensed into habit or automatism. We humans experience such shifting thresholds when we fluctuate between periods of habitual behavior as we wash during the morning and more intense periods of sensitivity, thinking, and decision when an intellectual issue perplexes us, a paper excites us, a love affair is in the offing, a new film challenges an old perspective, or the results of a scientific experiment surprise us.

So I speculate that periods of volatility and sea change become operative in numerous systems but that the capacities of feeling and internality have *emerged* at some time rather than finding expression in all entities and processes. "All the way down" does not point only to a micro-macro difference but to variations among diverse processes such as tectonic plates, ocean currents, species evolution, embryonic searching, plant perception, collective animal behavior, and collective human pursuits. It may be unwise, however, to place such differentials on one line governed by a common measure. Perhaps modes of complexity in some domains are different from those on others, as when one species is capable of intense, variable olfactory experience and another exhibits complexities of visual experience. You could train me intensively, but I will never be able to sniff out cancer the way some dogs do.

To explore such intuitions further, again, would be to engage at least two lines of test: coming to terms with the understandings in biology, climatology, oceanography, and physics of the relevant processes and asking to what extent each mode of understanding is capable of rendering intelligible the emergence of human capacities such as consciousness, judgment, and creativity without reducing them to epiphenomena. Our friends in the natural sciences often forget the pertinence to them of the second question. But if their sciences fail to render the latter processes intelligible, then there are parts of nature they do not comprehend. To the extent that is so their accounts of other processes may be defective too.

What is needed, then, is investment in a double process by which we move back and forth between findings in a specific science and attention to the most reflective readings of human cultural experience. Such a double-entry approach resists the one-way route some scientists demand, by which they propose a scientific theory and we adjust cultural theory to fit their propositions. It also resists obdurate desires of those within the humanities who seek to seal themselves from the findings of natural science. The idea is that the earth and cultural sciences need each other, that the boundaries between them are better construed as porous membranes that flow in two directions than either floodgates flowing in one direction or iron walls of separation.[36] These explorations by Euro-American thinkers can also be complicated further by close comparisons to, say, Amazonian perspectivism and Tantric Buddhism.[37] A triple process, then, is needed, as I discuss further in chapter 6.

A To-and-Fro Movement

One strategy Whitehead deployed to support process philosophy with respect to nonhuman processes was to identify subterranean dimensions of human experience that complicate strong notions of conscious human agency as they also extend the space within which human thinking and agency occurs. The human, it turns out, is less "human" on some registers than the devotees of anthropocentrism imagine. Accordingly other aspects of nature may be more human on an extended notion of humanity. The more unique or exceptional you find humanity to be, the more difficulty you face in finding ways to render human agency, freedom, consciousness, and creativity compatible with either species evolution or the vitalities of a host of organisms. And to eliminate all traces of freedom from those organisms would make it very difficult, perhaps impossible, to delineate a credible vision of human freedom.

Thus Whitehead attends to the tacit awareness of body position and perspective that accompanies, informs, and limits human vision, smelling, touching, thinking, and deciding. He is sympathetic to exploration of how active agents in the human body, such as bacteria, viruses, electro-chemical-neuronal connections, and hormonal secretions, flow into perception, mood, and thinking, helping to organize them. He is even alert to how posture and facial expression fold back into mood and demeanor. He is thus open in principle to how diverse *ingressions* of external elements into the body (such as bacteria, viruses, stares, hits, caresses, rhythms, nourishment, carcinogens, sounds, smells, and colors) help to compose experience before it reaches the abstract level of further and conscious processing.

Such background elements do not squeeze out agency, as long as you comprehend them to be interacting micro-agents rather than merely blind determinants. Rather they *complicate* agency by amplifying the number and type of conscious and unconscious elements that compose it. They extend agency as they also confound hubristic theories of human exceptionalism.

Let's pursue this tack beyond the examples offered by Whitehead. Tools are more than tools since they are both used by the working agent and fold back into the subjective organization of the user. Thus when Braille is used its use increases brain activity in the occipital lobe usually reserved for visual processing. The thinking capacities of the subject are thus altered. There is also suggestive evidence that the processes by which prehistoric humans used flaking to fashion tools extended brain capacities in specific directions.[38] Tools, again, are both used and fold back into the subjective capacities of users. Another example is how musicians, after long practice, display increases in the volume and subtle wiring of the sensorimotor cortex, enabling them in turn to refine their performance skills to a yet higher level in a self-amplifying circle. Or consider how a brilliant patch of yellow agitates the nervous system, even before we identify it by the concept *yellow*, with the visceral charge flowing into the lived meaning of the term. Or take the movement back and forth between the complex fingering of guitarists, the increased volume and plasticity of a brain region promoted by it, and the resulting capacity of the musician to become yet more creative. A micro-amplification machine of fingers, musician, guitar, and improvisation.

Another discovery in neuroscience is how damage to the hippocampus limits the ability to lay down new recollections but does not seem to affect the ability to lay down new motor memories. And recent evidence that olfactory receptors are distributed on the skin and internal organs of human beings as well as in the nose increases vastly our awareness of the range of responsiveness both to the outside and to the complex internal bodily connections established by nonconscious, relational sensitivity.[39] The discovery suggests that human organs enter into tacit modes of communication with the outside world and with each other below the register of conscious recognition. These processes help to compose human agency and are perhaps susceptible to those tactics of the self that Nietzsche and Whitman pursue.

Whitehead, at any rate, was a philosopher of human agency as a complex assemblage of micro-agents culminating in consciousness, with these micro-agents extending through and beyond the brain; he pursued this adventure well before people such as Deleuze, Bennett, Haraway, Connolly, Malafouris, and Massumi followed suit.[40] The searchlight of consciousness into the workings of its own experience is weak, Whitehead says. It misses "millions upon millions of centres of life in each animal body."[41] The weakness of the searchlight is partly due to its limited powers and partly to the fact that the processes it shines its light upon are themselves often cloudy and opaque. They become crystallized as experience unfolds. So complex *processing* of micromodes of feeling, thinking, perception, desire, and judgment are in play well before they reach consciousness for further work. *Such an account seeks to illuminate various aspects of nonhuman nature through the exploration of affinities with subterranean features of human life. And the other way around.* As Whitehead put it, we need to "construe the world in terms of the bodily society and the bodily society in terms of the general functioning of the world."[42] The above examples exhibit some of the dependencies and entanglements from which the creed of entangled humanism will be crystallized in chapter 6 as a corrective to the doctrines of sociocentrism and human exceptionalism that have haunted Euro-American thought for too long and disrupted its capacities to enter into relations of dialogue and agonistic respect with other living traditions.

Such a reading also allows us to clear up a common confusion about the Whiteheadian (and Nietzschean and Deleuzian) readings of nonhuman elements that help to constitute human agency. Theorists in the Cartesian and Kantian traditions resist such interpellations—as well as the "invasion" of neuroscience into zones previously reserved to phenomenology. They fear that each new element discovered beyond the reach of human self-consciousness must operate as a *blind determinant* of thinking and judgment; to them the admission of such processes into *agency itself* would automatically curtail the space of that agency. But strong intentionalists and human exceptionalists rush to make such an assumption because *they inadvertently import their own deterministic readings of all nonhuman elements into every such process.* According to Whitehead and others consulted here, however, *these very processes enable and help to complicate human agency rather than simply acting as blind determinants that squeeze it out.* Better put, perhaps, some condition agency, others enter it, and still others thrive in a rich zone of indiscernibility between these two crude categories. Life is enriched by exploring such zones of indiscernibility that are too often blocked by a binary, static logic. Such a logic squeezes creativity and becoming out of engagements with the world.

So far I have expanded the reach of experience and agency into the nonhuman, dissented mildly from Whitehead's agenda to place experience and perspectivism in every nonhuman process (panexperientialism), embraced Whitehead's account of micro-agencies below consciousness that help to constitute human agency, and explored some subliminal activities and microagents that inflect modes of human agency. Do these lines of pursuit provide a springboard to explore a more recent development, the idea that human brain activity expresses some characteristics of quantum activity at play in other nonhuman processes?

Quantum Brain Processes?

In a stimulating chapter of *Reinventing the Sacred*, Stuart Kauffman presents a speculative case in favor of the human brain being a quantum system hooked into other systems. He claims that much of that theory is potentially testable. If this claim can be rendered plausible it might count as another, crucial step in reducing the apparent gap between moments of criticality in some inorganic processes and moments of criticality in human thinking and judgment. The point would not be to eliminate significant differences of degree between such processes, for otherwise phase transitions in brain processes and in ocean currents would be identical, but to advance the case for a series of dissonant continuities and bumpy temporalities to challenge the sense of a unique, radical emergence of one mode of being, life, from another that is totally different in kind: nonlife. Kauffman is, in effect, giving life to the Eddington project in a new way.

Many neurobiologists, Kauffman says, present a "classical" reading of brain processes, as found in theories of artificial intelligence, for instance. This commits proponents either to a kind of tacit dualism or to identify consciousness as an epiphenomenon reducible to other causes in principle. Rejecting both views while seeking a new naturalistic account of consciousness, Kauffman explores a third alternative.

"The idea that drives me" in thinking about brain processes, he says, "concerns the transition from the quantum world of merely persistent possibilities to the classical world of actual physical events."[43] Keeping in mind that the physicists' use of the following terms are the opposite of how cultural and political theorists often use them, a quantum process can move from the *coherence* of multiple tendencies on the way to a *decoherence* in which a single result unfolds. However, decoherence does not proceed according to classical mechanisms of causality. It "decoheres" into an idea, thought, concept, or feeling that emerges from "the 'fog' of propagating possibilities." The decoherence involves "the intersection of the quantum system with the environment."[44] That decoherence occurs is one thing; how it occurs remains something of a mystery to scientists even today.

After dealing with objections to the idea that a quantum brain would have to function at temperatures different from that of other quantum systems—apparently photosynthesis proceeds at the right temperature—Kauffman articulates his key speculative hypothesis: "The conscious mind is a persistently poised quantum coherent-decoherent system, forever propagating quantum coherent behavior, yet forever also decohering to classical behavior."[45] By "classical behavior" he means the specificity of a thought, decision, or perception.

Kauffman contends that classical issues of mind/body and the nonlife/life transition might be eased if this speculative theory turns out to be credible. I think they would be eased further if at least some of the processes of decoherence under way are also understood to involve *teleo-searching processes that help to resolve, say, incipient thought processes into specific ideas.* This would move the "external" theory of quantum process closer to the tacit experience of the creative element in thinking when some new idea, tactic, or sensibility bubbles up for review. A creative result is not something an agent consciously intends before enacting it, otherwise it would already be instantiated and lack the element of creativity. Creativity often emerges in an unexpected situation out of rhizomatic intersections between several teleo-searching, subperceptual drives below consciousness; or better, in a situation where several such orientations reverberate back and forth between participants. What comes from these vibrations back and forth is a result that is reducible neither to a prior intention nor to classical causality nor to chance alone. The intuition of creativity suggests the need to modify classic notions of the masterful agent and blind matter.

If that is true, quantum brain processes would now point in one direction toward some nonhuman quantum processes and in another to complex modes of human experience set in convoluted body-brain-culture relays, that is, in rhizomatic relays between entities and processes of different types. Such a finding may lend support to the idea of bumpy temporalities, in which traces of experience sink rather deeply into nonhuman processes and some aspects of nonhuman processes bump into the constitution of human capacities. Could it thus help us to further reconfigure the debate between radical emergence and panexperientialism?

In running with Kauffman on the quantum brain, I do not endorse positive affinities he may have to neoliberal economic theory. Those two lines of inquiry, while sometimes drawn together, can also move in very different directions, as we have already seen. Indeed an ecology appropriate to today is at its best when it attaches such a theory to care for the world and pursues a politics designed to break the stranglehold of neoliberalism.

Creativity, Extinction Events, and Attachment to the World

Colin McGinn, an analytic philosopher of mind, holds (with Kant) that when we act we must presuppose ourselves to be free agents capable of doing otherwise, but when we consult the authoritative findings of modern physics there is nothing we can do to vindicate that perspective from a scientific point of view. The "we," for him, is composed of humans who transcend radically the rest of nature because of our capacities of consciousness, language, and freedom. Whereas Kant sought to resolve this "antinomy" by recourse to the necessary postulate of a higher Intelligence beyond human understanding, McGinn calls himself a "mysterian." He holds two incompatible views and never expects the sharp contradiction between them to be resolved. They can't be resolved because the image of blind matter he attributes to contemporary physics is set in stone. You are a crackpot if you deny that image of science, and you are at odds with ineliminable assumptions lodged in your own experience if you deny the element of freedom in human life. He does not mention perspectivalism in some nonwestern cultures, but it seems clear that he thinks they reflect pre-Newtonian modes of thought that must be corrected. Mysterianism is the only viable response.

Confronting Strawson's version of panypsychism, McGinn calls it "complete balderdash," "Hippyish," and "stoned," while also disparaging the long hair Strawson sported as a graduate student.[46] Nice, tight arguments by the analytic philosopher. Since the mystery would indeed become more tractable if the "physical" side of the equation were modified, as Strawson seeks to do, one wonders how long the repetition of such dismissals has set the frame of the acceptable and the heretical in this sector of analytic philosophy.

My current thinking is to resist key elements of McGinn's mysterianism, since evidence in favor of searching capacities in both simple organisms and species evolution is credible and can help us respond to the mind-body problem in human life. I also contend that what counts as "liveliness" sinks deeper into the order of things than classical humanists and McGinn acknowledge. But how far? I am divided against myself on this question. Traces of experience may infect every process, at least sporadically, as Whitehead and Strawson say (in different ways), or some fields may periodically enter plateaus that express *volatility* but convey little or no traces of striving or *experience*. My thinking on this issue is poised in uncertainty.

Such a stance edges me a bit closer to McGinn along one dimension, making me admit an element of uncertainty as to whether experience "emerges" from processes that do not possess it or whether traces of experience find expression in all entities. My current intuition is to say that numerous transitions are in play, ranging from processes without feeling to those with significant feeling. I locate one key line of transition (a bumpy temporality) in a zone well beyond the master line McGinn draws between creatures with vertebrae and the rest of the world.

My perspectivism reaches through human cultures to a large variety of organic processes and beyond. But to date it does not extend to all large, inorganic processes. Some fall below that line. McGinn projects one mysterious line; others project panexperientialism. I project a series of bumpy temporalities that periodically cross over into each other in ways that continue to be mysterious. My approach suggests the need to extend our subjectivities into and toward other subjectivities that have heretofore been alien or opaque to many outside the Amazon and various practices of Hinduism and Buddhism. The latter traditions have much to teach us. The approach adopted here, however, also means that we may encounter processes that are opaque in principle because they do not contain elements of subjectivity. Tectonic plates provide an example. They may be explicable only from the outside because they do not have an inside. Since they move in small fits and starts until a conflagration occurs, even outside explanation is apt to encounter practical complexities of slow movement punctuated by transitions.

Exactly where the lines of differentiation noted above are located remains shrouded in uncertainty and obscurity to me. I concur with Whitehead that speculation is unlikely to be eliminated entirely from this endeavor, though the cutting edges of speculation will shift over time.

So now you would have some zones of periodic volatility (criticality) with little or no internality, zones of periodic criticality with variable modes of internality, and zones of complexity expressive of consciousness and reflexivity, along with bumpy intersections between them. Additionally human consciousness is now seen to be limited in its capacities of introspection, its capacities to discern nonhuman subjectivities, and its powers of reflexivity. These limits, in turn, can be stretched to some uncertain degree through techno-artistic experiments and micropolitics, with such practices working on lower, active modes of agency that flow into consciousness without being reportable by it. Some such tactics might be unconscious, as the flaking study by Malafouris suggests. Others might be mediated by consciousness, as when you prime your dream life before going to sleep or expose yourself to a spirituality that challenges affect-imbued beliefs installed deeply in you. I concur, again, that the notion of bumpy emergence expressed in the above formulations contains a speculative element; it might well undergo revision in the face of new experience, new scientific evidence, new techno-artistic experimentation, or more refined engagements with non-Western cultures that have been engaging these issues and questions for centuries.

To be clear, the reference to differing zones of complexity does not refer only to a macro-micro line, the kind of division some quantum theorists speak of when they identify volatility and indiscernibility in quantum particles that are canceled at the macro level. The bumpiness speaks also to different modes of internality within large processes: no internality projected onto tectonic plates, perhaps a minimal degree in an ocean current, a complex process of searching in an embryo, and modes of reflexivity in human life. Even this statement may mislead, since, as Viveiros de Castro too asserts, different *types* of awareness available to organisms of different sorts are not helpfully placed on a single continuum.

The mosquito may place itself at the center of things as it sees and smells you only as a warm source of blood; when you slap it you may sense that it has not given your perspectival powers a fair shake. Or take the comparison between a human and an octopus. Some octopi have small brains (or cortical nodes) in each of their eight arms; each seems to act with some degree of independence from the central brain; and yet they coordinate. Octopi squirt ink to confuse their prey; their skin is very light-sensitive; they are venomous; and they can squeeze into tiny crevices because the only hard part of their body is a small beak. They are more complex than other cephalopods in their line of development, but does it make sense to compare them and human beings on a single scale? The Voice from the Whirlwind missed something in omitting the octopus from its litany. Perhaps, then, it is better to adopt a more rhizomatic image of complexity today, adjusting each line and its offshoots to its own conditions of being and becoming—a human would not fare well in a coral reef even if it could breathe; its arms would be clumsy appendages—as you take into account the platforms from which that line has evolved.[47]

You can assert that one entity is more "complex" than another if the second required the first as a platform from which it could emerge. But to say that does not necessarily commit you either to a single line of complexity or to project a cosmic trend in which things express an inexorable tendency to move from lower to higher complexity. Indeed if you study the history and possible future of extinction events you may be moved to follow Nietzsche and Deleuze in dropping the presumption of a deep propensity in the world to ever growing complexity. Moreover, as already suggested, even to say X is more complex than Y in one way does not commit you to saying that it is more complex tout court. The capacity for sonar detection of some species may enable them to evolve new complexities that are simply not available to those stuck with human vision.

Back to the late modern Inquisitor, McGinn, who poses a compelling question: What difference would it make *if* the external accounts of natural processes were revised to project variable modes of experience into them? Well, it would sure help us cope with the mind-body problem. Doing so, it would also make what I call an ethos of cultivation more plausible to many dualists who have heretofore demanded a command model of morality because no other model was conceivable to them.[48] It might even give us hints, as we saw in chapter 3, about how to cultivate an admirable ethic of critical responsiveness to being.

Perhaps McGinn and I have both been too literal in posing the issue of what difference it could make to proceed beyond the image of blind nature. Perhaps I should both affirm belief that experience sinks far deeper into the biosphere than McGinn accepts (as I do) and periodically act *as if* additional forces such as tectonic plates, ocean currents, glacier flows, waves at the seashore, and so forth are also inhabited by some degree of feeling and purpose. This would not take the exact form of the *as if* postulates advanced by Kant. His were putatively necessary postulates, and the latter become a possibility you enact as if they were true to ascertain what difference such actions make to your sensibility. To act periodically as if these aspects of the world are implicated in experience may set us on a path to appreciate and care more deeply how closely we are entangled with them. Perhaps, indeed, such *as if* enactments can deepen commitment to this world and open doors to experiments that further modify future beliefs in this domain. As we proceed the zones of indiscernibility between those classical notions of life and nonlife may continue to grow. I am indebted to both Viveiros de Castro and Anand Pandian for these thoughts, though I hold neither responsible for them.[49]

The very articulation of such a possibility helps to foment creative experiments that may render it more or less persuasive. Unlike Strawson, I doubt that an argument of *entailment* is apt to succeed on this front. I agree with Whitehead that an element of *speculation and experimentation* is probably ineliminable on this issue, though its cutting edges may shift over time. An *as if* postulate folds into practices of speculation and experiment. The experiment showing how yeast feels both quiescence and pain supports Whitehead's claim that feeling flows much more deeply into the organic matrix than either dualists or classical materialists had assumed. Another experiment showing that certain beetles can mimic the smells and sounds of an ant colony, so the ants accept their invasion and even feed their larvae, moves in the same direction. The cutting edge of speculation now shifts, and the cutting edge of contestation between perspectives does too. Kauffman's speculations about quantum human body and brain processes could, if supported further, also help to locate human brain and nonorganic quantum processes on a larger field of bumpy transitions.

It is possible that such explorations back and forth can help us to *feel* differently about human relations to nonhuman processes and to the rest of the cosmos than the most famous Euro-American alternatives—dualism, exceptionalism, organic gradualism, and blind materialism—have encouraged to date. That is the issue I pursue in closing, reentering an inquiry encountered in the previous chapter before the issue of panexperientialism was placed actively on the agenda.

One objective of deep ecology was to draw us away from the theme of a nonhuman world without meaning toward one in which we become reattuned to organic self-balancing tendencies within nonhuman processes. The processes I have been exploring, however, do not quite work that way. Interruptions occur periodically, and the long- or short-term balances that do arrive—a climate pattern persisting, an ocean current stabilizing, a pattern of drought persisting, a glacier stabilizing, a rapid shift in species evolution becoming consolidated—are often precarious and not always congruent with the interests of human cultures closely bound to them. In a world composed of multiple, intersecting systems of becoming a new stabilization may sometimes disrupt human life, as we already saw in several examples of climate change reviewed at the onset of this chapter. Often the beneficent and adverse effects are distributed asymmetrically across regions, races, genders, economies, religions, and classes. Some partially self-organized periods of *destabilization and restabilization* could wreak havoc upon several regions, as when rapid, radical climate change occurs, or the ocean conveyor system stops, or bitter struggles between regions following climate-induced migrations lead to a holocaust. Such possibilities cut against classical ideals of organic belonging at the same time that they contest the vision that organic philosophies treat as their main opponent: the image of a dumb world with blind causalities that either reduces mind to classical causality or postulates a magical "anthropic exception" among humans. But these images are becoming more dubious by the day. Does process philosophy, as amended, deepen a call already percolating to extend attachments to this world without demanding recourse to the attractions of either blind gradualism or organic holism?

As I will review in chapter 6, both the nineteenth-century geologist Charles Lyell and the evolutionist Charles Darwin authoritatively postulated temporal gradualism with respect to species and geological changes. But such an assumption is very difficult to sustain today, with our awareness of several mass extinction events and periods of rapid change in climate. After each extinction event the next phase of evolution forked in a new direction, spawning rhizome-like patterns incompatible with the image of a linear, progressive evolutionary process culminating with European civilization at the top of the tree. And we are now participating in the "sixth extinction event."[50]

Such events, when considered in conjunction with the explorations of distributed modes of agency pursued here, jolt a series of competing and complementary traditions of Western sensibility. I am not saying that they render *impossible* any of the following: theophilosophies of a providential world, those of a world that tends regularly toward greater complexity, those of a world in which relations of tenderness between diverse entities eventually overcome other tendencies, those of blind gradualism in nature, or those of cosmic human entitlement and human exceptionalism. I do suggest, however, that closer awareness of a bumpy history of climate change and extinction events does jostle each such story. It may encourage more of us to build more volatility, liveliness, bumpiness, and degrees of uncertainty into our lived cosmologies.

Suppose you find yourself trending toward such a modified process perspective, replete with the uncertainties clinging to it. There thus remain existential issues to plumb. You might respond to awareness of such periodic interruptions with, say, severe disappointment or even radical nihilism—the latter disposition bumping out of the initial shock of disappointment in the mastery or organic image you had previously projected. Or you might become an absurdist in theology. Or you might develop an ontology of the lack, in which everyone must always project a fullness of attainment going forward and must always encounter loss when it fails. Or you might respond to the jolts by folding into life a deeper appreciation of how rare the planet earth is. You might appreciate the complexity of human life; identify with the impressive entanglements between regions, humans, animals, bacteria, chemicals, and things; care about how fragile things are; internalize a call to work on ourselves to augment threads of attachment to being as such. I embrace the last pursuit, but as a pluralist I also welcome into a critical pluralist assemblage those who are moved by the others. The task is to make the case for the response you embrace while keeping doors open to other orientations compatible with formation of a critical assemblage. I focus on the first task now and add the second to it in the next chapter.

A process cosmology of differential, intersecting tiers of bumpy temporality replete with a medley of nonhuman subjectivities is thus compatible with more than one mode of existential response. As Euro-Americans work on each other to overcome the disappointments accompanying the loss of heretofore hegemonic Euro-American orientations, is it possible to deepen appreciation of the attractions and sweetness of life on this rare planet? Who will be the priests, rabbis, poets, visionaries, singers, philosophers, activists, and preachers who help us to do that work?

Today, perhaps, more constituencies are prepared to challenge the imperative to mastery that infuses capitalist institutions and the desire to belong to an organic world that has functioned as chief adversary and twin of that demand. During the era of the Anthropocene new generations in several places are forging *reflective attachments* to a broad range of people, nonhuman beings, and planetary forces with whom they are entangled. Appreciation of diverse entanglements challenges visions of both detached mastery and organic belonging. Attached entanglement, better, transfigures the sense of primordial belonging rather than rejecting it out of hand. It involves both *extending* appreciation of entanglements and *speculating* upon the cosmic upshot of these imbrications. To deepen and extend a spirituality of attachment is to respect nonhuman beings and forces with which diverse cultures are imbricated without insisting that all of them must be predisposed to our welfare in the first or last instance. The quest to reconfigure spiritual attachments is, I think, a major motive force behind the surge of interest in philosophies of panexperientialism today, as it opens avenues of exploratory communication between humanists and scientists with traditions of perspectivism outside the old centers of capitalism.

Such explorations could make a critical difference to politics during the current era. The goal is to counter cultural orientations oscillating wildly between the stances of mastery, studied indifference, disappointment, and aggressive nihilism with an ethos of reflective attachment to a world that is rich in diverse meanings and purposes. Such an ethos is difficult to forge if you are suffering intensely under the yoke of poverty, prison, racism, exploitation, imperialism, ill health, or old age, though there are noble examples of precisely such occurrences.[51] The task, however, becomes an acute responsibility for those who have so far escaped the most extreme deprivations. An ethos of attachment linked to furious modes of transregional ecopolitics. Such a counterethos, as it is forged, becomes infused into experiences of identity, self-interest, awareness of regional asymmetries, notions of responsibility to nonhuman species, orientations to the uncertainty of the future, attempts to challenge the hegemony of neoliberal capitalism, and cross-regional organizations.

Again the contending senses of *belonging* to an organic world, being *detached masters* of a blind world, or sinking into *passive or aggressive nihilism* in an empty, meaningless world may now devolve toward pursuit of reflective attachments to a multifarious, entangled, dangerous world, a world in which disparate modes of feeling, meaning, and purpose are connected through bumpy continuities, the investigation of which dramatizes numerous worldly entanglements, the identifications of which require radical challenges to predatory, extractive capitalism, the multifariousness of which includes nonhuman agencies, the exploration of which may deepen appreciation of the nonhuman aspects of human being, the being of which sets conditions of possibility for the modest bouts of creativity we prize, and the differential fragility of which calls us to reconstitute technocapitalist orientations to being, becoming, and politics.

By moving through and beyond complementary images of human exceptionalism, geogradualism, organic belonging, sociocentrism, uber-human intentionalism, and a blind world subject to human mastery we encounter an alternative more consonant with the still surprising event of the Anthropocene. If affirmations of this world find expression in what I call *the politics of swarming*, several constituencies may plumb affinities of spirituality that range across regions, creeds, and social circumstance. The *creedal differences* now become objects of debate and reflection, while the *spiritual affinities* feed enlarged assemblages of action. An accumulation of political protests across fronts and regions could culminate in cross-regional general strikes to target states, corporations, churches, media, university trustees, neoliberal ideology, the ethos of human exceptionalism, investment priorities, and established infrastructures of consumption that together resist, defer, obscure, or delay affirmative responses to the current planetary condition. It may be timely now to explore such an improbable necessity.

CHAPTER 5 THE POLITICS OF SWARMING
AND THE GENERAL STRIKE

So we challenge practices of neoliberal capitalism, gradualism in geology, neo-Darwinian versions of species evolution, conceptions of freedom locked into markets, strong intentionalism, sociocentrism, agency confined to human beings, and assumptions of a world either predisposed to human mastery or organically disposed to us. So what? What has all this to do with organizing to resist and overturn an extractionist capitalist history that haunts the world, if very asymmetrically, across world regions, races, and classes? My sense is that a variety of forces is converging creatively today toward distinctive images of activism, ecology, and freedom. None of those images is brand new, as we shall see.

But an extended "we" may be in the works, a "we" creatively composed of diverse constituencies set in a variety of world regions, faiths, classes, and other subject positions. Each invites others to enter into a loose assemblage as it also retains a distinctive sense of time, place, belonging, suffering, and possibility. A "we" that is a complex assemblage of dispersed constituencies rather than reducible to a class, a nation to be, a shared religious creed, or a world government in the making. A "we" in which many participants see through the histories of extractive capitalism, attend to differential modes of suffering promoted by it, pursue attachments to this world, and do these without projecting a future promise that is too smooth or untrammeled. Those who come to terms with a cosmos composed of multiple force fields entangled with human beings without being strongly predisposed to their mastery are apt to be skeptical about old capitalist, communist, and nationalist ideologies. Each gives off a hollow ring today.

When people speak about a future replete with volatilities, as I have done in the previous paragraph, it often sets a prelude for realism and acceptance of things: accept the capitalist world of production, investment, commodities, and oppressions in its awesome power while adjusting it mildly, or accept a world of states in military competition while striving to modulate its violences, or accept the human condition as made up of self-centered individualists whose activities are coordinated through markets, and so on. And yet many things work against such acceptances today. Today we—the "we" is, again, invitational—often recognize that the planet itself consists of a series of interacting, partially self-organizing, open systems that periodically go through rapid changes on their own. Often a dramatic change in one mobile system, say, that huge extinction event 250 million years ago that wiped out 90 percent of life, triggers new modes of self-organization in other modes of being, altering the pace and direction of species evolution.

Disruptions across heterogeneous systems sometimes turn out to be beneficial to specific human constituencies. At other times they are destructive to our habitat, as have been the recent leaps from tobacco viruses to soy viruses to bee infestation to a decline in pollination of crops. So laugh off Fox News and the Koch brothers, who tell you that climate and other force fields have often changed on their own and then imply either that nature is a benign source for us of natural resources and absorption of human waste or that natural changes mean that it is too late to do anything about climate. They are right that there have been such bumpy changes, but that increases rather than decreases the oppressions and dangers generated today by fossil fuel regimes.

One of the critical facts of our time is the acceleration of climate change amid growing awareness of human entanglements with multiple beings and forces with diverse lives and tendencies. Today it is wise to scale back utopian images of human perfection while simultaneously upping the ante of militancy against extractive capitalism and the world order it promulgates. We belong to a bumpy planetary condition, even a cosmos, that infiltrates us as it also impinges upon us in multiple ways, that is not predisposed to a future of human perfection, that calls us to accentuate militancy of several types, and that is worthy of attachment. Advanced capitalist states have made the greatest human contributions to contemporary climate change, and the effects of those changes are distributed very unevenly across the globe and within hegemonic regions. Both dimensions must be kept in mind when the question of counterstrategies is addressed.

The Politics of Swarming

Today those in the old capitalist states often face a dilemma of electoral politics. This is most dramatically operative in the United States, but it also applies elsewhere to varying degrees and in different combinations.[1] (1) The logic of the media-electoral-corporate-neoliberal-evangelical-racialized-filibustering-gerrymandering complex makes it extremely difficult to address a broad time horizon in politics, to express cultural attachment to the earth, or to address the Anthropocene within the grid of intelligibility electoral politics makes possible. The scandal focus of the media, the ability of corporations to take unilateral market initiatives and protect them by exercising veto power within the state, court decisions that allow unlimited and anonymous use of corporate money in campaigns, state gerrymandering of seats and the use of filibusters, concerted actions to make it more difficult for minorities to vote, the relative isolation of racialized urban areas, the strategic role in elections of the undecided who are often the least informed—all of these work to make electoral politics dysfunctional. I hope you are not surprised by that statement.

But (2) to forgo electoral politics on the issues of ecology would be to cede even more power to the radical Right. In the United States, at least, it would add yet another institution the Right can deploy to enact and enforce an extreme agenda. In an era replete with neofascist potential we thus must both participate in electoral politics and break the political grid of intelligibility it secretes.

The dilemma of electoral politics in the States helps to render invisible to its citizens environmental destruction that hits indigenous peoples and racialized urban centers hard. Indeed the dilemma is attached to a larger world assemblage that renders invisible or unimportant the slow violence of environmental degradation plaguing poor people on the Arabian peninsula, island states, farms in the American Midwest, indigenous Amerindians, microminorities in Africa, poor farmers in Japan, and indigenous populations in Australia, as a worldwide corporate-extractive-state complex attacks vulnerable territories. The extractionist assemblage imposes dislocations and suffering on those who cannot easily publicize widely what is happening to them as they suffer the effects of corporate invasions in long slow time. Cancer from the earthquake, tsunami, and nuclear disaster in Japan, the displacement and killing of Ogoni in Nigeria, the decimation of the Bedouin in Arabia, the cancer outbreaks after the Union Carbide disaster in India, racialized neglect of urban areas before and after Hurricane Katrina, the campaign by the Vedanta bauxite-mining corporation to take over indigenous territory in India, the slow sinking of Nauru and other Pacific islands, the timber projects that take away habitat and create flooding in the mountains of Indonesia, the role of drought in propelling the Syrian civil war and poverty in the sub-Sahara, the effects of fracking on several areas in Canada and the United States—these merely exemplify the casualties of slow violence that have been charted so well by Rob Nixon.[2] China is choking on slow violence as movements of protest are mobilized even despite the great danger in doing so.

First a corporation moves into a zone outside the centers of capital with its vast public relations machinery and glowing promises of affluence for all. Then there is population displacement and impoverishment that often falls below the radar of the neoliberal press. Then an "incident" occurs that may receive attention before it fades away as the populace faces long-term displacement, impoverishment, and health issues. Slow violence is systemically imposed violence, out of sight of the most influential media. Brief flashes of attention given to it are soon buried under the latest scandal, new war, terrorist attack, economic crisis, electoral campaign, or other shocking event. Slow violence draws its power from persistent, predatory corporations aligned with corrupt state regimes acting on weakened, dispersed populations. It sometimes operates outside the categories of legitimate crisis accepted by popular environmental groups. And fast, blatant violence is at work too in the rapid dislocations people face when a war to protect oil sources decimates a whole area, or a new conglomerate rolls into a town or locality. The toxic effects and traumas of those wars, in turn, manufacture slow violence for decades or longer. Check out Iraq.

How to negotiate such issues in an era when the situation is urgent, progress is slow, and several democratic states face their own dilemmas of electoral politics? One clue may be provided by honeybees when they search for a new hive site appropriate for 10,000 or more bees. The hive is neither ruled by a queen nor herd-like in its search. As Thomas Seeley shows in *Honeybee Democracy,* a few hundred female scouts check out possible sites; each returns to give a complex dance showing the location and attractiveness of its site; the dances are augmented by pheromonal secretions that activate bee energies; other scouts check out the attractive sites; gradually a quorum builds up through the give-and-take among multiple site assessments; and finally the assemblage gathers to fly to the new site. Seeley construes the beehive on the model of the human brain, another decision-making assemblage without a central coordinator.[3]

Perhaps in the contemporary situation too a politics of swarming provides the most promising pursuit out of a bad lot. You multiply sites and scales of political action through swarming movements, moving back and forth between creative role experimentations in churches, worksites, consumption localities, investment, universities, research, teaching; you organize worker collectives and university enclaves where possible; you participate in new social movements, some of which are inspired and informed by earlier scouting activities; you return to electoral engagements once the movements have crystallized; and you accumulate these disparate energies and creative insights until a citizen movement becomes possible across world regions. Not all scouts engage in all these things all the time—just as no honeybee visits all possible hive sites—but resonances between them nonetheless begin to crystallize. The politics of swarming, then, is composed of multiple constituencies, regions, levels, processes of communication, and modes of action, each carrying some potential to augment and intensify the others with which it becomes associated. I will start in the area I know best and work out from there. Since the United States has long been a top offender, that may not be too bad a starting place.

Take role experimentations that stretch out creatively to other connections and movements as they also work on the visceral register of cultural life. Such practices operate between individual behavior and collective assemblages as they activate role shifts within institutional settings. Foucault inaugurated a series of thoughts and experimental actions in this domain with his exploration of the "specific intellectual." The specific intellectual is not a philosopher who advances a universal image of truth and presents it to a waiting state or populace. The specific intellectual is one whose technical skills and specific capacities form a niche that have become strategic during this era. The specific intellectual secedes from a quest for universal acclaim to incite attention to hidden violences and injuries and to excite modes of response to them. You may be a physicist during an era of nuclear peril or the meltdown of a nuclear facility, or a prison official during a prison strike, or an African American anthropologist during an urban crisis between the police and urban youth in the States, or a psychiatrist during a time of gay protest against the medicalization of sexuality, or a political theory professor during a strike of nonacademic employees, or a gay worker in a corporation that is reviewing its benefit policies.[4] The task of specific intellectuals is to draw upon their specific expertise, citizenship capacities, and strategic location during a key period to call into question ingrained responses to that occasion. Specific intellectuals seek ways to reconsider the habits that have governed them as they also use their expertise and strategic position to call into question rules of normalization governing prison life, sexuality, psychiatric illness, nuclear stalemate, family life, extractionist practices, or racial definitions.

Specific intellectuals are scouts who periodically find themselves pressed—by their location in a bureaucracy, the protests they encounter, their skills as writer-activists, or cracks in the logic of the sciences in which they participate. The situation and niche encourage them to become activists on behalf of a cause that is crystallizing. Antinuclear activism, the reconstitution of sexual norms, the revamping of gender practices, prison reform, challenges to the death penalty, the rebirth of racialized urban zones—all of these can and have been mobilized, propelled, or augmented by specific intellectuals who work on themselves as they also help to mobilize a larger populace and to represent the situation to the media.

A series of territorially dispersed writer-activists such as Rachel Carson, Wangari Maathai, Ken Saro-Wiwa, Arundhati Roy, Indra Sinha, Anna Tsing, Naomi Klein, and Bhrigu Singh creatively dramatize eco-events of slow violence outside the old capitalist centers that are too often shielded from people living in the areas in which predatory corporations thrive.[5] Such activists support the spread of specific intellectuals well beyond zones Foucault had in mind.

The movement back and forth between these types and larger constituencies can become bracing. Such to-and-fro movements change specific intellectuals as they also help to mobilize larger, heretofore dispersed publics. Foucault anticipates some of this: "A new mode of the 'connection between theory and practice' has been established. Intellectuals have got used to working, not in the modality of the 'universal,' the 'exemplary,' 'the just and true for all' but within specific sectors, at the precise points where their own conditions of life or work situate them (housing, the hospital, the asylum, the laboratory, the university, family and sexual relations)."[6]

The point today is that the Anthropocene broadens and extends the ways that people in multiple subject positions can operate, not only as specific intellectuals but more generally as *specific citizens* drawing upon subjugated knowledges and strategic locations to work on the institutions in which they are set and the habits governing those institutions. If you are a student in the inner city, you might join protests to relieve urban blight, rework the infrastructure, and bring jobs to your neighborhood. If religious, you might bring new visitors, issues, and themes to your church, mosque, or temple. If a scientist or writer in India, Bangladesh, Tuvalu, Miami, or Brazil, you might publicize actively the effects the Anthropocene has on your area because of the CO_2 deposits left first by Western, extractive, capitalist states and now by a wide range of capitalist societies. If a dissident writer in Nigeria or the Arabian Peninsula you might dramatize the depredations imposed upon indigenous people directly and the rest of the world indirectly by the organization of corporate-extractionist-state complexes in those regions. If a dissident economist in America you might dramatize both the severe effects of eco-neglect in urban areas and the positive effects that a series of ecofriendly collectives could have in rural and urban areas. If a middle-class consumer you might participate in the farm-to-table movement, join urban farming collectives, buy a hybrid, or join a zipcar collective and tell others why; you might join campaigns to create bike lanes and rapid-transit systems and subsidize solar panels in your region, put up solar panels if you can afford to do so, or install more ecofriendly yards and gardens. If a teacher, you might change the content of the courses you teach or the issues you publicize, shift a portion of your retirement funds to sustainable investments, or write for a blog like *The Contemporary Condition*. If a skilled mechanic in a small town you might join a repair club in which volunteers rebuild and recirculate old appliances and furniture. If a Catholic priest you might publicize the encyclical on climate of Pope Francis to your parish; if a Catholic nun you might bring Nuns on Wheels to urban areas where the effects of climate change and urban poverty congeal together. If a climatologist, oceanographer, geologist, or paleontologist you might increase the intensity of publicity about the effects of the Anthropocene in different regions. If a tech geek you might form or join a company to perfect solar power, increase the power and recyclability of batteries for electric cars, redesign mass-transit systems, publicize new possibilities on Facebook, or build ecofriendly houses. If the logging company comes to take away your forest you might join with others in hugging those trees until the publicity presses the company to withdraw. And so on, endlessly.

Each role experiment—and all in aggregate—is radically insufficient to the scope of the problems, as so many institutional social scientists and others waiting for a revolutionary moment will tell you every day. They make you feel good but do not resolve the worldwide issue, couch objectivists love to say. You may have shifted a few role performances, but your authenticity is suspect until the system is transformed, some revolutionaries and right-wingers may chant across their lines of division. Or, later, Now that you have dropped out to gain purity you have lost any ability to make a difference anywhere, all these parties might sing in chorus. Bypass such attempts to place you in a double bind, the first bind of which is to neutralize the desire to take any action and the second of which is to demoralize you so that you do not expose publicly how the first bind works. The effect of such a double bind, when not identified and resisted, is to render specific citizens zombies who obediently play their assigned roles even when they know that those roles project a future that cannot be.[7] So one task of the scouts is to pursue micropractices of creative experimentations, as you invite potential allies in multiple subject positions to do so with you. You might soon become part of a rhizomatic complex with considerable growth potential, as constituencies in multiple places find that the issues and problems they pursue connect them to people in other places, with other creedal propensities and with other subject positions.

As you proceed, avoid joining *too intensely* in those all-too-familiar games of mutual accusation within the Left. Those are the games in which a few seek a singular reputation at the expense of all others; they work against formation of the militant pluralist assemblage needed today. In a critical pluralist assemblage constituencies will vary not only in the social positions and creeds from which they come but also in their degrees and modes of activism. That is an indispensable feature of such an assemblage, even at times when you seek to inspire yourself and others to more intense modes of activism. Whenever possible in such an assemblage it is wise to look for inspirations to draw from others as well as points in need of criticism. If neither is available, pass them by if and when possible, to allow the focal points of positive intersection to sing more richly. A *pluralist* assemblage of multiple actions.

The power of such preliminary modes of action is in part anchored in the cumulative effects they generate. But—as suggested in the discussions in chapters 3 and 4 on how daily activities help to organize the visceral registers of habit, belief, assumption, and mood—*an accumulation of such role experiments also works on the molecular or visceral registers of cultural life.* They thus may prepare us to embrace more adventurous collective activities when opportunities arise. They foster a spirituality of freedom through experimentation. You may now join a more active social movement, drawing upon connections to others and augmenting the visceral energies that have already been mobilized. A movement in one region may find itself borrowing tactics from those in others, joining with them where and when it is feasible. To and fro, back and forth.

As relays between different scales of action accumulate and accelerate, a new *event* will surely erupt, such as radical protests in third world countries against the entitlements assumed by rich countries that generate the most carbon emissions; or a devastating hurricane, a severe drought, a crisis in water supply, or a new series of wildfires; or vicious action by privileged states to resist pressure on their borders by refugees trying to escape the very conditions these states have helped to create; or protests in racialized urban areas against the pollutants, degradation, contaminated water, underfunded schools, and unemployment imposed upon them; or a rapid acceleration of glacier flows; or vigilante violence by the Right against nonviolent protesters; or a dangerous deceleration of the ocean conveyor system; or a marvelous new invention that enables the rapid advance of sustainable energy to more rapidly replace the extractionist cultures that plague us. Indeed several of these events could coalesce in a perfect storm.

Now to the extent movements back and forth between actions across regions and scales have already been put into play, the stage may be set to mobilize cross-regional general strikes. However, if such preliminary movements have not yet crystallized, the same events could well generate neofascist responses in several countries seeking to guard their old senses of self-entitlement. For we live in a dangerous time, when this or that crisis could erupt and powerful forces firmly committed to the old ways could intensify right-wing demands to return things to the old days through an intensification of violences already in place. The problem is that the old days are gone forever, so efforts to reinstate an old order can only intensify modes of discipline, repression, and scapegoating. The stakes of a swarming approach are high.

The Politics of the General Strike

Several thinkers can be drawn upon to explore the politics of a general strike appropriate to the current era. Along with Maathai and Klein, Georges Sorel, Mahatma Gandhi, Eugene Holland, Bruno Latour, and Pope Francis are some of the figures from whom I draw sustenance. Some talk about creative activism without exploring the distinct sources and distributed effects of climate change. For others the urgency of climate change moves front and center. The idea is to engage these adventurers comparatively to see if we can forge an idea of the general strike appropriate to the contemporary era. Jim Hansen, a distinguished climate scientist, could well be added to this list. He recently concluded that intense media activism and civil protest are needed to spur changes in ethos and policy. He is a contemporary example of the specific intellectual in which Foucault invested hope.[8]

I have sometimes been told that the prophecy of crisis is not a good way to motivate people to pursue positive, collective ends and that repeated reiterations of a crisis mentality dampen readiness to deal with actual issues. Such warnings are at least half true. Manufactured crises and scandals—one of the ways through which the twenty-four-hour media are maintained—are a big part of the problem, partly because they divert attention from real issues and partly because they encourage other fools to say that *any* discussion of crisis, even if real, is a bad idea. I dissent. Today production of collective motivation to act may require both intensifying diverse attachments to life on this rare planet and pursuing militant cross-regional citizen actions to ward off a planetary crisis in the making. If it reaches full fruition, the uneven suffering it brings will surely intensify border struggles and ratchet up bellicose military actions. The problem, then, is that a crisis *is* in the making, that it makes the poor suffer more than the rich, that it hits low-lying, poor countries that have made the smallest contribution to this result harder and sooner than rich countries, and that it fans resentments within rich countries as their most bellicose constituencies increasingly sense that the world is less disposed to their priorities than is demanded by the roles they enact, the faiths they express, and the ideological investments they make.

I have also been told that any vision of a general strike is dated. It may have applied to an earlier revolutionary era in capitalist states when class divisions concentrated masses of workers together in factories, or to a colonial time when an implicit nation needed to be freed from imperial control—but not to today. I believe nonetheless that this old vision needs to be updated and recrafted to fit an era in which climate is an overarching issue, some of its most serious effects are set on slow time scales, rich states have made the most significant contribution to it, several poor regions suffer its worst effects, and urban areas in rich countries loaded with racialized minorities and poor people also live on its cutting edge.

Let us consider Sorel first. Sorel distinguishes between a local strike that aims at limited objectives, such as better working conditions, higher wages, and job security, and a general strike that spreads more widely and demands a more fundamental reordering of the world. It is the latter he addresses. He enunciates the *myth* of a general strike in which anticipated violence against capital functions to sharpen class divisions.[9] He is valuable in calling our attention to how such a beacon (or myth) can sharpen needed energies and divisions even before the action is taken. He was not perturbed by those in his day who said that the actual class structure did not fit the sharp division he sought to produce. The goal was to sharpen class divisions by the promise of syndicalist violence. There is also something to his division between a local labor strike aimed at bread-and-butter issues and a general strike aimed at a more radical shift in the order of things.

Nonetheless his thinking is limited for the contemporary condition. The master division between labor and capital is pertinent but insufficient. More porous and shifting divisions need to be mobilized during the contemporary era. We need to mobilize a militant *pluralist* assemblage drawn from different classes, world regions, religious creeds, age cohorts, and gender practices. This feature of the new militancy may drive some Marxists away from the idea, even some who have given up the goal of a socialist, productivist society organized by collective domination of nature. But new situations require new modes of thought and action, as one of Sorel's heroes, Henri Bergson, would no doubt have seen more sharply than the devotee of class violence himself did. Sorel indeed thought that the clarification of class differences through the myth of a general strike was most apt to occur during a period of prosperity, not in the interlocked world of radical inequality between and within regions we inhabit.

He wrote his most important book before the advent of fascism, and today we face the risk of neofascist reactions to the perils of climate change. Indeed today, as before, advocates of a general strike will doubtless be accused of violence even when they eschew it. Sorel's celebration of revolutionary violence is thus apt to be counterproductive during an era of potential fascism. Finally, while a strike must include a class dimension as it aims at a more eco-egalitarian world, that goal must be contoured to fit the circumstances of the Anthropocene. It must speak to the need for radical revisions in the very idea of a civilization of productivity and material abundance. Despite these limits, Sorel teaches us how a general strike can serve as a beacon to mobilize constituencies.

This is perhaps where Gandhi enters the scene.[10] Gandhi grasped how a colonized territory must prepare for militant action while eschewing collective temptations to violence. You can strike, but you are unlikely to maintain either momentum or integrity if you slide into violence. The slide of one faction of the New Left in Europe and the United States into violence in the late 1960s after a period of initial effectiveness may teach the same lesson. So Gandhi teaches us how to act militantly while disciplining ourselves to avoid violence, treating nonviolent militancy as both an intrinsic obligation and a strategic strength.

Gandhi was a devout Hindu who believed in a higher power and rebirth. Does he demand that the needed disciplines always be tied to Hindu faith in a higher power from which to draw energy and courage? I don't think so, at least not at this stage in my reading of him. He is open to diverse constituencies drawing upon different sources to pursue a common end, as long as they discipline themselves to refrain from violence while confronting the forces of authoritarianism and violence. During his time he pursued efforts to forge positive ties between Muslims and Hindus in the same country, eventually being severely disappointed in his country and himself for failing in that objective.

But what can *nonviolence* mean today? To me it means a strong presumption against unleashing bloodshed joined to strategic willingness to set up barricades, close down factories, initiate new collective businesses, block highways, curtail consumption, participate in investment strikes, and so on if and when the time is right. Does it mean a willingness to go to jail to prove the sincerity of your action to opponents and the undecided? That is a situational issue to be determined as you focus on the strong presumption against violence as bloodshed. We go to jail if filling jails with protesters also promises to dismantle public support for established priorities. Timing is everything. We resist it if that promise is inoperative. We do not need to see ourselves as moral purists on these issues, since political action is composed of interwoven ethical, political, prudential, and tactical considerations. I imagine Gandhi would not like that last sentence.

Gandhi also celebrated the spinning wheel as a village mode of production that simultaneously protests the imperial law that cloth must be bought from England, activates positive energies, provides the poor with sustenance, supports the strength of the village system, and challenges the hegemony of dominant modes of production and consumption. Spinning was one of the ascetic disciplines by which people could improve their ability to provide for themselves and to work on cultural dispositions to fashion a positive ethos of material austerity. He advised all members of the Congress Party to spin a little every day and to buy clothing that had been spun in the villages. He hesitated to be active in the Congress Party unless this was done. The practice of spinning in Gandhi's time may be compared to the politics of role experimentations in our time.

We too need to cultivate an ethos of positive material austerity as we work to shift simultaneously established modes of extraction and the infrastructure of consumption in rich states. The latter must shift state subsidies from carbon-based and high-energy commodities to modes of agriculture, food supply, health care, travel, entertainment, retirement, and so on that reduce inequality and support ecological goals.[11] Sorel, by the way, made fun of the spinning wheel, committing himself to a syndicalist mode of high production and consumption that is difficult to sustain during the Anthropocene. Today, as will be discussed soon, we can work to stretch the role expectations in which we are set, doing so to improve modestly the ecological outlook through the cumulative effects of such actions and to shift by these acts the molecular dispositions to thought and action that inhabit us. This is one of the key ways the genius of Gandhi is relevant today.

Gandhi, moreover, displayed the creative *theatrical* talents needed to mobilize a mass movement, as when he led the huge march to collect salt at the seashore in direct disobedience of English law that salt must be bought from the empire. He carried his handful to the authorities to demand arrest for having broken the law. Brilliant.

Gandhi's actions resonate with a later series of environmental actions elsewhere, such as the creative protests led by Maathai in Kenya. In the 1970s and 1980s she led women who had seen their land decimated first by British imperialism and then by neocolonial authoritarianism. Maathai's doctorate in biology stood her in good stead in these struggles, even as it licensed some authorities and local men to demean her as arrogant. The protesters first planted oak saplings on lands designed by the regime for tourist development and gated communities. They incited the ire of the regime until they were arrested. Those arrests backfired.[12]

Maathai's activism speaks eloquently to the intersections of role performances and ecological movements I have been elaborating. When local people complained to her about the government's policies promoting deforestation she both agreed and countered: "The government was selling off public lands. . . . However, I felt strongly that people needed to understand that government was not the only culprit. Citizens too, played a part in the problems the communities identified. . . . You're allowing soil erosion to take place and could do something about it. You could plant trees." Out of the innovation in local citizen actions of planting trees in public settings and publicizing it, a women's organization grew that eventually became the Green Belt Movement. It became an effective, though dangerous, movement of protest, publicity, and positive enactments against government-corporate cronyism. "This personal responsibility became collective as communities managed their environment better."[13] Eventually over two thousand women's groups were formed, helping to establish nurseries in Kenya and beyond. When it was time to become more militant against the state to fend off the destruction of a major park in the heart of Nairobi, that network provided a base of publicity, organization, and protection from which to proceed. The politics of swarming.

One thinks here too of sparks that travel across regions, such as the American civil rights movement that was led by Martin Luther King Jr. and indebted to Gandhi, and the inspiration that King offered Maathai after her visit to the States. Sparks and stories traveling across territories and time. Temporal and regional crossings initiated below the radar of state- and global-centered discourses.

Or think of the "tree huggers" in the Himalayas whose tactics spread to the United States and Indonesia.[14] These tactics had both Gandhian and feminist roots. One spark even flew to my neighborhood, when my partner, Jane Bennett, guarded a tree scheduled to be cut until the phone company changed its mind. It still shades us as we walk to the coffee shop. Activist writers of the next generation will spread such stories and fit them to new situations, drawing upon the brilliance of predecessors in doing so. Each tactic was a creative intervention when it started, and the travels it inaugurates express creativity too.

Klein's work resonates with the spirit of Maathai, particularly in chapters 9 and 10 of *This Changes Everything*. There she reviews protest movements in several regions against destructive coal and fracking technologies. These movements, in China, India, Canada, the United States, and elsewhere, speak to one another. They link together ranchers and indigenous people, students and the elderly, and peasants and urban parents in new pluralist assemblages. Recent drives to divest universities, cities, retirement funds, nonprofit foundations, and the like from carbon investments express one of these lines of development. They help to dramatize the health effects and dangers of extraction, to encourage the institutions involved to move to clean energy themselves, to delegitimize extraction industries, and to foment broader campaigns to tax them to pay for production of clean energy grids in place of subsidizing them. As communication between them grows across regions, the protest and divestment movements pave the way for the cross-regional general strikes to be organized.

Let's cut back to Gandhi for a moment. There are also limits to his perspective. His responses to the issue of race were perhaps not sensitive enough to racial struggles elsewhere, particularly with respect to African Americans. He also seemed to misunderstand the nature of the fascist threat in Germany, a phenomenon that scrambles the politics of militant nonviolence when it is in power. His assertion that God had punished Indians for their treatment of the untouchables with the Bihar earthquake of 1934 is also worrisome.[15] And his pursuit of the collective goal of chastity, while being patient with those who did not live up to its demands, deserves reassessment. Perhaps today we need to appreciate the theatrical genius of Gandhi as we fold erotic elements into creative political energies. No reason to let conservative TV dramas and capitalist advertising monopolize the energies of eroticism. We need today, perhaps, an amalgam of Gandhi and Pussy Riot.

Gandhi's aim was to create a new nation in India by a mass movement to expunge England as an imperial power and to overcome the internal Hindu treatment of untouchables. The nation, with the corollary fantasy of a world of nations, may be part of the problem today. We need to foment innovations that press upon states and corporations while transforming classic ideals of the nation into vibrant systems of egalitarian pluralism. We must draw upon forces that express and appreciate the minoritization of the world rather than building walls to resist it. This is particularly pertinent today, when climate change already contributes to intense migration pressures, placing old ideals of a world of nations under incredible pressure. What is needed today are critical assemblages constructed from minorities of multiple sorts connected across regions and domains. During an age of minoritization along multiple dimensions, pluralism provides an essential precondition of the general strike rather than an impediment to it. Only those who underplay the historic role of spontaneity in periodic collective modes of action, despite all the evidence to the contrary, will miss this point.

We draw from Maathai, Klein, and Gandhi a strong presumption against bloodshed joined to a readiness for militancy. And we—the "we" is, again, plural and invitational—seek to attach those presumptions to the acceleration of citizen militancy across regions to press states, corporations, churches, universities, the media, international agencies, and everyday consumers to respond to the Anthropocene. In an era when the radical Right regularly accuses protest movements of violence—and often enough orchestrates such appearances as white police often do with respect to young blacks—it is doubly important to publicize far and wide that cross-regional general strikes will be militant but will avoid bloodshed.

Consider, then, Holland's sublime idea of a slow-motion strike.[16] As I understand it, the slow-motion strike is a nonviolent process by which workers in a variety of capitalist states progressively generate collective production units, particularly in zones of capitalist failure or neglect, and in which these collectives relate to each other through impersonal market transactions. This takes the distortions and exploitations created by private capital out of the market equation, Holland thinks, allowing markets themselves to cleave more closely to Hayek's image of self-organized market rationality. Hayek had a good idea of how unconscious coordination could proceed, Holland suggests, but he tied it to the hegemony of private capital. What is needed is a slow-motion general strike that issues in a communist mode of market life as it devolves capitalist ownership into a system of worker collectives. Self-organizing markets without private ownership.

This too is a complex argument, which I cannot give full justice to here. I very much appreciate how Holland distills a fecund, operative "minor Marxism" from Marx's tendencies to royal science. I learn from him how the "early" processes of primitive accumulation in the consolidation of capitalism are still very much operative today. What about a slow-motion general strike? I embrace it as part of a larger agenda. Indeed the active role experimentations at a variety of sites can be thought of as contributive to a slow-motion strike, with Holland's project of worker collectives providing a dramatic and significant instance of it. The slow-motion strike, however, is most effective if it operates in tandem with swarming movements that energize it and perhaps issue eventually in a hotter cross-country strike. All are needed to respond to the asymmetrical, interfolded fragility of things today. What else makes a slow-motion strike both pertinent and insufficient?

First, noncapitalist markets would be self-organizing, but there is still no guarantee that they would spontaneously generate collective rationality. There is no simple equation between self-organization and spontaneous rationality, even in markets composed of worker collectives. Different collectives, with inevitable differences in relative advantages and disadvantages, would still have to decide how much surplus to reinvest and what uses to make of the reinvestment. They would also have to decide between production alternatives. Differential advantages and risks would thus accrue across collectives. The issue of first and third world priorities would not be resolved automatically by a proliferation of worker collectives.

Second, patterns of consumption display an important element of autonomy too, supported by state actions. Consumption patterns in old capitalist states both embody self-organizing traits and propel the established social infrastructure of consumption in self-defeating directions, as Fred Hirsch has shown in brilliant detail in his classic study of consumption.[17] So there remains the huge question of how to reconstitute the collective *infrastructure* of consumption and the collective *ethos* of consumption so that we can move toward a world in which a positive austerity of material desire and more equal ways of fulfilling those desires come into view together. Consumption provides a promising target of political action because it has a degree of autonomy and because changes in the infrastructure and ethos of consumption can make such huge contributions as they also recoil back on modes of production.

Third, there will be myriad legal and illegal efforts by corporate giants tied to mammoth states to stymie a slow-motion strike, as previous organizers of consumer collectives, nonprofit insurance schemes, consumer boycotts, antiwar movements, antiracist movements, and labor union movements have discovered to their dismay over the past 150 years. This will require activists to try to influence the state in their favor even as they also try to revamp the priorities of state power.

Fourth, a slow-motion communist strike, as currently conceived, does not explicitly factor in the real power of a variety of nonhuman, partially self-organizing systems entangled with market and other cultural processes. When this larger constellation is emphasized you see more dramatically that no single self-organizing system is self-contained, that all face the prospect of periodic volatility, that impersonal market rationality is inadequate to itself, and that the idea of a smooth communist horizon in the possible future expresses a version of sociocentrism that cannot remain plausible today. This means that states with at least formal modes of public accountability will be needed to help respond to the effects of urgent natural events, such as violent hurricanes, extended drought, crises of water supply, rapid transmission of diseases, rising ocean levels in low-lying areas, reconstitution of the power grid, and so on endlessly. It means too that states may be needed to help finance or subsidize large-scale projects, such as production of new energy grids, shifts in the infrastructure of consumption, and subsidies to those collectives that pursue long-term consumption changes. It means, above all, that we are entangled in larger nonhuman worlds that exceed our capacities of mastery and demand several modes of collective organization to respond to the contingencies they engender.

If these dimensions are folded into the idea of a slow-motion strike, it may become clear how role experimentations in other domains, social movements, and consolidation of a movement toward hotter, cross-state strikes can and must augment each other. I suspect that Holland could support several of these points.

Now that I have read a more recent, unpublished piece by Holland entitled "To Believe in This World: Debt Strike," I see how our visions have moved even closer together.[18] He now supports a debt strike that will be more confrontational than a slow-motion strike, while supplementing it. The connection between a debt strike and a climate strike is this: to the extent that an irrational infrastructure of consumption fosters a debt economy—for instance, impelling students to take out huge loans to go to college, pressing parents to send their kids to private schools, creating multiple pressures on behalf of expensive suburban living—a debt strike, shifts in the state-supported infrastructure of consumption, and an ecofriendly economy go together.

Latour has examined the Anthropocene itself closely. Consider the new lines of political division he visualizes in his Gifford lectures, "Facing Gaia." On one side you have the humans, the bifurcation of nature and culture, the modernists, the abstract scientists, the theo-escapists. To Latour this diverse, cross-territorial constellation increasingly faces a cadre of the earthbound, carriers of a Gaia geostory, labcentric scientists, and new secularists. Thus he foresees the composition of a new "Schmittian division" at the planetary level between friends and enemies.

This latter cadre, barely under way, embraces the Anthropocene as a defining event of this time; it admits that we cannot dominate the earth; it acknowledges the absence of a providential cosmic order that could intervene to save us from ourselves at the last moment; it suppresses fantasies of escape to another planet or divine place, as the need to save a place on this rare planet for the earthbound becomes vivid. It adopts a new secular image and treats the sciences as key allies in the struggle with those who defer action in this world or dream at the movies of another world. And it challenges those secular modernists who continue to emphasize the past we have escaped to avoid staring at the possible future looming before us.

I learn from Latour. He inspires me. I suspect there is a lot to the Gaia story as modified by Lynn Margulis, when she retreats from calling it an organism to emphasize its character as a set of intersecting, self-organizing processes that mobilize the atmospheric conditions of life on earth and retain a limited margin of self-sustainability.[19] I concur that the two long-term and competing sociocentric stories of mastery and providence need to be challenged together. I also agree that I need to find more ways to exorcize that strain of climate skepticism persisting in me that Latour says invades most of us, including him, who talk about the problem more than doing things about it, who profess belief in it without making role and political adjustments that express the belief. Belief, he agrees with a long line of pragmatists, is invested in performance as much as in what you say. I do worry, however, about the Schmittian division he has identified. I will thus inflect the Latour perspective a bit rather than saying yes or no to it.

Let's start with his new secularism. I suppose that the cosmology I embrace is closer to that of Latour than to several other ontotheological creeds in play. But if you also emphasize, as I do, how creed and spirituality are interinvolved without either being entirely reducible to the other, such an agreement does not exhaust the issue. My sense is that a struggle over the importance of the Anthropocene is being waged today *within* Christianity, Judaism, Islam, Hinduism, and variants of nontheism at least as much as between any of them and something called "the new secularism." How so? Well, each creed expresses a set of formal understandings, say, of a personal God, or of impersonal transcendence, or of radical immanence in a world of becoming. And each is also the site of spiritual investments not entirely exhausted by its formal creedal confession. The nest of culturally infused drives from which a creed is abstracted is not captured entirely by the conscious light of a creed. For instance, you and I may diverge in creed, share a sense across that difference that each creed is contestable in the eyes of others, and, the clincher, respond spiritually by seeking ways to negotiate connections across creedal difference. An Augustinian may thus accept the doctrine of omnipotence and salvation and infuse that doctrine with either an appreciation of its contestability and care for the diversity of this world or, say, deep resentment of alternative doctrines and the contemporary intrusion of the Anthropocene. An immanent naturalist may resent the world for lacking a salvational god or affirm it for the sweetness and abundance of life it makes available amid the risks and dangers it presents.

If you explore the interinvolvement without equivalence between belief and spirituality you also sense how negotiation of spiritual affinities across diverse, lived creeds can help to pave the way for creative construction of an energetic, pluralist assemblage on behalf of the earthbound, a constrained image of Gaia, and militant responses to the Anthropocene. I sense that Latour and I move toward each other on this issue, and I should emphasize here how much I appreciate his fecund image of "the earthbound."

I also doubt that scientists divide on this issue neatly across the distinction between abstract and lab-centered types, though Latour, again, may not believe that as strongly as he sometimes asserts. Some lab scientists may not care that much about climate change, and some abstract scientists may care a lot even though their accounts of it vary from Latour's. Spiritual tendencies as well as diversities in scientific creed make a difference here too. Latour and I concur that other lines of social division, such as class, education level, gender, sexuality, age cohort, the media, and ethnicity, do not line up on the issue neatly for similar reasons; that is one reason contemporary social science is sometimes so crude: it tends to ignore affinities of spirituality in politics across creedal, class, and other distinctions. Since Latour himself seeks to touch our spiritualities almost as much as to shift our cosmic creeds, I doubt whether what I am saying is deeply at odds, as it were, with the spirit of his message.

But isn't spirituality itself infused with belief? You adopt Augustinianism but play up its commitment to love more than others do its position on the punishment of heresy? Yes. Spirituality is bound to creed and imbricated with a creedal community. But spirituality also infuses belief with variable degrees of *intensity* and tendencies to action, so that your intense gratitude for the human predicament may contrast with resentment of it by others *of* this condition as they perceive it in broadly similar creedal terms. Spirituality thus gives a specific edge to belief and action; its intensities bathe the *quality* of participation in and beyond creedal communities whether they be religious, professional, local, scientific, entrepreneurial, or educational. Pope Francis, Bhrigu Singh, Latour, Klein, and Bill McKibben may express selective affinities of spirituality across significant differences of onto-creed. That is why arts of the self and constituency micropolitics are as important to the quality of a political movement as creedal sharpness.

If creed, spirituality, and practice are interinvolved but not equivalent it may be high time to break the analytic/synthetic dichotomy into *degrees* of analyticity. Brian Massumi radicalizes such an approach by transfiguring the logic of the excluded middle into a logic of the *included* middle.[20] The former logic was invented by Aristotle, who sought to fix the state of the universe. The latter logic, one proposed in fact by the great logician Whitehead, is more congruent with a universe of becoming in which strange (to us) mixtures periodically occur and new becomings emerge. So a series of fixed binary distinctions, such as that between mind and body, thought and matter, life and death, human and animal, intentional agency and determined conduct, wild and cultivated, now devolve into differences of degree. The zones between them may inhabit an element of wildness or noise. It is in such zones of indiscernibility that much of the creative action arises. Such a perspective may trouble proponents of logical empiricism and rationalism, but, hey, that is to the good. It encourages us to occupy those zones of indiscernibility between questionable categorical divisions where the vitality of things occurs. Latour sees this when he says that many profess belief in the Anthropocene, but the reality (intensity) of that belief is mild by comparison to the pursuit of personal health, higher income, reputation, a good education for the kids, and so on. Belief, spirituality, and action are linked by obscure connections that slide between the analytic/synthetic dichotomy and the law of the excluded middle. I think I have been channeling Latour as much as adjusting him here.

To crystallize the importance of pursuing affinities of spirituality across differences of creed in order to forge a critical assemblage appropriate to the contemporary condition, consider the recent entry by Pope Francis into this scene. Here are a few things Francis says in *Laudato Si': On Care for Our Common Home*:

> There is a tendency to believe that every increase in power means an increase of progress itself . . . as if reality, goodness and truth automatically flow from technological and economic power as such.

> We fail to see that some are mired in desperate and degrading poverty, with no way out, while others have not the faintest idea of what to do with their possessions . . . leaving behind them so much waste which, if it were the case everywhere, would destroy the planet.

> Finance overwhelms the real economy. . . . Some circles maintain that current economics and technology will solve all environmental problems and argue . . . that the problems of global hunger and poverty will be resolved simply by market growth.

> Doomsday predictions can no longer be met with irony or disdain. We may well be leaving to coming generations debris, desolation and filth. The pace of consumption, waste and environmental change has so stretched the planet's capacity that our contemporary lifestyle . . . can only precipitate catastrophes, such as those which even now periodically occur in different areas of the world.[21]

With these statements, and more besides, Francis throws the weight of the Catholic Church—with its impressive presence in Europe, North America, Latin America, and other places—behind rapid action to respond to the entanglements between regionally distributed poverty and the dire effects of the Anthropocene.

There are numerous points of faith, economic creed, and political priority at which I diverge from Francis.[22] I do not confess an omnipotent, personal God. I am not a devotee of the Trinity, though I have come to see how it provides *one way* to embrace the complexity of selves and culture, including an appreciation of the element of mystery in both. I embrace a woman's choice with respect to abortion. His commitment to the primacy of heterosexuality, while softened from that of his predecessors, remains way too strong. I resist the patriarchy of the Church and the doctrine that rules women out of candidacy for priesthood. He has begun to relax the creed of papal infallibility, though it would be salutary if he took it on more radically. Maybe he will. He also embraces faith in an organic world presided over by God, a world disrupted mostly by ruthless market processes and inordinate consumption demands; I contend that several nonhuman processes possess considerable vitality and volatility on their own, so that organic critiques of the demand for world mastery do not provide the strongest critiques of it to pursue. He talks mostly about markets, technology, and wasteful consumption, while I say, with many others, that those forces must be linked more closely yet to the institutions of neoliberal capitalism within which they operate. He looks to the strengthening of international institutions to cope with climate change, while I think it is even more important to ignite cross-regional citizen movements that press dominant states, corporations, banks, universities, international organizations, and churches into action at the same time. If the strengthening of international institutions occurs and these movements do not become more active, the door is open for neoliberal hegemony over international institutions.

And yet I do admire this pope, across these differences. While Pope John Paul II labeled people like me who do not believe in a personal God "nihilists," Francis resists such formulations. He also acknowledges that several strains of Christianity in the past treated scriptural discussions of human dominion as if they meant human domination and mastery over the earth rather than deep respect for the diversity of living beings. Most significant, he addresses his text to "all people of good will," whether they embrace a Catholic creed or, it seems, *any other* confession of a personal God. He pursues affinities of spirituality across multiple differences in creed.

Francis also understands that those regimes most eager to go to war to protect historic entitlements kill millions of innocent people, wreak devastation on ecologies of the world, and delay new attempts to respond to the Anthropocene. Living in the United States I must supplement the pope's point by emphasizing that the U.S. oil, coal, evangelical, Republican machine deploys war talk and wars in ways that protect its entitlements and severely set back a host of progressive political movements. The underlying drive is to do anything it takes to maintain American entitlement in a world in which such entitlements must in fact be redefined and curtailed. That is the spirituality we are contending against.

Francis speaks first and foremost to Catholics, but he also addresses Hindus, Jews, Buddhists, indigenous peoples, and nontheists, without trying too hard to convert them to his creed. He thus pursues relations of agonistic respect across creeds, relations in which each party articulates publicly the contestable creed that *in*forms it as it also pursues lines of communication and coordination with others with respect to urgent issues of the day. You pursue agonistic respect when you replace the old secular pretense that people can always leave their faith in the private world to adopt a neutral discourse of reason in the public world. Of course you know that some will refuse the invitation. But you make the invitational move. Francis acknowledges the reasonable contestability of his faith in the eyes of others.

So Francis confesses the creed of his church; he understands public life to be regularly embroiled in creedal issues that transcend the quaint, secular division between public and private life; he remains open to possible shifts in the priorities of his own creed as new issues and unexpected situations arise; and he pursues lines of spiritual affinity with afflicted constituencies who care about the world and confess different creeds. He himself believes "that the world came about as the result of a decision, not from chaos or chance, and this exalts it all the more."[23] But he pursues connections to those whose positive spiritualities are anchored in the very creeds he contests. He brings an appreciation of deep pluralism to the issues of the day.

Francis inspires a cross-regional assemblage of constituencies of many sorts to take action in response to the urgency of climate change. He might encourage some proposed actions, tolerate others, and find yet others to be too dangerous or destructive. That is what participation in an active pluralist assemblage on the move means. You diversify ideas and actions within it rather than demanding to preside over it as pope, authoritarian party, ruler, or unquestionable prophet.

Such an assemblage may break up or break down over key questions, but it also may grow. Indeed the attraction of such a critical assemblage is, first, that it is less likely to replicate the dogmatism and authoritarianism of some of the very movements it opposes; second, that disparate constituencies can inspire each other to action within it; and, third, that creative action by one constituency in a fraught situation may foster creativity by others as they riff off that strategic innovation.

Perhaps it is wise to listen again to how Francis works on the devotees of his faith and reaches out to others who could join him in this cause without participating in his creed:

> This rediscovery of nature can never be at the cost of freedom and responsibility of human beings, who, as part of the world, have the duty to cultivate their abilities in order to protect and develop its potential.

> If we acknowledge the value and the fragility of nature and, at the same time, our God-given abilities, we can finally leave behind the modern myth of unlimited material progress. A fragile world, entrusted by God to human care, challenges us to devise intelligent ways of directing, developing and limiting our power.

> In this universe, shaped by open and intercommunicating systems, we can discern countless forms of relationship and participation.[24]

Cross-Regional General Strikes

To the extent such spiritual struggles are waged within and across regions, states, religious communities, scientific practices, families, union gatherings, student meetings, gender relations, election campaigns, blog postings, and university courses, they may provide us with clues about how to wage them better. The hope is to forge a militant, cross-regional pluralist assemblage in which the next disturbing event encourages large minorities in a variety of subject positions to organize cross-regional strikes. The strikes will be more effective to the extent they impinge upon the economic and moral life of states, churches, corporations, universities, and so on from the inside and outside simultaneously: strikes that are both general and cross world regional lines. A bracing event is probably needed to spark the actions because it enables us to translate the diffused *sense* that concerted action is needed into embodied interconstituency *drives* to act. We are entangled beings and interwoven constituencies.

Such a strike will involve withdrawal from work and travel joined to mass reductions of consumption above the levels needed for subsistence. It will also be marked by intensive lobbying of key institutions, such as legislatures, churches, unions, universities, corporations, farmers, foundations, retirement funds, parties, international agencies, and localities. The cross-regional action could be enacted for a defined period on the first occasion, combined with a promise to renew it if the relevant institutions do not initiate a specified series of interim actions. The actions demanded could include promises of a rapid shift in the eco-priorities of numerous nonstate institutions, radical state and local projects to reorganize the power grid, a radical reorientation of subsidies in the infrastructure of consumption, action to relieve debt in third world countries and student life, support for worker collectives, financial support by the old capitalist states of other regions seeking to undertake eco-actions, media publicity to reorient the public ethos of investment and consumption, and hundreds of billions in mitigation and adaptation payments from rich to poor countries that have suffered inordinate damage. Cross-regional general strikes build on the momentum of swarming social movements already in motion to press hegemonic states, corporations, and other institutions to redefine their priorities more rapidly and radically. One of its powers is that *it acts on states and other institutions internally and externally at the same time.* When consumers in Japan, Australia, India, China, and Germany boycott goods made in the United States and the United Kingdom until specific actions are taken, they bolster the power of critical constituencies in the latter states and help to protect them from punitive actions.

Such a new cross-regional movement can draw selective inspiration from other creative movements, such as the Green Belt movement in Kenya; the Arab Spring; the antipollution drives in China; women's suffrage in the 1920s; the 1926 general strike in Britain; the 1937 sit-down strike in Flint, Michigan, that stopped scabs from coming in the back door and consolidated the American labor movement as an effective force; antilogging movements in Indonesia; Tiananmen Square; several instantiations of the civil rights movement; minority eco movements in Nigeria; Pussy Riot in Russia; multirole experiments and institutional pressures emanating from the LGBT movement; the cross-country divestment movement against apartheid in South Africa; the Gandhian drive to free India; the widespread, spontaneous student and faculty strikes after the Kent State shootings in May 1970; the Occupy movement; and the Black Lives Matter movement. The point is to enliven social movements on several fronts, to respond to a new event with cross-regional citizen strikes, and to fold modes of creativity into these actions to enable them to spread further.

Multimodal preparations, a dramatic event, cross-regional citizen strikes, stringent interim demands. In the spring of 1972, 1,300 students, faculty, and allied citizens in western Massachusetts enacted an illegal sit-down strike at

Westover Air Force Base to protest a new escalation of the Vietnam War by Richard Nixon. Most participants had actively protested the war earlier, but the event of escalation inflamed us as it did numerous other constituencies inside and outside the United States. The question now was not whether we would escalate the protests but whether we would be wise enough to do so in ways that were not apt to backfire. The meetings about what to do were intense; divisions were sharp between those who called for violence, those who called for nonviolence, and those who wanted to wait for a revolutionary moment. I chaired a hastily called UMass ad hoc faculty meeting, and we came slowly to a judgment of what to do. The call from the floor for a sit-down strike at Westover gradually met with the support of a vast majority, and we eventually joined students and faculties at other schools in the valley to enact it. There was considerable support in the wider Amherst community. The militant action taken there was replicated spontaneously in many areas inside and outside the country. The spontaneous spread of militancy in response to an ugly event. In cumulative effect these actions rattled authorities and helped to turn the tide of public opinion against the war, even though it wound down for two more long years.

With respect to the Anthropocene, such strikes will involve a host of loosely coordinated constituencies acting within and upon several regimes at the same time. If the combination of massive publicity about the Anthropocene, the escalation of social movements already under way, and new activating events coalesce to set the stage, such loosely coordinated actions may hold considerable promise. Work in advance to publicize how our side will avoid violence, remembering how some on the other side are eager to accuse you of violence in order to demoralize, isolate, arrest, beat, or kill you. They have the guns, media, military, judges, and many university presidents to draw upon to try to defeat and demoralize you if your numbers are small and your strategy is unwise.[25] Macho tactics are thus not the thing in this situation, but concerted, furious action to dramatize the issue, to press multiple institutions, to inspire the undecided, and to place pressure on dominant institutions from inside and outside at the same time.

Indeed each time such an event is enacted, it will be accompanied by a series of other creative activities: festivals, new use of the social media, art that dramatizes the situation, satires, and so forth. These accentuate and accelerate the movement in question.

Let us agree in advance that the mobilization of loosely coordinated cross-regional strikes is, well, *improbable*. The odds are that an insufficient number of strategically located actors (i.e., constituencies, institutions, individuals) will heed the call in time. Indeed it may seem to be a strike aimed at saving the future rather than demanding specific benefits now. But, as many of the movements noted above already show, history is full of militant collective movements that aim at future, diffused ends even more than a list of specific benefits. Moreover the effects of the Anthropocene are already being experienced in many places. Check out Miami, Tuvalu, California, the Arctic Circle, the melting Bengkel glacier in China, the sub-Saharan region, and Bangladesh for starters. So let's agree that such an event is improbable and that its very improbability suggests the need to bypass crackpot realism. Crackpot realists gauge the probability of an event and adjust their actions accordingly. They fail to ask what might happen if they fail to challenge the odds. Above all, they fail to connect the needs of the day to modes of publicity and action that could speak to those needs. The most pertinent question, then, is not whether such rolling strikes are probable. It is whether they can become live *possibilities* that speak to urgent *needs* of this time. Spectatorial modes of optimism and pessimism are thus insufficient to the situation. The task is to help each other heed the danger, hear the call, intensify spiritual affinities, and mobilize to act.

It might seem to some that the agreements reached at the Paris Conference in December 2015 militate against the need for such actions. These agreements were reached just as this study was going into production. They are an impressive start but do not come close to pressing all regions and states to take sufficient action fast enough. And numerous constituencies will lobby against them, including first and foremost the Republican Party in the United States.

Even if, as seems very unlikely, cross-regional strikes do not prove necessary to spur massive changes over a short time in the global organization of capital, entrenched state priorities, infrastructures of consumption, and the established ethos of investment, their projection as a vision may still accentuate the needed alliances. Sympathizers who argue against such specific actions may be prodded to reconsider what actions they will take. That is a debt we owe to Sorelian insights.

The divisions we pursue are more porous, horizontally organized, uncertain, and soft around the edges than the top-down politics of sovereign decision loved in different ways by Schmitt and Lenin. Schmitt wanted to exacerbate differences to disrupt horizontal connections and to strengthen a bellicose, top-down state. As I read him, he sought to drive wedges in society to exacerbate threats to sovereignty and to force exclusionary state decisions. We seek to enliven and radicalize horizontal connections across several constituencies and regions in a variety of different circumstances. Some participants will be in a position to enact all elements of the strike; others will be able to support it in this or that way, such as organizing consumption boycotts aimed at outlier capitalist states or pressing the institutions to which they belong to divest from all fossil fuel investments. The most dramatic division we seek to exacerbate is between neoliberal ideology, the transnational oil-coal-gas combine, the right edge of evangelicalism, old-timers on Fox News, and bought climate scientists who face a vibrant pluralist assemblage energized by young and old people in a variety of regions and subject positions. Many either outside the old capitalist states or in their urban centers face the most adverse consequences of the Anthropocene while having made the least contribution to it. This asymmetry itself, if publicized and dramatized often and loudly enough, can provide incentives to join a cross-regional movement crystallizing in general strikes. The new constellation, again, will deploy blog, Twitter, and Facebook communications, be inspired by dynamic music and theatrical events, and promote contagion across class, gender, creedal, ethnic, professional, and world regional lines. During these strikes there will be dancing in the streets out of joy in the diversity of life and attachment to this rare planet.

It is pertinent to note how the prospect and reality of sparking events speaks to the politics of freedom and attachment today. As prospect, a strike helps dispersed participants to coalesce into a new assemblage as they resist the destructiveness of extractive hypercapitalism. Doing so dissolves the sense of being neutralized by the everyday practices of capitalism into the prospect of acting collectively on its priorities. Doing that, more constituencies in a variety of dependent subject positions are encouraged to become more active citizens in reshaping the future. If creative citizenship is a key element in the practice of freedom, such periodic movements enact one of its contemporary conditions of being. For citizens today need to act across state lines as well as within states to meet the contemporary demands of freedom.

The initial goal is to impose a set of interim demands upon a variety of states and allied institutions, responding in each case to the history of perverse activism by established corporations and states that produced the current crisis. Freedom, as collective action mobilized by a rolling cross-regional assemblage. Many participants will act out of injury and anxiety about the future. Doing so, some will see themselves belonging to a cosmos composed of multiple force fields that simultaneously enable them to be and pose differential dangers to the human estate and the numerous beings with which it is entangled. Some will connect such a larger sense of attachment to a benevolent God, others to an immanent divine, and others yet to an immanent cosmos of becoming without divinity. Under the shadow of the Anthropocene the practice of free citizenship involves the creative pursuit and consolidation of affinities across regions and creeds to speak to new conditions of being.

One problem with a multiregional, pluralizing, swarming strategy that crystallizes in cross-regional strikes is that the movement may take too long to mobilize as the irreversible effects of the Anthropocene accelerate. This too constitutes a live dilemma. In a world of tragic possibility there is no guarantee that the need to act will be matched in fact by timely action. If and when such a mobilization crystallizes, uncertainty will also be high. Such uncertainty is essentially embedded in the nature of democratic tipping points. But even those dangers and uncertainties are not as great as the slow violence of unattended climate change, with its acceleration of differential suffering, forced migrations, and violent conflicts. To paraphrase a great thinker: The task of life is to become worthy of the events you encounter. A major event of this time is the accelerating burn of climate change.

CHAPTER 6

**POSTCOLONIAL ECOLOGIES, EXTINCTION EVENTS,
AND ENTANGLED HUMANISM**

In *Slow Violence and the Environmentalism of the Poor* Rob Nixon asks why, in light of all the eco violence done by predatory capitalism to people and places both inside its disposable zones and outside its centers, postcolonial thought has historically tended to bypass environmental issues. He cites Edward Said, Stuart Hall, Frantz Fanon, and others whose work, valuable in so many ways, failed to place environmentalism front and center. Here is what he says:

> Edward's Said's *Orientalism*, the most decisive text in the rise of postcolonial studies, appeared in 1978, just two years before Ronald Reagan's election. President Reagan oversaw, domestically, a massive rollback of environmental regulation and, internationally, proliferating cold war conflicts from Angola and Mozambique to Nicaragua, from the Horn of Africa to Laos and El Salvador. Crucially, in terms of postcolonial skepticism toward environmentalism that was cemented during the 1980s, few American environmentalists showed any interest in linking Reagan's transnational imperialism to socioenvironmental degradation in the global south. Instead, most American environmentalism became inwardly focused: on wilderness preservation, on wielding the Endangered Species Act against developers, and on saving old-growth forests.[1]

In other words, environmentalism and postcolonial studies, particularly in the United States and the United Kingdom, tended to head in different directions under the onslaught of Reaganism, Thatcherism, and several decades of neoliberal assault following in their wake. This combination encouraged environmentalists to narrow their focus territorially and to concentrate energy on wilderness projects and wildlife protection. It invited postcolonial theorists, often enough, to think of environmentalism as a white, middle-class issue focused on Europe and the United States. Two ships passing in the night, as ocean acidification intensified.

There have been numerous exceptions, as we have already glimpsed and are about to see further. But as Nixon and other recent writers have shown, the dominant propensities at work tended to render the exceptions less visible and to create a hole in environmental studies and public eco-awareness in the old capitalist centers. Those holes and blindnesses found expression in white eco-orientations to poor urban centers and in areas outside the metropoles.

To cite one example of eco-urban neglect in the United States, in 2011 the neoliberal governor of Michigan, Rick Snyder, placed Flint (my hometown) under the control of an emergency manager. During that period the city—with a high proportion of poor African Americans and poor whites—switched its water supply from Lake Huron to the Flint River to save money. While the river had improved in water quality after the withdrawal of General Motors and decades of being used as a dump for GM waste, it still contained large amounts of lead and other dangerous contaminants. Citizens in the deindustrialized city became activated and sued the state once they tasted and saw the foul water. But the state claimed the quality was high. By the time external investigators confirmed very high lead levels the city's youth had suffered perhaps irreversible damage and the pipes had become so corroded by the foul water that even a belated shift to a cleaner water supply was insufficient: the clean water was now contaminated by the corroded pipes it flowed through. This eco disaster, we can be confident, would likely not have occurred if the class and race composition of the city had fit that courted by Governor Snyder. The dismal record of eco damage in poor sections of most American cities verifies the assumption that these are the last areas protected by state and urban policies.[2]

Those located in poor urban centers regularly face the most eco-risk and damage. For example, predictions that heat waves are going to come more often and last longer will make life particularly hard on poor urban constituencies. For those living without air-conditioning in zones saturated with pavement and brick the deleterious effects of such changes will be dramatic and severe.

The focus of many Anglo-American activists on deep ecology and wilderness studies was perhaps explicable under the assaults from Reagan and Thatcher. But these points of concentration have been *doubly* limited. With exceptions, such as care to avoid destruction of Amerindian sacred places, they did tend to focus, as Nixon says, on Euro-America and on notions of deep ecology that assume nonhuman, planetary processes are pointed toward stable equilibrium if and when the human imprint is lightened.

Nixon himself focuses on the environmentalism of the poor outside capitalist centers, and a host of activist writers is rapidly closing the gap in postcolonial theory. Engaged perspectives find valuable expression, for example, in the work of Nixon, Dipesh Chakrabarty, Bhrigu Singh, Anna Tsing, Sankaran Krishna, Anatoli Ignatov, and Naveeda Khan.[3] Thus in a superb chapter of *Friction*, Tsing shows how one locality in Indonesia was transformed into a "frontier" by the combination of predatory transnational logging corporations, a cooperating state regime, and a minority of corrupted locals who had themselves been dislocated by a previous onslaught. This frontier is not virgin territory; it is a previously organized rural area exceeding capitalist categories of property, commodity, and investment now rendered wild and susceptible to venture capital, hypermasculine domination, and new displacements: "Frontier men and resources . . . are made in the dynamics of intensification and proliferation. Confusions between legal and illegal, public and private, disciplined and wild, are productive in sponsoring the emergence of men driven to profit, that is entrepreneurs, as well as the natural objects conjured in their resourceful drives. These men and objects are contagious, recharging the landscape with wildness and virility. The frontier then appears to roll with its own momentum."[4]

Frontier stories of the American West even travel to Indonesia, where they inspire new actions and casualties. As a young boy I watched movies portraying frontier images of the American West, not realizing until I was older what "frontier" life did to peoples already there. Now counterstories in both places are also traveling, as Tsing so eloquently portrays them.

Using close ethnographies, Tsing teaches how a series of distinctions between wilderness and cultivation, field and forest, private property and public domain, settlement and hinterland, weeds and garden, and local and global slide over critical activities going on in the "gaps" between those pristine categories. Much of the sustenance of locals in the Meratus Mountains, for instance, takes place in the gaps between our categories, even more so before massive logging companies rolled in to free-cut those areas and generate uncontrolled flooding. Some of the fruit the locals harvest, for instance, comes from seeds they have thrown into the edge of the forest after eating the fruit. Forest as neither garden nor wilderness.

Tsing reviews a series of local struggles with transnational loops, hoping that they might be amplified further by publicizing and extending them. She is very familiar with the risks of broadening activist connections in order to resist the transnational-local combines through which habitat destruction and profit outflow have been organized. But she concurs that such risks must be run today, given the multiple scales on which frontier exploitation occurs. She hopes that it is possible to pursue them without merely extending Western imperial power.

In reviewing one fight to save the forests around Manggur, a village in the Meratus Mountains, Tsing elaborates the diversity of understandings and priorities from which that effective assemblage was built. "Nature lovers" drawn to the region from the national capital, environmentalists from the provincial capital, and villagers "collaborated" with each other. But they did not all share the same understandings or priorities. Some treated the trees themselves as living beings with perspectives to be taken into account. Others construed the forest as a collection of objects with priorities for use given respectively to villagers, tourists, and a nature reserve with little village presence. All of these perspectives were ranged against the plundering policies of the logging company, its local cronies, and its transnational investors. Even the idea of a village came under critical scrutiny from some locals who did not identify as villagers. Out of this medley of voices and pressures a critical assemblage was formed that, in this case, turned back the logging company. Even some maverick organizers of capital played a positive role.[5]

The emergent assemblage did not become a unity, let alone a community; it became a moving complex of interests, concerns, and critical perspectives with a few shining points of affinity and commonality. All, for instance, opposed the logging company, but some pursued a wilderness ideal, while others sought to retain the forests as living sites of human-forest-animal-plant intersection. Even the victory did not look the same to all the parties involved.

Tsing writes as one who places a "hair in the flour" of neoliberal stories on one side and notions of pure wilderness on the other.[6] Several hair balls, perhaps. She is moved by the locals in their struggles against corporate depredation. She adores "nature lovers" from the cities, even if she does not share the purity of the wilderness perspective that moves them; she is inspired by the activism they pursue and the larger assemblages they help to foment. Her own writing moves others to explore lines of collaborative activism. Engaged ethnography, forming a part of the assemblages on which it reports.

Such inquiries show in detail how northern transnational corporations recruit displaced local adventurers to produce new "frontiers," that is, disrupted and disorganized spaces in which displacements and confusions become happy hunting grounds for venture capital. Get in. Get a quick profit. And get out before things fall apart. Let others try to pick up the pieces. That false gold bubble in the mountains Tsing reviews represents a perfect example of such an ugly game.

Tsing identifies sites, then, at which counterassemblages have been and can be built. She writes in a poetic style that invites us to attend to ecologies closely and encourages us to extend our own modes of activity. She loves to talk about stories that travel from one world region to another: frontier stories, stories about creative strikes, and stories about tree hugging, moving across regions and acquiring new tonalities as they do so. Her stories invite comparison to the assemblage of disparate protestors that have gathered together in the American West as ranchers, white parents, Native Americans, and national environmentalists—replete with different stories and priorities—coalesced in a pluralist assemblage to oppose the Keystone pipeline. That pipeline was primed to connect dirty Canadian tar sand oils to New Orleans by a continent-wide pipe that would damage Native areas, hurt ranchers, produce more climate warming, feed into the fossil fuels corporations' addiction to a future built on oil, and, above all, threaten the huge Ogallah Aquifer that provides sustenance to several western states. A Republican president, if elected in 2016, will be eager and ready to reverse President Obama's decision against this pipeline.

Do such studies also address the self-organizing powers of large planetary processes that intersect with multiple regions in different ways? Let's look at an exemplary contribution by Chakrabarty. In a groundbreaking essay published in 2009, Chakrabarty writes of his effort to come to terms with climate change, "I realized that all my readings in theories of globalization, Marxist analysis of capital, subaltern studies, and postcolonial criticism over the last twenty-five years, while enormously useful in studying globalization, had not really prepared me for making sense of this planetary conjuncture within which humanity finds itself today."[7] Many of those studies had assumed that human culture is largely internal to itself, with "the environment" mostly playing a background role or operating on culture only to the degree culture operates on it They were organized around coming to terms with the ways a center exploits the periphery and with explaining internal contradictions in a mode of production.

Chakrabarty asserts that Stalin's 1938 essay on nature and culture condensed a larger set of views along this dimension. Stalin wrote that "changes and development of society proceed at an incomparably faster rate than the changes and development of geographical environment. . . . Changes in geographical environment of any importance require millions of years, whereas a few hundred or couple of thousand years are enough for even very important changes in the system of human society."[8]

Moreover, Chakrabarty says, the historic pursuit of human freedom has often been linked by dominant voices in the West to pursuit of human separation from, or even domination over, nature. He draws on Bruno Latour to challenge these perspectives, as he moves toward what I call *entangled humanism.*

Thus Chakrabarty in no way lets capitalism off the hook, particularly the transnational capitalist companies that extract fossil fuels in vulnerable, manufactured "frontiers" outside the easy reach of transnational media, as they leave behind innumerable casualties of slow violence. Postcolonial ecostudies are critical in coming to terms with such combinations. And extractive capitalism forms the cutting edge of those forces, even if it does not exhaust them. So accounting for the new era in which various cultures emerge as more active geologic forces cannot be done, Chakrabarty agrees, by reference simply to "humanity" or to a generic "species" drive. That language covers up radical differentials in how this geologic force was produced, how it is maintained, and the radical asymmetries in how its effects are distributed. But focusing on capitalism alone, while much better, also underplays the different responses of different capitalist regimes, lets state communism off the hook, downplays the role of some religious groups that have fervently supported such activities, and ignores long-term Western trends that are not entirely the product of capitalism.

I concur with Chakrabarty on these points. We need to rethink human freedom, rooting it partly in small and large nonhuman processes. Histories grounded in cultural internalism are sadly deficient. Neoliberal capitalism is a very aggressive force today in fostering climate change and ocean acidification, with its evangelical and oil partners in the United States making that country the most dangerous outlier in responding to the issue. And zones outside the northern centers of capitalism suffer inordinately from the slow violence those companies help to disseminate. Sure, China has recently surged ahead of the United States and Europe in CO_2 emissions, and India is not far behind. But the Euro-American constellation—two rather small territories even when considered together—accounts for about 52 percent of the world's cumulative emissions. When you check out the per capita carbon imprint, the situation is even more dramatic, with the United States well ahead of all other states and regions. You must add too that desolate urban zones within capitalist centers and indigenous "reservations" on its margins are sites of slow violence. Chakrabarty would surely accept these points.

I do have one worry, however. Chakrabarty identifies cultural forces that have become geological. He also sees that the assumption of gradualism with respect to geological processes themselves is exaggerated as he attends to cyclical shifts in the tilt of the earth and the earth's wobble. He does not seem to accept a notion of deep ecology in which eco stabilization would become automatic if the human imprint were lightened. But he also may not attend closely enough, to numerous self-organized, nonhuman *amplifiers* that operate within these planetary cyclical constraints and make huge differences on their own. They do so particularly in response to the acceleration of capitalist triggers created by fossil extraction strategies, deforestation, and carbon emissions. My sense is that Nixon and Naomi Klein, each with invaluable contributions, may concur in downplaying the role of amplifiers and thus the rocky history of rapid changes that have periodically occurred in climate, glacier flows, and the ocean conveyor.

Today at least a three-way process of intellectual exchange is needed, or better, overdue. Euro-American environmentalism and postcolonial ecostudies must inform each other so that environmentalism acquires a density and reach that tracks that of transnational neoliberal corporations, crony regimes, and international agencies. On top of that both need to address the work of new geologists, paleontologists, glaciologists, oceanographers, evolutionary biologists, and climatologists who have exploded the notions of planetary gradualism earlier generations in those very fields had adopted. Their work adds depth, range, and complexity to ecological studies. Of course these traditions themselves sometimes need critical attention, some of which I have tried to pursue in chapters 2 and 4. But eco thinkers today need to move back and forth among three modes of inquiry, allowing each in turn to inform and sometimes challenge the other two. Drawing the humanities and the earth sciences into closer proximity in these ways may even help to broaden the spectrum of political activism emanating from the academy. In any event such threefold intersections enable us to come to terms with bumpy transitions in the past, to explore self-organized amplifiers within nonhuman systems today that can accelerate the climate effects of extractive capitalism, and perhaps help us to see better how cross-regional citizen alliances could work to challenge the hegemony of predatory, transstate, corporate complexes. Closer collaborations between the humanities and the earth sciences in the academy might make a modest contribution to such a larger assemblage.

With considerable help from others, in earlier chapters I touched on autonomous elements in species evolution, tectonic plate movements, glacier flows, bacterial flows, and ocean currents. Let's now take a look at recent research into a couple of species extinction events to see how they can illuminate our thinking further. The point is to examine bumpy intersections of heterogeneous force fields that generated radical extinction events to see how such events from the past might inform understandings of the contemporary condition.

Extinction Events and Bumpy Temporalities

Lyell, the great nineteenth-century geologist, and Darwin, the great nineteenth-century theorist of species evolution, were both gradualists about geological and species change. Living between 1797 and 1878, Lyell concluded that species and geological strata change very slowly. The "wild" theories of one predecessor, Cuvier, about a series of periodic "catastrophes" in nature led by the rapid extinction of dinosaurs, were to be rejected in the name of respecting the everyday grind of normal science over unfounded speculation about periods of rapid change. Darwin's own theory of natural selection and survival of the fittest underwent significant revision in 1871, with the publication of *The Descent of Man*.[9] There, as we have seen, he added aesthetic and sexual elements to the theory for the evolution of species with vertebrae, a teleodynamic amendment inserted into the heart of his theory that calls neo-Darwinism into question before the very formation of that theory. But he nonetheless retained a gradualist outlook about species evolution. He claimed, for instance, that the residues of body hair, the curtailed ability to smell, the capacity of some of us to wiggle our ears (I can), and the shape of our organs of locomotion express shifts over millennia from earlier formations that gradually allowed the evolution of humanity to occur. The rudiments connect us to a long evolutionary tree linked to slow geological change.

The themes of gradualism and evolutionary progress acknowledged extinctions, but evolution was seen to be gradual and tied to an overall advance in species complexity, with white humans in the British Empire at the top of the evolutionary pyramid. The sad irony is this: both Cuvier, who rejected evolution but accepted rapid extinctions, and Darwin and Lyell, who pursued tree-like images of evolutionary gradualism, advanced racist theories. Cuvier did so by positing eternal species ranked according to an eternal hierarchy. Darwin and Lyell did so by projecting an evolutionary tree along a dominant line of ascent. Two different images with similar cultural effects.

Early critics of gradualism, including Bergson, pounded away at the problem of how the evolution of one organ could be gradual and unilateral unless it was intimately involved with a set of other shifts in other organs. He thought about more rapid changes in entire organisms.[10] But Bergson's objections were generally thought to point merely to sore spots in the dominant theory that would eventually be ironed out by a gradualist image of the evolutionary tree. Better to retain the sore points than to insinuate a divine element of *élan vital* into a more bumpy and creative evolutionary process. The identification of symbiogenesis by Lynn Margulis and the introduction of theories of epigenesis and teleodynamism have posed more commanding challenges to neo-Darwinism.

The debate over gradualism surfaced only sporadically in the earth sciences until as late as the early 1980s, with gradualists holding the upper, "scientific" hand. Then an essay appeared by Luis Alvarez, a physicist, about the huge asteroid in Mexico that rapidly wiped out dinosaurs and several other species 65 million years ago.[11] About 50 percent of life disappeared. After a lengthy period of intense debate it became the established view. It is difficult to watch geologists on TV pointing to the thin line of glass-like sediment in the Black Hills of North Dakota that separates the periods before and after the asteroid hit without consenting to such a reading. Below the thin line are innumerable dinosaur fossils of different sorts; above it only a few turtles and crocodiles who survived the onslaught.

Here was a mass extinction event over a decade or so followed by a slower turn in the future trajectory of evolution. If other such instances were discovered, species evolution would now look more like a series of interacting, bumpy temporalities than a single, linear evolutionary tree set on a gradualist trajectory.

More examples were quickly found. There was the near extinction of life as such 250 million years ago, when up to 90 percent of life succumbed over a period of perhaps 20,000 to 200,000 years. There was another major extinction 450 million years ago and another yet around 200 million years ago. Human beings faced a monster volcano 75,000 years ago. And there was the final extinction of Neanderthals around 28,000 years ago. Today extractive capitalism is a prime mover and shaker in a new mass extinction event moving very fast;

it is triggered by fossil fuel use, a new era of rapid climate change, ocean acidification, and the loss of evolutionary niches for a variety of species.[12]

Studies of past extinction events doubtless have been spurred by recent
awareness that rapid climate change is occurring, making it wise to check out
other such events in the past. Can the previous events help us to cope scien-
tifically, politically, and existentially with the current situation? Let's look a
bit more closely at just two such events: the great extinction event 250 million years ago and the more recent decimation of our kissing cousins, the
Neanderthals. I tiptoe into this literature as an amateur entering a domain of
inquiry that is unsettled and yet highly pertinent to the human sciences, the
humanities, and ecopolitics.

Two Extinction Events

Up to 90 percent of life was extinguished during a short period in geological time 251 million years ago. The causes of this devastation are still being
debated; indeed it became an object of close exploration only recently. Hy-
potheses of another major asteroid impact have been advanced but seem to be
based on scant evidence. One scenario links the event to a series of methane
bursts that occurred after a period of rapid global warming, itself caused by
volcanic eruptions in Siberia (the Siberian Traps) releasing huge amounts of
CO_2 and other gases into the air. The "repeated eruptions" may have warmed
the air over the Antarctic Ocean enough to lift the ice cover over methane
fields there. Michael Benton, a palaeontologist and earth scientist, contends:

> Release of carbon dioxide from the eruption of the Siberian traps led
> to a rise of global temperatures of 6 degrees Celsius or so [about 11 de-
> grees Fahrenheit]. Cool polar regions became warm and frozen tundra
> became unfrozen. The melting might have penetrated to the frozen gas
> hydrate reservoirs located around the polar oceans, and massive vol-
> umes of methane may have burst to the surface of the oceans in huge
> bubbles. This further input of carbon into the atmosphere caused more
> warming. . . . So the process went on, running faster and faster. The
> natural systems that normally reduce carbon dioxide levels could not
> operate, and eventually the system spiraled out of control, with the big-
> gest crash in the history of life.[13]

As the repetition of "may" suggests, this is a speculative theory, though there
is evidence to support it and the event itself now seems undeniable. The evidence of a double whammy followed by a series of self-amplifying processes is

stronger than that so far offered in support of other theories. Moreover there is solid evidence of another methane burst 55 million years ago, with severe effects of its own.

The possible pertinence of an event 250 million years ago to today is two-fold: it shows how triggering events, followed by a series of amplifiers, can issue in devastating results, and it calls attention to independently stated concerns today that the breakneck pace of global warming could once again release methane bubbles now covered by ice or previously sedimented under a cool ocean. Indeed the temperature increases during that period are close to those now projected for 2100 if nothing radical is done soon to reduce the human input of CO_2 into the atmosphere.[14] One difference, however, is that there are 7 billion people on the planet now—up from a mere 10,000 around 60,000 years ago, shortly after a crisis, only 5 million in 800 BCE, and 3 billion a mere sixty years ago—and there were none when the great mass extinction occurred.[15] We are playing with a wildfire and it is playing with us.

A second event is closer in time and mode of life. Around 28,000 years ago the last of the Neanderthals were extinguished. If you are over fifty you are likely to have assumed (as I did) that they disappeared either because they were vanquished by *Homo sapiens* or because they were not intelligent enough to survive the competition for stable supplies of food and resources. We *Homo sapiens* are so smart. That story paints a triumphalist view of humanity (or of one of its types) in a way that recalls the old story, before the discovery and dating of that huge asteroid cavity in Mexico, of how dumb dinosaurs bit the dust. Both stories reinforce a vision of *Homo* triumphalism on the way to new triumphs in the future.

The emerging picture is rather different, though it too is pockmarked with uncertainties filled with speculation. According to Clive Finlayson, the *Homo sapiens*–Neanderthal split began 600,000 years ago, after which each evolved into its "classical shape." They occupied adjacent land for a while in the Mideast, where some intraspecies sex and reproduction occurred. The evolutionary pattern after that was bumpy for each type, not corresponding to any smooth image of evolutionary progress. As the climate cooled 125,000 years ago Neanderthals were pressed to retreat to warmer areas. Why? They had larger brains than *Homo sapiens*, though it may well be that the ratio of cerebellum to cerebral hemisphere differed between the two groups. For instance, one Neanderthal site in Jersey (currently an island off the shore of England but once part of an isthmus connecting England to the mainland) reveals that they organized complex hunts for woolly mammoths by forcing them into stampedes until they fell over a high cliff; then they cut up, barbecued, and ate them, while warding off other predators. Such a feat involved extensive foresight, improvisation, and organizational skill.[16]

The changing climate combined with their stocky build to make life tough on Neanderthals. That build had suited them for warm periods when they could hunt large animals on the edges of forests and plains. But warming wiped out the large animals—or forced them elsewhere—and the Neanderthals were pressed to move south to find food consistent with their body type. They could not, for instance, chase down animals on long hunts or adopt too active a nomadic life.

The last hurrah for the Neanderthals occurred on Gibraltar, an area that retained its warm weather longer. They lived there for 125,000 years, as the remarkable layers of temporal evidence on the Gorman Cave show. "By 40,000 years ago their homeland had been pinned back to the Mediterranean, southwest France, and pockets around the Black Sea. The acceleration of cold and unstable conditions after 37,000 years ago reduced the range even further, leaving a major stronghold in southern and eastern Iberia and pockets in northern Iberia, the Atlantic seaboard to the north. . . . By the time we reach the end of our period, 30,000 years ago, the only Neanderthals left were in south-western Iberia."[17]

Between 28,000 and 24,000 years ago the remnants became extinct, perhaps from a disease that wiped out the weakened few remaining on the Iberian peninsula. Finlayson's thesis is that dissonant conjunctions of body type, hunting methods compatible with that type, the loss of large animals, and rapid climate change did in the Neanderthals. As he puts it, there was a lot of luck and contingency in how things worked out. By that I think he means that while each of the force fields in play—climate change, migration patterns, body type, hunting instruments, type of game available, pace of evolutionary change—was in itself explicable, the amplifying conjunctions created situations that rapidly favored some groups and threatened others. Even if you add, as I would, a teleodynamic element to species evolution that makes each new stage in evolution only partially explicable in principle, the fate of the Neanderthals was shaped by a series of conjunctions and the variable speeds at which they occurred.[18]

We did not triumph over the Neanderthal in a stable environment, nor did we wipe them out in a series of genocidal battles. Our weak, slim body type, ability to forage and go on long hunts, resultant emergence of village sources of vibrant activity, and invention of projectile hunting launched growth in the *Homo sapiens* population on the cold plains that helped to protect the subspecies from the ravages of disease and climate change. What if the climate had entered a rapid warming period? Or if that warming had produced new and highly contagious diseases? Or if a new series of volcanoes and methane bursts had occurred? *Homo sapiens* might not have been as lucky a species as it was in fact, though the fate of the Neanderthal might have been severe too.

Are we the Neanderthals of today, packing 7 billion people onto the face of the earth during a period when climate change is rapid, fossil fuel use is still growing, and the prospect of future conflagrations is likely between those trying to emigrate from low-lying zones and militant countries aggressively protecting more favorably disposed territories? If the Neanderthals in fact had a narrow line of escape they did not find or luck into—an idea that is uncertain, the apparent one now available to *Homo sapiens* is thwarted by the forces of transnational fossil fuel companies, neoliberal capitalism, the infrastructure of investment and consumption in several states, the drudgery of everyday life for so many, the right edge of evangelical theology, the media's limited aspirational projections for poor and working-class people, popular denialism, temptations to use nuclear weapons, and even an abstract belief by many in the United States in particular in climate change disconnected from living drives to political action.

Aggressive and Passive Nihilisms

Humanist exceptionalism, to rework a theme drawn from Charles Taylor, is the idea that we are either the one species favored and nourished by God or a divinely unprotected species so superior to other forces and beings that we can deploy them endlessly for our purposes.[19] We have language, rights, dignity, meaning, consciousness, creativity, artistry, and endless entitlements; they are either useful to us as "objects" or so inferior that we do not need to think about them intrinsically. The long debate in Euro-American philosophy between utilitarianism and Kantianism was largely a debate within what I am calling humanist exceptionalism. So too was that between capitalism and communism. Sociocentrism, cultural internalism, and humanist exceptionalism complement one another despite their differences; they provide the shifting matrix within which a series of limited debates and omissions has occurred in Euro-American states. To varying degrees all have been out of touch with human entanglements with a volatile world that increasingly makes things fragile—even if very differentially—for people in several world regions.

Some have argued that humanist exceptionalism formed a bulwark against nihilism. By identifying with human exceptionalism you resist the drive to drain all meaning, purpose, morality, and artistry from life after "the death of God." You invest it in human flourishing. Of course Nietzsche would not accept such a reading, since he sees close bonds between the specific monotheism of divine omnipotence and the humanism it helped to spawn as both opponent and complement. But we do not need to tarry now over that well-worn issue.

My question is rather different: Do the remnants of sociocentrism and humanist exceptionalism—in both their divine and secular expressions often concentrated in northern capitalist states—run the grave risk of becoming new modes of nihilism in those zones during the current planetary era? If so, what are the possibilities of overcoming humanist drives to nihilism? To pursue this question I inhabit and revise Nietzsche's account of nihilism. I both draw sustenance from his account and freely work on it during an era he might have been prescient about but did not anticipate specifically.

Nihilism, the sense that all meaning has been subtracted from the world, emerges when a set of urgently needed beliefs and meanings are sorely threatened by events and new interpretations. The culturally imbued need might be the belief that God infuses the world with divine meaning and providence, or that Christ will soon return, or that eternal laws of the world are all knowable by us in principle, or that humanity is uniquely made in the image of God, or that the world is an organic whole to which we belong when we tread lightly on it, or that history is set on a progressive trajectory of mastery over nature with possible positive outcomes we can vaguely discern on a singular horizon, or that we are the only ones who make a substantive difference on the planet. If and when the culturally infused need is intense and belief in its actuality is threatened, nihilism emerges as a real force.

Nihilism is the sense that one or more of these demands is indispensable to give life meaning but that it in fact is not available. Since elements of belief and unbelief express differing degrees of complexity in different body-brain subsystems, and since these subsystems are connected by multiple relays and loops to the world and to each other, expressions of nihilism find both individual and cultural manifestations.

One expression is the emergence of aggressive nihilism. Today the temptation to aggressive nihilism comes not only from threats to the existence of God or from the loss of a sense of organic belonging; it also emerges from a palpable sense that a new planetary era throws familiar, institutionally anchored projections of progress and abundance into jeopardy over a short period of time.

Aggressive nihilism responds to shocking evidence that the course we are on is self-defeating by radically upping the ante of deniability, by attacking the messengers, and by doubling down on the exact activities that exacerbate the problem. "Drill, baby, drill," the lively, young vice presidential candidate repeated at every election stop in 2008. And "Frack, frack, frack us" is the new demand. The most extreme form of aggressive nihilism may be inhabited by whispers: "Either we retain our current world entitlements or we let the whole thing collapse." In the United States the fossil fuel companies, the right edge of neoliberalism, Fox News, the Republican Party, and the right edge of evangelicalism take the lead, often inspiring each other to new levels of extremism. Indeed it is not just that the fossil fuel companies demand a future built around those fuels; the long-term investments they make to ensure a supply of such fuels twenty or thirty years from now lock them into this vision of the future.[20] So the self-interest of oil magnates and investment banks plays a major role here. But if a somewhat broader atmosphere of aggression were subtracted from that social calculus, these forces would become much more susceptible to isolation and defeat. A conspiracy theory is thus pertinent but insufficient to the times.

The biggest danger of aggressive nihilism is that it will carry the day until it is too late, delaying responses until irreversible changes take over. But there is a second, more subtle danger attached to it. The repeated critique of aggressive nihilism by eco critics, while important, also allows many others to fail to come to grips with the passive nihilism that may haunt us to different degrees. For we too may grieve the loss of a world that can be no longer. I mean to suggest that many Euro-Americans still recovering from the loosely intercoded tendencies to sociocentrism, cultural internalism, humanist exceptionalism, and planetary gradualism reviewed earlier are vulnerable to the disease of passive nihilism today.

Passive nihilism involves a two stage process. First, the nihilists had invested profound meaning in a set of institutional practices and aspirations. That meaning might be invested, say, in institutional faith in a providential God, or practices of consumption, investment, art and production built around human exceptionalism, or practices presupposing sociocentrism, or some combination of the above. Now things happen that begin to hollow out faith in those beliefs and practices. More and more people lose faith in them, but continue to participate in them. They can find no route to replacement. [21]

"Nihilism," Nietzsche says, "as a psychological state is reached . . . when one has posited a totality, a systematization, indeed any organization in all events, and a soul that longs to admire and revere some supreme form of domination and administration."[22] Your faith in your own value has been grounded in a set of conscious beliefs and affectively dense molecular preunderstandings that have heretofore rumbled together. But now, for whatever reason, the flow between these two registers has become blocked. You lose conscious belief, but continue to be attached to old residues of it. We have walked to the edge of passive nihilism. Existential anxiety intensifies.

The complexity of the relation between the forfeited beliefs and their persisting residues is worth examining. "The philosophical nihilist is convinced that all that happens is meaningless and in vain; and that there ought not to be anything meaningless and in vain. But whence this: there ought not to be? From where does one get *this* meaning, *this* standard?"[23] The second-order sense and cloudy demand is located in molecular residues heretofore connected by neuro flows to the onto-perspective now subdued at a refined cognitive level. The new blockage within and among us now becomes a source of anxiety and passivity. For both selves and cultures consist of multiple, interacting layers and flows, with cloudy, culturally imbued affective purposes and feelings at visceral levels flowing into slower moving, more refined processes in ways that can either strengthen or weaken those processes. My discussion of drives and instincts in earlier chapters is consistent with such a view.

We also communicate mimetically across molecular tiers, through gestures, tonality of voice, bodily stance, the unconscious choice of words, stutters at untimely moments, visceral responses to smell, and intensities of response to daily stress: the visceral or molecular dimension of life operates within the social structure of selves and cultural processes.[24] Fox News works on the collective visceral register, often trying to translate passive nihilism into aggressive nihilism.

In passive nihilism persistent residues from past understandings and expectations now inhibit people from moving beyond a vague sense of loss, even if they no longer believe in the world that has been lost. Passive nihilists are weakened, anxious beings who doubt a providential God, or human exceptionalism, or sociocentrism, or climate gradualism. But they do not invest in alternative paths of meaning, responsibility, and activism partly because stubborn residues within and between them resist those investments and partly because they sense how disruptive political efforts would be to transform the institutions expressing them.

These residues inhabit the lower registers of experience. They consist of culturally imbued proto-thoughts invested with dense affective intensity. The lower registers thus subsist below the ready reach of clean representation, argument, or reflexivity. The old pathway now persists in the same direction as heretofore, but its ingression into the refined zone has now become blocked. We do not *know* this register in itself. Our interpretations dramatize in one way or another a set of incipient processes, doing so to sound them out by ascertaining which way people turn once this or that dramatization is offered.[25]

That is why it is too crude to talk about "performative contradictions" here, since the heterogeneous registers in question are both connected and operate at different speeds, degrees of intensity, and levels of sophistication. Rather, disparate processes that had once been wired together now create static when the channels of flow between them are stymied. Energy is sapped. Critical theory needs to reduce its reliance on the performative contradiction as a master tool of critique. Such a demand underplays the messiness of an undesigned world with heterogeneous connections of multiple sorts, including those between different brain subsystems marked by variations of intensity and complexity.[26] There is an old saying in neuroscience: "Neurons that fire together wire together." Not a bad way to think about the cultural formation of habits and motor skills. But another slogan may fit the dissonance addressed here: "Disparate affect-imbued cognitive registers that had rumbled together can sometimes become jumbled together." Passive nihilism.

Nietzsche seeks to tap such uncanny blockages through dramatization; he also seeks to move the molecular register of cultural life through the kinds of arts of the self we reviewed in chapter 2. Buddhists do so through mindfulness and lucid dreaming. Deleuze collectivizes such constituency engagements through micropolitics. Fox News works relentlessly on this cultural register in a destructive way. One issue of passive nihilism during the late stage of the Anthropocene is whether and how to recraft such molecular flows and the blockages they can foment. The exploration of role experiments in chapter 5 represents one effort to do this very work. Since there is never a vacuum on the visceral register of cultural life, ignoring it cannot suffice. Working to modify it is both daunting and more promising politically.

My sense is that in old capitalist states today the shock of the planetary—when linked to the massive alterations it calls for in productive and extractive practices, the organization of consumption, profit-making enterprises, military priorities, and established cultural meanings—fosters seething seedbeds of passive nihilism in several corners of life. These find variable expression in established investment portfolios, dominant research profiles in the academy, established consumption practices, some churches committed to divine omnipotence, and politicians trying to win votes from harried citizens who try not to think too much about the planetary condition. Not always the outright denials pushed by aggressive nihilists; more often explicit admission and tacit evasion.

It is a dangerous and volatile time. But passive nihilism may tremble with multiple potentialities, some pointing toward an even more morose resignation, others to evolution into aggressive nihilism, and others yet to new investments of meaning, purpose, and drive in a world that no longer fits, if it ever did, the world pictures in which dominant capitalist institutions have been invested. And, as previously noted, several institutions are locked into such pictures even if the role bearers have begun to doubt them. Both Pascal and Nietzsche may need to be reworked to some extent today. During the Anthropocene, Pascal's wager over the existence of God has morphed into one over how many places of human habitation can survive if old and new capitalist states remain on the same trajectory. Nietzsche's voluptuous gratitude for existence in a universe that is not highly predisposed to human hegemony must perhaps morph into care for the exigencies of the future joined to furious opposition to forces that work to lock so many who have not contributed to the result into it.

Entangled Humanism

During this era it is certainly not enough to reject humanism. Such rejections, standing alone, are all too apt to fuel new variants of aggressive nihilism within several old capitalist states, variants that can be dramatized to say, "It will be over soon, so let's take care of ourselves and a few others as we ridicule modes of political activism anchored in the squishiness of interspecies entanglements and worldly care." Or: "Let's oppose finding places for refugees on the grounds they are dangerous even though the climate changes we have helped to introduce do and will contribute to those migration pressures." Today perhaps it is wise to try to *transfigure* the old humanisms that have played important roles in Euro-American states into multiple affirmations of entangled humanism in a fragile world. Such a transfiguration can then work hand in hand with the strategies articulated in chapter 5, including those role experiments designed to work on the visceral registers of cultural life.

One such transfiguration of humanism acknowledges a world composed of innumerable entanglements, including:

The ancient bacteria imprisoned in human cells (mitochondria).

Other bacterial micro-agencies in our guts that influence moods flowing into our higher brain.

The reptile brain within us that has evolved to forge a series of dissonant lines of communication with the world and more refined brain zones.

Our internal relations to the Neanderthal and Denisovan.

Incorporated drives nested within and between us that send affectively imbued proto-thoughts into consciousness and also influence behavior and communication directly.

Myriad modes of interspecies symbiosis and disease jumps.

Cultural relations with innumerable species with perspectives of their own.

A history of capitalist exploitations within and beyond the core territories of its origin.

Shifting entanglement with the planet's gravitational pull as the Antarctic shelves melt at a rapid rate and a larger proportion of increase in ocean height occurs in the temperate zones.

Numerous imbrications with the planetary, partially self-organizing capacities of climate, glaciers, ocean currents, water-filtration processes, bacterial and viral flows, and species evolution.

These entanglements are of multiple types. Many have been appreciated in some places and traditions for centuries, particularly outside the confines of that division of the world into subjects and objects that major traditions in Europe have elaborated and "minor" traditions inside and outside Europe have protested. So it may be that the entangled humanism that grows out of the encounter with a new time can also place its adherents in northern, privileged territories in a better position to enter into thoughtful exchanges with eco-centered traditions in other places.[27] Certainly modes of human and nonhuman perspectivism found in India, the Amazon, Indonesia, Ghana, and other places offer ripe possibilities for creative exchange. Such exchanges will not, of course, mean that all parties become entangled humanists. It may mean, rather, that attempts to respect differences of creed across real differences will improve as the debates continue and spiritual affinities across the differences are explored.

I do not advance entangled humanism as a new universal that should be accepted by everyone everywhere. Rather it is offered as a revision of doctrines of human exceptionalism and sociocentrism that have previously carried so much weight in northern capitalist states. My hope is that such a transfiguration will allow entangled humanists to forge relations of agonistic respect with other traditions that also challenge exceptionalism and sociocentrism in distinctive ways. The findings of entangled humanism are also increasingly consistent with those of contemporary ethological sciences. They too reject a world split between human subjects and objects. Such knowledges are marked by mobile boundaries of remainder, noise, uncertainty, and creativity that exceed them. These infuse and impinge upon us as we do upon them. Such remainders, too, must find a place within entangled humanism.

Some variants of entangled humanism may embrace a god or gods of entanglement; some may be nontheistic; some may pursue an immanent divine, and some the theme of an immanent naturalism that is never apt to understand the world completely.[28] Every which way, seeking positive entanglements with other traditions concerned about exploitation of world ecologies.

Entangled humanism of the sort pursued here strives to acknowledge without existential resentment the constitutive imbrications and interdependencies noted above. Such an affirmation does not, certainly, undercut resentments against class domination or racism; rather it seeks to surmount resentment against the most fundamental terms of human existence as such as it fights against class domination and racism.

The spiritualities encouraged by entangled humanism tilt everything they touch, without trying to eliminate strains of belief and faith that appreciate the power of the Anthropocene from other angles. Pluralist proponents of entangled humanism seek to pursue affinities of spirituality with supporters of other creeds also concerned about the urgency of today. We are, in aspiration, deep pluralists who pursue affinities of spirituality across creedal differences as we recognize that powerful forces work implacably to defeat those combinations. We certainly do not assume that every constituency seeks to become part of the critical pluralist assemblage we embrace.

Entangled humanists also acknowledge limits to the human ability to feel, perceive, think, know, judge, and respond in a world teeming with a variety of human and nonhuman modes of perception. But, as numerous ethnographies and techno-artistic experiments have revealed, we do not know in advance exactly where and what those limits are. We may be able to stretch our capacities of experience enough to inhabit the experiential edge of other species, such as whales, hippos, vultures, crocodiles, octopi, plants, yeast, and crows, without becoming attuned to any completely. Such modes of experiential augmentation intensify awareness of interspecies entanglements.

To take merely one example, the drive to extinction of the vulture in India is fueled by the proliferation of a new drug for cattle that is toxic to vultures. Their extinction would shut down a symbiotic relation wherein they scavenge dead cattle, the scavenging protects the populace against disease, the cleaned bones provide the poor with items to collect and sell as fertilizer, and the feral dog and rat population is kept within manageable limits.[29] Is it possible to imagine more about the lifeworld of the vulture? Perhaps experiments in aerodynamic flying, peering through binoculars at a grassland from high perches, tearing meat off a carcass, and the cultivation of new smells could be joined to interpretive studies to take us to the edge of vulture experience? Not merely to think differently about vultures but to inhabit the edge of their life experiences and to infuse those experiments more into the visceral or molecular registers of being? I need such infusions because my soul remains haunted by boyhood movies in which buzzards hover on dead trees when death is in the cards for a western villain or hero. I see now that they were waiting to eat, and that the way they eat cleans things up, but I do not yet feel that way in my bones.

Entangled humanists are thus wary of transcendental arguments that pretend to fix the boundaries of interspecies experiential engagements once and for all, given the numerous defeats of such attempts in the past. As multiply entangled beings we seek periodically to stretch the visceral habits of perception and identification from which our cultural judgments are forged; to work on congealed drives within and between us by tactical means to open common sense to new modes of experience, experiment, and attachment; to extend knowledge of other species by confronting work in allied fields; to enliven the existential dimension of life; and to expose ourselves to new events that may rebound on those endeavors.

But what else makes this a creed of entangled *humanism*? As entangled humanists struggle to become worthy of the events we encounter, we also give a recurrently problematized degree of priority to the human species in its interdependencies and imbrications with other beings and forces it neither masters nor owns. We thus affirm care for the human estate in its worldly entanglements as we also stretch that care beyond the scope of human exceptionalism and toward other species with whom we are entangled. We care about humans as we incorporate into ourselves more actively appreciations of how members of other species care about themselves. Thus the symbiotic relation to the vulture is valued in part because of appreciation of how it cares for itself, in part in care for a species that is ugly to many of us, and in part because its practices decrease the spread of rabies and anthrax to poor people living in rural India.

Entangled humanists pursue neither a morality of purity nor a pure horizon of community. Such projections are too closely associated with extreme human entitlements and too inattentive to planetary forces. To be clear, the humanist dimension in entangled humanism means that as we become more aware of other modes of experience we both extend the net of species appreciation more widely and learn that we must cast our lot with some species more than others. The difficult questions, to be answered in part by cultural ethnologies and ethological studies, are which.[30]

To take a fraught example: the attempt to save the whooping crane by encouraging imprinting on crane-costumed humans and the use of ultralight aircraft to teach the fledglings migration patterns is noble in intention and responsive to the human causes of the potential extinction of that species. Such activities can even teach us how our own molecular registers become organized. But the experiments also pose a series of difficult issues about the use of captive birds for egg laying and of other types of crane as captive egg-sitting surrogates. The point is to dig into interspecies entanglements in each situation to inform experimental action. It is way too late merely to leave the world alone.

The questions are these: How to renegotiate complex entanglements during a late period of the Anthropocene? How to construct a militant pluralist, cross-regional assemblage that pursues ecological actions at multiple sites and seeks to isolate its opponents? These tasks include revitalizing positive affinities of spirituality across differences in creed; pursuing role experiments to readjust church, consumer, teaching, entrepreneurial, work, scientific, blog, parenting, and electoral priorities to respond to the new condition; broadening awareness of eco protests in several regions too often outside the gaze of Euro-centric environmentalism; and organizing cross-country general strikes to press states, corporations, churches, universities, localities, consumers, and investors to pursue a series of rapid changes in their institutional priorities. As we move back and forth between new role investments and the other engagements it is well to remember that the first pursuits make a cumulative difference in themselves when diverse constituencies practice them. *They also work on the molecular dimensions of cultural life and communication.* They work on molecular propensities to perception and prejudgment. Micropolitics is thus fundamental to entangled humanism without being sufficient to it. Correspondingly macropolitics too is critical; its affirmative possibilities are most apt to come alive when it responds to citizen mobilizations in different regions at the same time.

Doubtless several issues remain. I pursue only one now. Do the positive affinities of spirituality pursued here themselves fold a strain of passive nihilism into the mix? Does a subliminal tension between these professions and the sensibilities inhabiting them project the possibility of a new turn in the future when we should in fact come to terms nobly with the irreversibility of human extinction along with numerous other species with whom it is entangled?

That is what Guy McPherson, a climate scientist, would say. Extinction of the human estate is already in the cards, according to McPherson. The amplifications now under way have become irreversible. It is time to learn how to die with nobility.[31] McPherson has not yet told one old guy how to inform his children, partner, students, grandchildren, and Facebook friends about such an implacable future.

It may well be that Fred Pearce would contest such a prognosis, as he concentrates on how new processes of wilding take place as old species lose out.[32] Perhaps. But he does not sufficiently gauge the violent potentialities of the old capitalist states as migration pressures intensify from regions hard hit by changes they did not produce. Once you address the possible imbrications that could emerge from the acceleration of climate change, urgent drives to migration, the rise of neofascist responses in old capitalist states, and the temptation of bellicose states to use nuclear weapons, McPherson's prognosis cannot be dismissed out of hand. Pope Francis and I concur on that point, as we saw earlier when he counseled against treating "doomsday prophecies" with ridicule and contempt. Nonetheless I assume that we are not there yet.[33] I assume that there is time to make a real difference and to avoid the worst. *I assume.* To say that is to acknowledge that my view is lodged in uncertainty and that it contains an element of hope.

McPherson's generic formulation does tend to erase or deface radical differences in the degree to which specific regions and constituencies experience these effects now and will do so in the future. Perhaps the greatest danger is not species extinction per se but the decimation of some regions, intensified migration pressures, and resulting regional tensions that foment new wars.

I would rather think that the modes of creativity expressed by the politics of swarming and cross-regional general strikes could ward off the greatest dangers. What's more, I would rather think that after interim actions have been taken to ward off the worst, new modes of creative experiment will find ample expression in the technical, ethical, and political domains of life in ways that further adapt various regions to the new planetary condition. Such assumptions are partly grounded in shaky counterevidence, partly in historic examples of creative action during other difficult situations, and partly in molecular protests against the prospect of a bleak future. Do traces of passive nihilism thus fold into them?

Well, I cling to entangled humanism in a way that suggests that this attachment is under threat during a fragile time. I will do so as long as I can, while acknowledging that the clinch expresses molecular identification with a revised future itself in jeopardy.

From whence comes this "I would rather think"? Is it sparked by a clash between residues from a previous humanism and shaky attunement to a new condition, a clash that, if conjoined to care and creative actions of the right sort, could encourage more of us to pour energy into emergent, militant, pluralist assemblages? Beyond such a conjecture, I can't say. Let's give the politics of swarming and cross-country general strikes a try; then, if such an improbable necessity proves impossible to enact, it may be time to move to the next items on the agenda.

BRADLEY J. MACDONALD: Before we delve more specifically into the issues and ideas associated with your current work, I would like to pause on an interesting confluence between your early work and the establishment of the Caucus for a New Political Science. As you know, the Caucus was established in 1967 to critique and revamp what was considered the increasingly *antipolitical* character of political science in a world shaken by the third world insurgencies, the rise of the New Left, struggles for African American equality, and a growing discontent with the militarization of global life seen in the Vietnam War. For members of the Caucus—and for fellow scholars sympathetic to its organizational and ideological thrust—the discipline was defined by a myopic methodological commitment to behavioralism, a rather limited reigning conception of pluralism, and a supposed "value neutrality" belied by the deep connections between political science scholarship and existing political power.[1] What I find fascinating is that your early work was clearly part of the growing discontent associated with the insurgent goals of the Caucus. In your first work, *Political Science and Ideology*, and in your subsequent edited volume, *The Bias of Pluralism*, you are clearly aligning yourself with this growing critique of mainstream political science. As you note in an essay published in *The Bias of Pluralism*, "A definable 'critical temper' finds increasing expression within the 'left wing' of political science (and allied disciplines) today and I seek here to identify and support the main thrust of that temper."[2] With that said, I would be curious to get your sense of how you now view your early work written during this tumultuous period. In what way were you sympathetic with the goals of the Caucus as a young scholar, and how did you see your theory in this context? Moreover, how did this early "critical temper" continue to animate your subsequent theoretical development?

BILL CONNOLLY: I was a young assistant professor when the Caucus organizers met at an APSA [American Political Science Association] meeting in 1967. To many of us, who were already participating in protests against the Vietnam War and supporting civil rights, the staid, professional character of much of political science was disturbing. Detached behavioralism, a consensual notion of settled pluralism, "value neutrality," and professionalism all reinforced one another. Or so it looked during this period to the son of a factory worker in Flint, Michigan, coming to graduate school and, soon, the profession. *Political Science and Ideology* was first written as a dissertation before the Caucus was organized and then published as a book in 1967. It argued that the assumptions and test procedures supported by behavioralists unconsciously load the dice in favor of treating a tame version of one-dimensional pluralism as the only viable description of the United States. That description implicitly operated as an ideal too. Ideal and reality were thought to converge by the pluralists, so not much needed to be done. In exposing the ideological underpinnings of the official test procedures I was also showing how American critical theorists such as C. Wright Mills and Peter Bachrach were not the only ideologues in town. The line of differentiation between science and ideology now became more contestable than it had seemed to Robert Dahl, Daniel Bell, and Seymour Martin Lipset. A second goal, drawing upon Karl Mannheim and G. H. Mead, was to craft an approach that both overcame scientism and enabled social scientists to be responsible, engaged intellectuals. This outlook was soon complemented in a superb essay by Charles Taylor. He showed not only how we bring biases to inquiry (he accepted that too) but how every explanatory theory carries with it a set of normative secretions for judgment and action.[3] Debates over the logic of explanation and tests are also, then, debates over the constitution of the good society.

As a young theorist at Ohio University teaching four courses a term I felt excited about teaching and yet isolated in the discipline. It was with a sense of relief and hope, then, that I attended my first Caucus meeting. My recollection is that Mark Roelofs and David Kettler were important movers and shakers at that meeting. It was very well attended and many people spoke. I did not. The gist was that the professionalism of mainstream political science demeaned and punished the very activism needed at this historical juncture; further, it served to shroud the activities of those who spouted professionalism and worked for the CIA. We needed a new political science, participants agreed, because the professionalism, behavioralism, and "value neutrality" of the day made too many cautious and compromised others. The aura of narrow professionalism, of course, was an aftermath to the havoc McCarthy had wreaked on the academy in the previous decade. For instance, the chair of my dissertation committee at the University of Michigan—where behavioralism was then being consolidated—was supportive of my work, but he also periodically warned me against pushing this or that theme "too far." James Meisel had fled Germany during the advent of the Nazi era and later witnessed the emergence of McCarthyism in the States. He had a dramatic fund of experience to draw upon.

The ups and downs of the Caucus are superbly covered in the essay by Clyde Barrow you have noted. I can only add to it by saying that the emergence of the Caucus was bracing to a whole generation of young scholars and critical theorists. In my case, it helped me to discern how the critique in my first book had been unconsciously tempered by a false anxiety that I stood alone in the world, as I looked over my shoulder at how professionals might dismiss what I said. Looking back, I sense how this anxiety short-circuited to some degree my engagement with C. Wright Mills, the bad boy of sociology during the 1950s and 1960s.

Such an interiorized background may work to deflate exaggeration. But it can also confine experimental thinking and bold exploration. My next two books, *The Terms of Political Discourse* and *The Politicized Economy* (with Mike Best), were, I believe, more exploratory. They were prodded, supported, and enabled by the charged atmosphere provided by the New Left and the Caucus. My sense is that this atmosphere of energy and support was very helpful to many others as well.

I was, at David Kettler's behest, included on the Caucus list of Council candidates for the APSA election in 1969. Christian Bay was the Caucus candidate for president. Robert Lane, a political scientist who shared some values with the Caucus, was the politically savvy choice of the establishment. Bay lost, and I of course lost big. I also recall how, at one fraught APSA Business Meeting, Sam Huntington stood up to say that we were forces of totalitarianism and should be treated as such. I was more stunned than I should have been. It is important to remember how the work of David Easton and Robert Dahl was positively affected over the long run by Caucus activism. Sam Huntington, however, held firm right up through *The Clash of Civilizations*.[4]

After the razor-thin defeat of Peter Bachrach for APSA president a couple of years later, I supported the faction contending that the Caucus should no longer contest APSA elections. We should, rather, create a parallel association to support scholars who combine activism, teaching, and political research. Such a combination would allow us to test through live experiments the positive possibilities residing in the regime rather than limiting our "tests" only to actualities already in play.

Again, the most important legacy of the Caucus, to me, was its success in legitimizing and inspiring critical thinking, writing, and action within a profession that had been organized around different expectations and demands. That is indeed an important legacy to appreciate.

BJM: In my reading of your theoretical trajectory, you seem to reach a certain political intensity in your aforementioned work with Michael Best, *The Politicized Economy*, a critical threshold that, of course, reflects the theoretical and political concerns associated with that period in the development of the democratic Left. As a "threshold work," it seems to be at once an important marker of where you had been traveling as a political theorist up to that point (in a sense, representing a culmination of one's initial journey and a temporary home for one's political subjectivity), but also, as may be expected, a limit-state that had to be transformed, transgressed, or, at the very least, reconceptualized and renegotiated, particularly given the new theoretical and political terrain you began to traverse from that point onward. In *Capitalism and Christianity, American Style* you indeed mention this work as an important conceptual building block for your current engagement with the conditions, character, and devastating consequences of neoliberal capitalism. For me, the central critical concerns of this early work are threefold: first, a trenchant critique of corporate capitalism as a structural impediment to both a truly functioning democracy and an egalitarian economic order; second, a forthright engagement with the limitations of the welfare state in that context; and, third, a willingness to entertain seriously an ideal of democratic socialism as a political horizon for change and transformation. Moreover, in the process of developing this multifaceted argument, you offer rather prescient discussions of the rise of income and wealth inequality, the increased proliferation of alienated modes of work, and the further entrenchment of ecological destruction in the wake of capitalist development (all of which are of central concern for radical theorists and activists today). In reflecting back on *The Politicized Economy*, what do you see as the most important analyses and critiques you developed there? What are the elements of that work which, while possibly providing a summation of your thinking at the time (a theoretical home, so to speak), needed to be rethought and reevaluated given the transformed social, economic, cultural, and political conditions associated with the beginning of the twenty-first century?

BC: *The Politicized Economy* was written at the University of Massachusetts when neoliberals in the Economics Department were eager to rid themselves of a young scholar on the Left, Michael Best. His eventual tenure, following the publication of this book and a period of tumult over the issue, led to the departure of key neoliberals and, surprisingly, to the appointment of several radical economists. They soon divided, of course, with Althusserians forging a strong caucus, and others, led by Sam Bowles and Herb Gintis, playing up historically distributed practices of political power. We were closer to the second group, even though our explorations of stagflation, worker alienation, environmental issues, and an emerging conflict between the pluralizing Left and the white working class focused the issues differently. This was true particularly in the last domain.

There are several things in that book that still shape my thinking. The first, perhaps, is that there is a political element in every aspect of economic life. For example, we spent considerable time charting the successful political strategy by which Standard Oil, General Motors, and Royal Tire worked to have twenty-seven cities in the 1930s dismantle their trolley systems so that the automobile would become a necessity of life and the state would devote its resources to road construction. We contended that capitalism and democracy could morph in several directions, depending in part on the volatilities of politics in corporate boardrooms, the workplace, elections, union activity, universities, consumption practices, and so on. While emphasizing the natural advantages of power capital had, we resisted formalist accounts of capitalism that focused on labor time as a master mode of explanation or defined capitalism as a closed, contradictory structure.

One of our concerns was the bind of the day in which the white working class was placed. It was caught in a pincer movement between corporate capital and the pluralizing Left. That bind, we thought, could pave the way for a fateful turn to the "neofascist Right" by a section of this class. We thus called upon the Left, still a force to contend with, to infuse its support of pluralization in the domains of gender, sexual practice, and race—which we also supported actively—with a more active class dimension. There would thus be a class dimension to affirmative action, state support for workers having a hard time making ends meet, changes in the infrastructure of consumption to reduce inequality, and so on. So you can see that we did not treat the "subject position" of the working class as settled. This call to the Left failed, and a turn to the right was indeed consolidated in a large section of the white working class. We did not anticipate, however, that a key engine of that shift would be what I later called the rise of "the evangelical-capitalist resonance machine," another rapidly formed, novel political movement not predictable through a structural reading of the system.

Another thing was our focus on the politics of consumption, something that was not at that time so common on the Left. We distinguished between "exclusive" and "inclusive" goods. The former are more likely to prevail when consumption processes escape extensive state involvement and regulation. An exclusive good provides satisfaction when a few receive it, but its satisfactions decrease and its social costs increase when extended to many. Moreover, the generalization of exclusive goods makes it harder for lower- and middle-income people to make ends meet, even if their incomes increase modestly. So they become less willing to support tax increases and social services. Inclusive goods reverse these priorities. They demand both the radical extension of direct state programs and greater regulation of corporate priorities. A public health care system, affordable public schools and universities, public utilities, public retirement programs, public postal service, public transit, public social security, public bike trails, and new turns in energy production are examples of the first. Regulations to increase car mileage and reduce emissions are examples of the second. The argument was that failing to move rapidly in this direction would both hurt lower- and middle-class consumers and add fire to the flames of worker discontent with both liberalism and the Left. Today I would add that you need to work on the infrastructure and ethos of consumption together.

We also focused on the relation between environmentalism and the construction of a viable Left alternative. We opposed both market environmentalism and any focus on the Left that concentrated simply upon equality and increasing productivity. Improving the environment would improve the health of workers and consumers and significantly reduce household expenses. Throughout the book we linked together a viable environmentalism and significant reduction of inequality in income and worker well-being.

We pursued democratic socialism. We also acknowledged that socialists still needed to devise a vision of socialism robustly compatible with freedom. By "freedom" we meant, vaguely, the ability of workers to organize and exert pressure on the state and corporations, the ability of workers to have a substantial voice within corporations, the ability of workers to reduce alienation on the job, the ability of consumers to participate in an economy that allowed them to make ends meet, the ability of people to speak and act freely in public, the ability of the electorate to shape the polity, and so on. We sought a practice of democracy in which work life participation and electoral representation were punctuated periodically by disruptive social movements.

We negotiated the issue of freedom by focusing on interim projects that could push the economy in new directions. We were impressed by the difference between liberal reformism and militant reforms that could open the door to yet more significant changes.

Looking back, there are key things we missed. First, we did not anticipate that the turn to the right in America would take the shape of an evangelical-capitalist resonance machine. That was, perhaps, not only because this event arose fast, as if from nowhere. It was also because we did not include religious and spiritual processes inside our readings of political and economic efficacy. We were still Left secularists of the sort I criticize in a later book.

A second limit was in our definition of the environment. We treated it as something capitalism acts upon in ways that damage it. But we insufficiently appreciated how nonhuman forces such as climate processes, bacterial flows, species evolution, ocean currents, tectonic plates, watershed self-filtration processes, and the like themselves express variable degrees of self-organizational capacity. We joined innumerable others on the Left, Center, and Right in tending toward what I today call sociocentrism. Sociocentrism plays up the causal primacy of social processes, while its proponents debate which ones are dominant. Its proponents tend implicitly to treat "nature" either as a set of processes that move on long slow time, or as a context that human exceptionalism allows us to ignore, or as a deposit of resources for human use, or as governed by divine providence, or as benign, stable forces to which we could be attuned if we only lightened our footprint. Arendtians, for instance, have generally depreciated bodies and nonhuman processes, and dialectical materialists have tended to think of the structures and crises of capitalism as internally generated.

On my current reading Mill, Marx, Weber, Keynes, the early Althusser, Rawls, Arendt, Habermas, Kateb, Shklar, Elster, Gadamer, Friedman, Keynes, and Hayek—disagreeing with each other in so many ways—nonetheless expressed differential tendencies toward sociocentrism. Mike Best and I barely began to puncture that bubble in our book—I note the discussion of self-organizing processes in the Great Lakes. But mostly we ran with the crowd in this respect, expressed in our quaint use of the term *environment*. An environment is a background that supports or hurts you. It is something you can support or damage. It is not a set of distributed force fields, and "it" does not *act* that much. Nietzsche, Whitehead, Deleuze, and William James—also diverging from one another in several respects—concurred in breaking with the crowd radically on this issue. So later did Bruno Latour, Donna Haraway, Brian Massumi, Jane Bennett, Karen Barad, Tim Morton, and I. One early exploration of the issue of active force fields by me appeared in a reading of the theophany of the Book of Job in an essay published in 1993.[5] What we need today is a conception of multiple, interacting force fields. Some of them may stay in a relatively stable state for a while and then go through a period of rather rapid phase transition. This happens in the zones of climate, ocean currents, and species evolution, for instance. The history of relatively rapid extinction events provides merely one instance of this double pattern. I still find it revealing how many twentieth-century readings of Nietzsche's "perspectivalism"—whether loving or condemning it—completely missed its extension of operational perspectives to a variety of nonhuman forces on the move that intersect fatefully both with each other and with a variety of human activities.

My current sense is that it is not merely necessary to modify socio-centrism to study climate change. It is also wise to do so when you study urban life, regional conflicts, military policy, racial politics, and the politics of inequality. My focus today is on the Anthropocene, where the limits of sociocentrism are glaring.[6]

Another way to put this point is to say that while capitalism, neoliberalism, communism, secularism, socialism, Christianity, social democracy, humanism, and Judaism were contending very unevenly with each other over the type of future to build, they were together racing headlong toward the destiny of the Anthropocene. By "destiny" I do not mean that which was foreordained; I mean the overarching trajectory toward which conflicting parties blindly tend, even as minor voices inside several camps protest against it. We may have to study Sophocles again to grasp the shape of the contemporary condition. I note that plagues and gods play active roles in his dramas.

BJM: I would like to pause a bit on the concept of the Anthropocene that you have raised and whose interrogation you currently find to be an important part of the deep political and theoretical commitments of your ongoing work. Your understanding of the way in which divergent positions associated with social and political life (be they linked to neoliberalism, socialism, Christianity, etc.) have all converged in reinforcing, in a deadly and devastating way, the human propensity to radically transform and disarticulate ecosystems, destroy species of life (both flora and fauna), and increase global climate change, seems to get to the inherent anthropocentrism of these positions. This is obviously a very long-standing critique of human discourses and practices as they affect ecological processes (e.g., think of the work of Aldo Leopold and, more recently, of the proponents of deep ecology, biocentrism, and ecocentrism). You actually use a slightly different term, *sociocentrism*. Indeed, it is very clear, as you intimate above, that in your most recent work [particularly *A World of Becoming* and *The Fragility of Things*] you now see the possibility of a more productive critical ecopolitical position arising from an awareness of the divergent force fields and modes of autopoiesis that swirl between the human estate and nonhuman estates, social systems and ecosystems. One question that arises is how this onto-figuration actually helps us to see the *political* nature of our contemporary ecological conundrums. That is, if humans are now displaced in terms of the ability to affect meaningful change in this respect (only one agent amongst many, let's say), if we can no longer assume an efficacious posture toward the very issues that we confront given the unexpected and emergent events that occur in our world, where does that leave us in our attempts to rectify and turn back our current Anthropocenic adventure? How can we be eco-egalitarian without being sociocentric?

BC: A tiger has us by the tail; we are swinging around without really coming to terms with the character of the Anthropocene. By the Anthropocene I mean the two hundred to four hundred years during which extractive capitalism has significantly modified atmospheric CO_2 levels, amplified radically by the "Great Acceleration" starting in the 1950s and continuing apace today. There is no guarantee that we will succeed in our actions if and when we do finally face up to it. The urgency of time. That is, indeed, one of the subliminal sources of second-stage denialism today. First-stage denial is the insistence by many evangelicals and neoliberals that the issue is not nearly as severe as climate scientists and the recent flood of climate marchers in many cities around the world contend. The second stage of denial is admitting the issue but continuing to study and act within old sociocentric categories. We need to confront both modes. The approach I adopt in league with thinkers such as Latour, Whitehead, Deleuze, Bennett, Barad, Nietzsche, and others does not carry any guarantees with it. It also does not aim at a pure regime of freedom or communalism or market individualism as it seeks to link ecological and egalitarian pursuits together. Engagements with the imbrications between capitalism and planetary forces drowns purity.

  A critique of sociocentrism does not mean the denial of human, collective agency. It means accentuated attention to how a variety of active nonhuman force fields interact with late modern versions of human agency in capitalism, social democracy, Christianity, and so forth, joined to active efforts to adjust our conduct to these volatile realities. If communism were still in force, we would add it to the list. The critique of sociocentrism also means paying attention to how the agency of microbes and so on enter into, help to constitute, enable, and limit human modes of agency. These are not simply nonagentic forces. They are microagents that help to constitute us. Without them we would not be agents. Human-nonhuman entanglements.

The argument in chapter 4 of *Capitalism and Christianity, American Style* was that several interim policies could make a real start toward eco-egalitarianism under these conditions. You start with political movements to change radically the infrastructure and ethos of consumption. Each helps to respond to the Anthropocene as it also reduces inequality. You then connect those changes to other strategies, such as state-supported subsidies for corporations in each domain of production that reduce the gap between the top and the bottom pay level of employees. Success by some corporations could then be treated as obligations others in that domain must legally meet. There are other examples as well. I recently added a discussion in *The Contemporary Condition* of how to construct an eco-egalitarian university so as to provide an example to other institutions. Of course, this plan is something few universities will now accept. Most of them are under the control of neoliberal presidents and boards. There will, however, be a discussion of it by the AAUP [American Association of University Professors] this spring (2015). Such projections provide a regulative ideal to place in relation to the hegemony of neoliberalism within the university.

It is also important politically to dramatize and amplify ways in which we are entangled with and attached to the larger world, even with its volatilities. That is the topic of the first interlude in *The Fragility of Things*; the theme is pursued actively elsewhere too. Many theorists shy away from such affect-imbued thinking, fearing that it appears naïve and weak to do so. But, as Nietzsche already showed at his best, it is very possible to join an enhanced love of this world to a commitment to positive action and to a tragic conception of possibility. That is exactly the combination I pursue.

Those provide preliminary elements. But your question points above all to the question of how to mobilize a political strategy appropriate to the Anthropocene if and as such elements are brought into play. Fair enough. I commend a swarming approach that finds its best expressions in the first chapter and postlude of *The Fragility of Things* and in a 2014 paper given at the APSA called "The Anthropocene and the General Strike." The strategic idea is to move *through* accentuation of attachment to the sweetness of life in an unruly world, *to* a variety of role experimentations that make a cumulative difference to the Anthropocene on their own, *to* more active participation in social movements, *to* renewed pressure on electoral politics, *to* a cross-country general strike that poses a series of stringent interim demands to states, corporations, churches, universities, international organizations, banks, consumers, and the like. Each of these modes of activity, once activated, feeds into, enables, and augments the others. A resonance machine in the making. That is one reason I get impatient with people who say (without textual support) that theorists like me are only interested in "micropolitics." We are, rather, partly interested in the efficacies of such practices, partly in how they help to deepen beliefs and connections as they grow, and partly in how they can be linked to a series of corollary macro-movements.

In their early essay on micropolitics, Deleuze and Guattari first explored its ugly role in the formation of German Nazism. They paid attention to movements back and forth between micro- and macropolitics in its emergence. Those who missed the dynamics of interaction pursued in that essay are merely responding to their own surprise about the inclusion of micropolitics as part of the larger matrix. The emergence of the evangelical-neoliberal resonance machine in the states I later explore in *Capitalism and Christianity* introduced an impressive array of micropolitical practices into churches, localities, school boards, TV religious shows, local elections, court cases, university trustee meetings, think tanks, and corporate boardrooms. Those burgeoning practices helped to bolster the success of their macropractices. Many leftists and electoral liberals were taken by surprise by that emergent machine because they ignored the role of micropolitics. I was too. But it has become, among many other things, an extremely powerful machine of racism, assaults on women, class inequality, and climate denial.

In thinking about a counterresonance machine I do not focus first and foremost on the *probability* that it will come into being. I focus, rather, on the urgency of the contemporary *need* in relation to contemporary *possibilities* of action. It is easy to be a crackpot realist, as C. Wright Mills called the realists of his day in the state, military, and social sciences. The more compelling thing is to gauge the severity of the overriding issues, the time dimension on which they are set, and the possibility of an emergent, swarming movement. Mills wrote an essay on the origins of the New Left in 1961 *before such a phenomenon became widely visible*. That is the kind of thinking and action needed today, more than probabilistic thinking stuck within current parameters of action. It is true that I doubt that the contemporary condition of finance capitalism, extreme inequality, and multidimensional pluralism is compatible with a classical model of working-class revolution, but a huge space yawns between that image and the established conventions of electoral politics.

Your question also asks, I think, what constituencies could speak to these issues. That is a critical and difficult issue, about which I only have exploratory thoughts. I do not think in terms of a centered movement governed by one core constituency or party surrounded by a series of satellite groups. That model better fits, perhaps, the era of Fordism. Today we need to construct a militant pluralist assemblage composed of constituencies in multiple subject positions. They will not all come from the same class or share the same onto-creeds. They will come together out of growing concern for the fragility of things, care for future generations, and attachment to a world that is larger than humanity. They will, that is, identify *affinities of spirituality* with each other across *differences of creed, regional location, and social position*—even as many continue to work on their received creeds and priorities in the light of new circumstances. Secularists, for instance, too often ignore promising intersections between them and activist proponents of this or that religious creed.

It is not that bearers of all creeds and social positions are potential participants, but a plurality of creeds and social positions do show differential potential here, including people from multiple classes and different regions. Taking the United States alone, [these include] blue-collar workers seeking jobs in green production, bureaucrats tied to progressive churches, green entrepreneurs, minorities seeing how urban life is undermined by eco-neglect and climate warming, students, professors, high school teachers, middle-class consumers thinking about their grandchildren, and so on. Bearers of several theological stances, remember, were actively involved in the most recent climate march. I can now even imagine that Pope Francis could come to support such a movement, though not his predecessors (Fall 2014). The possibilities to pursue can be enacted in part because creed and spirituality are interinvolved but not equivalent and in part because the modes of spirituality circulating within each social position are multiple too. If a multifaceted social movement becomes mobilized many of its movers and shakers will come from energetic, creative, younger contingents in each subject position. So multidimensional pluralism sets a condition of possibility more than an impediment for a swarming movement.

One key is new awakenings pursued through blogs, courses, marches, books, essays, films. New singers, bands, comedians, and dancers can help to energize such a constellation, as has been the case in the past.

If and as such multiply anchored, swarming movements become consolidated we may then be able to mobilize a cross-country, nonviolent general strike mobilized by the issues posed by the Anthropocene. One of the models of inspiration will be gay and lesbian movements of the past forty years or so, as they built up steam slowly on multiple fronts against the odds and then reached lovely tipping points. The examples of Occupy, the Arab Spring, and the Hong Kong rebellion may provide us with a few lessons too, even if all have met stringent opposition and some defeat.

It could turn out, certainly, that the needed constellation will not arise, or it might arise and be too late to stop the effects of the Anthropocene from triggering new civil and regional wars. On the other hand, if such swarming movements do become amplified, a new activating *event* could appear. Perhaps a group of vigilantes attacks climate activists. Perhaps a meltdown of this or that ice sheet occurs much faster than previously expected. Perhaps militants in poor countries organize massive protests and boycotts against rich ones for producing most of the ecological damage, so far experiencing little suffering from it, and doing the least about it. One or more such event could help to mobilize support for a cross-country general strike, especially if activists publicize the need for it. Need, the urgency of time, swarming movements, and new events. Those are the things to keep in view, once your vision of events includes and goes beyond the assumptions of sociocentrism. .

A critique of sociocentrism, of course, does not entail the denial of human agency or refuse to draw this or that insight from its most noble carriers in the past. I teach several of those thinkers and learn from them. Rather, it points to the fact that sociocentrism is *insufficient* to the world, that previous understandings and ideals need to be reworked, that spiritual attachment to the larger world must be amplified as we broaden our sense of entanglements, that new militant assemblages must be constructed, and that new strategies must be devised which draw selective inspiration from innovative actions in the past.

I do not have all the answers to these questions, and only in part because they require experimentation. The Anthropocene twirls us around by the tail. We become dizzy. Claims to either consummate explanation or a pristine strategy become implausible. Dizziness, up to a point, enables experimental action in response to changed circumstances. That is the mood in which to think and act today as we help each other to hear the call.

BJM: One of the most significant features of your most recent work, *The Fragility of Things*, is the consistent radical quality to its analyses of our human and world condition and its persistent advocacy for a variety of "militant" political actions, even if your form of critical theory tenaciously attends to *both* the micropolitical and macropolitical. By "radical," of course, we mean, literally, to attend to the deep foundation ("root") of our political life, be it arboreal or rhizomatic (to draw upon the wonderful differential articulated by Deleuze and Guattari). I agree wholeheartedly that leaving out the everyday, micropolitical dimensions of our political economic reality (in which we are always implicated in bodily reactions, emotional sentiments, affective relations, spiritual dimensions, etc.) is fundamentally problematic, particularly if we are concerned with actually changing our current trajectory. And it is very clear that you continually argue for the importance of linking these micropolitical practices and discourses to macropolitical structures, institutions, and axiomatics. To me, your consistent focus on the imbrication of these two political dimensions is what sets your critique of neoliberalism apart from other theorists and activists who are concerned with the same conditions associated with our global capitalist lifeworld. With this said, I would be curious for you to comment on how you see your critique of neoliberalism in relation to other versions circulating within radical theory, be they Marxist, post-Marxist, Foucauldian, anarchist, autonomist, feminist, or something else. What do you see as the strengths of your conceptualization and critique, and in what way does it attend to issues you think are lacking in other versions? Moreover, in what way does your critique of neoliberalism represent an anticapitalist position?

BC: I suppose my insistence that the partial self-organization of capitalist markets regularly bumps into a variety of other partially self-organizing systems, such as language evolution, social movements, climate processes, ocean currents, wetland self-filtration processes, sunspot activity, bacterial flows, and species evolution, is one relatively distinct thing about my perspective, at least in much of the human sciences. Another is, perhaps, the political importance I place on the question of challenging the effects of existential resentment in several constituencies during the era of the Anthropocene. I agree with other radicals on the issues of wealth distribution, income inequality, worker alienation, the politics of austerity as class war, and so on. But I do not project forward the regulative ideal of a smooth communist horizon or, indeed, any smooth horizon. When the agitation of several force fields of different sorts becomes accentuated, or as regional religious differences become amplified, you need to think about rapid interim responses to general issues. We must recall how few Marxists, Weberians, or Keynesians even thought about the primacy of the Anthropocene until, say, the 1980s or even later. But it was well under way. Their (and my) notions of human agency, social explanation, and natural processes were already out of synch with these developments. I suspect that many on the Left are now moving away from these earlier notions.

Perhaps one way to think about these turns is to locate the sort of thinking pursued here in relation to Marxism. A promising route today, it seems to me, is to deepen interchanges between Marxists touched by the Anthropocene and those I will here call left-Nietzscheans. Michel Foucault, Gilles Deleuze, Elizabeth Grosz, Jane Bennett, Eugene Holland, Brian Massumi, Wendy Brown, Thomas Dumm, and Maurizio Lazzarato all represent noble carriers of this latter tradition. What is more, many find themselves mixing and matching left-Nietzschean themes with some dimensions of Marxist thought.

For example, take the alienation themes in Marx. I embrace the young Marx's exploration of alienation from work and the products of work, but I then join those themes to Nietzschean explorations of alienation from mortality and, above all, alienation from the shaky place of the human estate itself in a world of becoming. These are sources from which the dangerous politics of *ressentiment* wax and wane. The Marxist modes of alienation need to be resolved, but the latter modes need to be *transfigured* until more of us become attached to a world that enables us to be and yet is not highly predisposed to either our technical mastery or organic belonging. We need to pursue relations with the world that are least destructive to our entangled relations with these other forces and beings, even as we appreciate the gifts they present to us. A radical reflection on complementary traditions of belonging is thus critical today. Some of those modes have been dominant in capitalism; others have found expression in opposition to capitalism. But they all need refiguration. So I neither reject the alienation themes in Marx as post-humanist Marxists did, nor do I find them to be sufficient to the contemporary condition.

Deleuze, Foucault, Holland, Lazzarato, and I also appreciate some "minor themes"—as Deleuze would put it—in Marx's mature reading of capital, for example, Marx's discussions of primitive accumulation, how the work day is organized, and the power relations that govern labor. But I would not articulate a labor theory of value oriented around "labor time" nor go with tendencies in his thought later carried by Althusserians toward a more formal, structuralist, antihumanist reading of capitalism. Capitalism—and the world in general—is too susceptible to periods of volatility, contingency, and surprise to make these promising routes.

Consider two points. The first is how Deleuze construes capitalism to be an "axiomatic," even more than first and foremost a mode of production. A capitalist axiomatic is composed of interacting and mutually constraining dimensions such as private profit, the priority of the commodity form, drives to make labor and nature into commodities, banking independence, and states that support these pursuits. So an axiomatic makes a big difference, but its constitutive elements can also morph and shift in surprising directions. It is also marked by other noises within and around it. Some axioms that were subordinate may gain new priority as things morph.

New axioms may be added in response to internal and external shocks that periodically disrupt things. Think of social security, unemployment insurance, and the enlarged role given to labor unions during the Fordist era. Or the reintroduction of slavery of children and women caught up in the ugly processes of trafficking. Or the way the Communist Party now presides over capitalism in China, belying the idea that capitalism and a competitive party system must go together. You can also think of the evangelical movement as a surprising axiom added to American neoliberalism in the late 1970s and early 1980s; it helped to enable the hegemony of neoliberalism and to set new cultural constraints within which the latter moves. Such elements shift in importance and degrees of primacy because of social movements of the day, new patterns of insistence adopted by capital, new responses by dispersed regional forces outside of capital, new ideological investments, and historic conjunctions between capitalism and nonhuman force fields with powers to morph of their own. Explanation runs into limits in principle here, in part because of the impact of exterior forces and in part because of creative responses developed by the relevant parties. Politics in a strong, dispersed sense of that word never disappears from a world in which a porous axiomatic is operative, excesses are in play, unexpected events arise, and periods of creativity are real.

I agree, then, as you stated in your thoughtful and generous review of my book in *Perspectives on Politics*, that it is insufficient to criticize neoliberalism.[7] It is not even enough to pursue positive alternatives, though that is always pertinent. It is also important to see how neoliberalism fits within and works on, as I would put it, a shifting capitalist axiomatic. It is particularly relevant to explore how the creative, ugly politics of neoliberalism has moved and shaken that axiomatic in directions that were not inevitable before it arose on the scene.

The second point is to review the processes of discipline and governmentality that have arisen within the capitalist axiomatic. Foucault paid attention to how disciplinary society arose within capitalist and communist states. He and Deleuze later explored how such modes of institutional discipline and normalization (firms, prisons, armies, schools, hospitals, etc.) have become supplemented by impersonal modes of population control. Their presentations of "control societies," "governmentality," and "biopolitics" are rich. Neoliberalism, you might say, emerges as a potent force within the orbit of these developments, helping both to foster them and push the welfare state into decline.

This is where Lazzarato enters the scene. In *The Making of the Indebted Man*, he appreciates the work of Marx, Nietzsche, Foucault, and Deleuze in critical relation to each other. But he says that today the impersonal logic of social control works more through debt and indebtedness than Foucault had foreseen. Put another way, the contours of the capitalist axiomatic have shifted once again, so that financial capital now relegates the Fordist regime of managerial capitalism, labor unions, worker strikes, and the welfare state to a secondary status. Finance capital is not epiphenomenal. It is real and efficacious. Workers, corporations, consumers, and states now strain unevenly under the sway of its speculative priorities, its containment of political movements under mountains of debt, its campaigns to drown the welfare state through selective state austerity, and its tendencies to create recurrent speculative bubbles and crashes that other sectors of the society must eventually absorb. It is not all-powerful, partly because of responses by other forces and partly because its leaders cannot control the long-term concatenations attached to the very practices they initiate.

I pursued a version of this theme about discipline and the rise of financial capital in the second interlude in *The Fragility of Things*. But Lazzarato has taught us much more about it. He draws upon the "minor" Marx, Nietzsche, Deleuze, and Foucault to trace these developments, even as he must also work on all of these figures. My main critique of Lazzarato is that he ignores the planetary dimension and the self-organizing capacities of multiple nonhuman systems. That is a huge omission today. If he had paid attention to those dimensions he could have shown how the rise of an intensely indebted populace poses yet another set of barriers against popular readiness to come to terms politically with the new spate of unruliness of climate, glaciers, ocean currents, and species change. My self-critique, however, is that I did not fold the themes he invokes sufficiently into *The Fragility of Things*.

Am I anticapitalist? I criticize the institutional priorities of capitalism in the ways specified above. But I also contend that our problems are partly anchored in existential and civilizational tendencies that are both immanent to capitalism and not its product or property alone. Hence, for instance, the distressing history of ecological devastation in communist states and the modern evolution of the Christian idea of dominion over the earth. And hence the importance of Nietzsche's groundbreaking explorations of how the politics of *ressentiment* can surge into modern regimes of different sorts when comforting existential assumptions are disrupted by new events. Today we must come to terms critically with widespread assumptions about nature, images of freedom, and modes of belonging that are not confined to capitalism alone: nature as a set of pliable forces to act on, material abundance as a prime goal of life, a nonhuman world that is predisposed either to our benefit or to our mastery, explanation as sufficient in principle to our condition. No economistic rendering of the contemporary condition, whether neoliberal, Keynesian, or Marxist, is sufficient to our time, though it is wise to fold selective insights from the latter two into a revised world picture.

If you draw Sophoclean insights into an affirmative vision of life you do not project the regulative ideal of any smooth, unfettered future. That is an all-too-human-centered image of possibility. I think Foucault, above all, arrived at such a sense of the fragility of things while initiating radical modes of critique. The idea is to affirm our entanglements with the larger world while pursuing interim responses that are eco-egalitarian in direction.

BJM: As a "militant" political theorist (drawing sustenance from Nietzsche, Foucault, the "minor" Marx, Deleuze, James, among others), you seem continually drawn toward thinking about the political practices that must be engaged and transformed if we are to bring about important goals associated with deep pluralism, eco-egalitarianism, and richer forms of democracy. This is not just a recent development in your theory; it resonates, as indicated in our discussion, in your early attempts to call into question the scientificity of political science itself. With this said, I would like to end our discussion with an inquiry into what you see as the political potential of theory today. In a sense, all *political* theorists deal with politics as an object of analysis, but they don't necessarily see their theorizing as part of the necessary struggle to transform and reconstitute our political world. My sense from your most recent work is that you do see an important role for theory itself in these urgent political practices. What do you see as the role of theory in relation to the important goals toward which you strive and, importantly, to the macropolitical practices that are necessary to institute these ideals?

BC: Political theory—and the disciplines to which it is closely allied such as anthropology, some currents in philosophy, global studies, interdisciplinary humanities programs—is once again under assault. Some forces in political science seek to marginalize it; many universities are cutting back on graduate and undergraduate programs in the humanities in general; and neoliberal drives in the country at large are very powerful. In thinking about this context it may be wise to consider what we do best and how we can work to maintain the depth of the intellectual enterprise. Perhaps we can think in terms of the work we do in our linked capacities as writers, teachers, blog writers, panelists, intellectual activists, and citizens. How each of these roles has its own integrity and yet can inform and ignite things in the others.

I note how your book, *Performing Marx: Contemporary Negotiations of a Living Tradition*, effectively linked strains of classical Marxist thought to a series of contemporary thinkers and issues. Ernesto Laclau, Antonio Negri, and the situationists are among the engagements I recall most vividly. The task of that book was to dig deeply into one theoretical tradition as you also work on it in relation to new thinkers, activists, and issues. Indeed, I think of Negri and the situationists, above all, as participants in the "minor tradition" noted earlier. They resist "royal or state theory," represented diversely by Plato, Augustine, Kant, and Hegel; tug on subordinate strains in the latter thinkers; work on them; and ask how drab and formal thought would become if these strains were lifted from it. They also accept infusions from royal theory.

We must work on the university to maintain our ability to dig as deeply as possible into the minor and royal traditions of political thought, as we show students how exciting, enlivening, relevant, and bracing such work can be. Periodically, what might be called *slow thinking* is required in political thinking, as you allow the ramifications of a new event to jostle some assumptions that have heretofore governed your thinking. New thinking comes out of such movement back and forth between work on an established theory, a new situation, and reflective hesitation in which conscious thought itself is suspended for a time to allow subsidiary processes of creativity to bubble up for further work. I have elsewhere compared that period of hesitation to dwelling like "a seer" in the midst of things. Theory is thus a multifaceted enterprise to nourish and protect within the academy. Protection implicates us, recurrently and unfortunately, in the micropolitics of university life and professional associations.

Teaching remains an anchor and source of inspiration. Here we expose students to diverse orientations on specific topics of cultural or political importance. This term I find it rewarding as students negotiate the contending perspectives of Hayek, Lazzarato, and the ecologist Clive Hamilton. They are thinking about Hayek's reading of capitalism in relation to the latter two. Next term I will teach a course on Sophocles and Kant, allowing a "minor" thinker of one era to bump repeatedly and obliquely into the thought of a profound "royal" thinker, one who continues to infuse the assumptions of several strands of contemporary political theory. (This makes it clear, I hope, that "minor" does not mean "unimportant"; it means different from royal theory, less oriented to an overriding system, and attentive to messy engagements with a plurality of forces and pressures in a larger world not necessarily predisposed to us in the last instance.) That course is gratifying, partly because the conjunctions forged between two disparate thinkers separated by centuries can bring out minor strains that otherwise might be missed in Kant.

Sometimes he did not pursue them, and sometimes he folded them into his larger philosophy. One example is the amazing work he launched but did not pursue on nonhuman organisms as self-organizing systems. Such textual conjunctions can also spark us to rework Sophocles to speak to late modern life.

Our writing and teaching, in turn, can be linked to the blog work we may do, to the academic issues we pursue publicly, and to our practices as citizens. For me, the blog *The Contemporary Condition* has been pivotal. Moderated by Jairus Grove, Steve Johnston, Tim Hanafin, and me, it enables a variety of theorists on the Left to reach a larger audience as they engage contemporary issues. One of my recent posts, for instance, called "Toward an Eco-Egalitarian University," identifies neoliberal drives in the university as it explores internal strategies to expose and counter them. The shameful proliferation and harsh treatment of adjunct faculty members is one topic in that post. Another post is called "The Politics of the Event," speaking to several issues we have discussed in this interview. Bonnie Honig wrote a great post explaining why so many American Jewish intellectuals now feel called upon to criticize Israel. Participants in that blog pursue a variety of topics, allowing their theoretical insights to find expression in the treatment of this or that pressing issue. Even Facebook provides a political catalyst sometimes. A group of academic theorists, led by Corey Robin, John Protevi, Bonnie Honig, and Bruce Robbins, recently inspired thousands of us to write public letters of protest to Chancellor Wise at the University of Illinois after she fired Professor Steven Salaita for "uncivil" remarks about the Israeli attack on Gaza. We lost the particular battle on behalf of academic freedom, but the effort still had some salutary effects. It publicized how deferential universities now are to neoliberal donors and trustees and how many now restrict academic freedom under the guise of promoting civility. The widespread academic boycott now under way against that university could also have effects on the tone and quality of academic life there and elsewhere, even though battles on this front are uphill.

Much more could be said. But those of us who see theory as a critical enterprise have several avenues available to link our thought to activism. Writing is an activism. This turn in theory is one reason it is under assault again today.

Saying all that, it is also important not to hold each other to too demanding a standard on these fronts. Better to appreciate what other people do as we make periodic calls upon one another when the occasion requires it. Otherwise, promising participants are driven out by a sense that they can never measure up to the impossible standards others set for them. Fox News loves to insist that critics who are not perfect in all their life activities are merely hypocrites. Their message: *You can stop being hypocritical only by accepting the prevailing order as they wish it to be.* But that would mean that almost all critique is hypocritical. We see through that as we acknowledge that we are implicated in the larger world we seek to contest on specific fronts. The gradual mobilization of a larger, cross-regional, critical assemblage may depend upon the ability to magnify internal invitations as we curtail the sharpness of internal accusations.

I entered the academy during an era when forces inside and outside it had been marshaled to push out exploratory, critical theory; the demand was to fold the social sciences into utilitarian modes of being. The rise of the New Left, in its broadest compass, and the Caucus for a New Political Science, very specifically, helped to challenge those pressures. Well, the old pressures have returned in a new guise.

Certain theorists become beacons for us as we think about how to allow each of our capacities to inform the others. Early on, for me and many others, Sheldon Wolin was a very important inspiration; he showed us how to salvage the theoretical enterprise under difficult circumstances, and he helped us to appreciate more deeply how crucial such an enterprise is to the vitality of life. Hannah Arendt played a similar role for others. Later Michel Foucault inspired and energized many, as we tracked how he oscillated between creative theoretical work, bracing interviews that expressed his political commitments more directly, and participation in social movements as diverse as psychiatric reform, prison reform, sexual diversity, and cross-state citizen efforts to respond to the boat people of the 1980s. There are other admirable beacons, too, such as Judith Butler's work on gender and sexuality and, more recently, the Israeli occupation. Each of these figures reminds us how the specific subject position you occupy periodically makes a call upon you in the face of a new event or a fixed, destructive norm. The call I hear most strongly today emerges from those dangerous intersections between neoliberal capitalism and a variety of nonhuman force fields with self-organizing capacities of their own.

ACKNOWLEDGMENTS

I am lucky to be surrounded at Johns Hopkins University by people who forge eco sensibilities into their teaching and writing. Naveeda Khan, Katrin Pahl, Paola Marrati, Nidesh Lawtoo, Anand Pandian, Nicolas Jabko, Bentley Allan, Mimi Keck, and Jane Bennett have all contributed to my thinking on the issues explored in this book. I thank them for both the examples of their work and the illuminating conversations we have had.

Recent and current graduate students in theory at Hopkins have played an important role in my thinking, calling attention to texts that were passing me by, posing criticisms inside and outside of class, and reading chapters of this book with critical and caring eyes. Jairus Grove, now teaching at the University of Hawaii, has been very important, and I thank him also for the indispensable role he plays in our blog, *The Contemporary Condition*. Anatoli Ignatov, who now teaches ecology at Appalachian State University, has been equally important. Derek Denman has read through the entire manuscript and made invaluable suggestions for its improvement. Stephanie Erev and Jon Masin-Peters have read chapters and called my attention to important texts as each also prepares a dissertation on allied topics. Nicole Grove, Kellan Anfinson, Tim Hanafin, Chris Forster Smith, Chad Shomura, and Nur Kirmizdag have also informed my thinking. A new set of students has been subjected to two seminars in which we engaged several of these issues and themes. Too numerous to list now, I prize their thinking and the convictions they bring to the world.

Eco-thinkers elsewhere have been very important to this study. Libby Anker, Tom Dumm, Steve Johnston, Emily Parker, Romand Coles, Claire

Brault, Richard Grusin, Brian Massumi, Erin Manning, Catherine Keller, P. J. Brendese, Smita Rahman, Mort Schoolman, Bonnie Honig, Kennan Ferguson, Bhrigu Singh, Kathy Ferguson, Roban Kramer, David Panagia, David Howarth, Lars Toender, Rupert Read, Alex Livingston, Mike Shapiro, Nathan Widder, and Kam Shapiro have all helped to inform and inspire my thinking, as numerous references in the text show.

I have had the opportunity to test these ideas in several settings, including the Neal Maxwell Lecture at the University of Utah, with Libby Anker and Kennan Ferguson as two thoughtful respondents; a section keynote at the massive Seizing an Alternative conference in Claremont in June 2015 on climate change attended by 1,500 people; the conference After Extinction at the University of Wisconsin, Milwaukee in May 2015; a talk at the Center for the Humanities, Wesleyan University, in December 2015; a talk at Amherst College in April 2016; lectures at the University of Copenhagen in the spring of 2016; and several papers at the APSA and WPSA over the past few years. I thank the coordinators and audiences at each. I would also like to thank the publisher of *Political Research Quarterly* for permission to republish a significantly revised version of "Species Evolution and Cultural Freedom," published there in June 2014, and the publisher of *New Political Science: A Journal of Politics and Culture* for permission to republish a 2015 interview with Bradley MacDonald, then titled "Confronting the Anthropocene and Contesting Neoliberalism: An Interview with William E. Connolly."

My work and mode of being continue to be influenced by Jane Bennett. We taught two seminars together on these topics, and her new work on modes of in-fluence that extend through and beyond human life informs themes pursued in this text. I thank her for being a living example of the kind of spirituality needed today, even if she does not like the word *spiritual*.

NOTES

Prelude: Myth and the Planetary

1. Mitchell, *The Book of Job*. I explored this story earlier in Connolly, *The Augustinian Imperative*, chapter 1. The two engagements doubtless overlap, but there and then the point was to pose a contrast between the conceptions of divinity, sin, morality, and grace of Augustine and corollary images in Job.

2. Mitchell, *The Book of Job*, 19.

3. Mitchell, *The Book of Job*, 22.

4. For a reflective presentation of the vision of a complex moral order see Gordis, *The Book of God and Man*. In *Job: The Victim of His People*, Rene Girard argues that Job's suffering is necessary to promote the artificial unity of the community; Job is a scapegoat. Perhaps he is, in part, but Girard reads all myths, except the sacrifice of Jesus on the Cross, through the lens of the scapegoat. He seems to believe that a definitive resolution of this struggle is available only within Christianity. And he does not ask whether the cosmic commitments—including our relation to nature—Job embraces may in fact be worthy of endorsement by others.

5. Mitchell, *The Book of Job*, 79, 80, 81, 83, 84.

6. For an account of the "evangelical/capitalist resonance machine" in the United States, see Connolly, *Capitalism and Christianity, American Style*. That study attempts to grasp how so many remain positively bonded to neoliberalism, even with its volatility. The book came out several months before the 2008 meltdown. I continue to think that it helps us to understand how the subjective grip of neoliberalism can intensify after it spawns a crisis. It also may help to explain one contemporary feature of American exceptionalism: why, in a world with several neoliberal regimes, and other modes of political economy too, the United States is the place where climate denialism is the most intense and most extensive.

7. Mitchell, *The Book of Job*, 85.

8. Mitchell, *The Book of Job*, 88.
9. Alley, *The Two-Mile Time Machine*, 120.

Chapter 1: Sociocentrism, the Anthropocene, and the Planetary

1. Foucault, *Discipline and Punish*; Foucault, *Security, Territory, Population*.
2. See Connolly, *Political Theory and Modernity*, especially chapter 3.
3. Connolly, *Political Theory and Modernity*; Johnston, *Encountering Tragedy*; Honig, *Democracy and the Foreigner*.
4. See Feit, *Democratic Anxieties*.
5. Flathman, *Freedom and Its Conditions*.
6. See Foucault, *History of Sexuality*, vol. 3; Connolly, *A World of Becoming*, especially chapter 2.
7. For a superb, brief review of the relation between Machiavelli and republicanism see Skinner, *Machiavelli*.
8. Berlin, "Two Concepts of Liberty," 158, 164–65, my emphasis. See also Dumm, *Michel Foucault and the Politics of Freedom*, where an excellent reading of Berlin on normality is offered as part of Dumm's critique of negative liberty. I am greatly indebted to his reading of Berlin.
9. Note, for example, how the Rawlsian ideas of neutrality with respect to the good and the difference principle are both operationally close to the Berlin position. He continues this line much later. For a thoughtful ecocritique of Rawls see Read, "Why the Ecological Crisis Spells the End of Liberalism."
10. Hayek, *Individualism and Economic Order*, 28.
11. Hayek, *Individualism and Economic Order*, 23, 24, my emphasis; Hayek, *Road to Serfdom*, 223–24.
12. See my critique of that assumption in Connolly, *The Fragility of Things*, chapter 2.
13. See Klein, *This Changes Everything*, chapter 8.
14. See Best and Connolly, *The Politicized Economy*; Connolly, *The Fragility of Things*.
15. See Connolly, "A Note on Freedom under Socialism," 461–68. The problem governing that early essay was that corporate capitalism quells the freedom of workers and consumers as it weakens the powers of the poor and unemployed it generates, while democratic socialism must come to terms with institutional ways to protect dissent and enable democratic modes of agitation. These issues remain. Here are the closing sentences of that piece: "While both advanced capitalist and socialist societies today mobilize their populations around the goal of economic growth, this increasingly irrational objective . . . seems to be an internally generated imperative of capitalism. It might not be so necessary to a socialist society. If this is so, it constitutes another consideration in favor of further exploration of a conception of socialism consonant with freedom" (471).
16. Marx, "The Critique of the Gotha Programme," 615, 616.
17. See "Amazon's Bruising, Thrilling Workplace," *New York Times*, August 16, 2015.
18. I want to emphasize that the classical ideal of communism is undergoing radical rethinking in some quarters in relation to the acceleration of climate change.

That is all to the good. A fine example is Wark, *Molecular Red*. Another text that identifies late revisions in the communist idealism of Marx, though without engaging his tendencies toward sociocentrism, is Balibar, *The Philosophy of Marx*. See also Moore, *Capitalism in the Web of Life*.

19. I note in particular Moore, *Capitalism in the Web of Life*; Cooper, *Life as Surplus*. These books absorb a notion of nonhuman processes containing self-organizing processes. Doing so, they take steps toward transfiguring the labor theory of value into a theory that pays heed to how new biotechnologies squeeze profit and capital from various aspects of nature. I am sure there are others pursuing this tack as well. I feel particularly close to the Moore book. It came out too late to be examined in detail in this study.

20. See Edelman, *No Future*. For a thoughtful critique of Edelman see Honig, *Antigone Interrupted*, chapter 2.

21. Tournier, *Friday*, 50.

22. Tournier, *Friday*, 50–51.

23. For one attempt to probe the powers of going back and forth between the perspective of the theorist and that of the seer who suspends action orientations to time, see Connolly, *A World of Becoming*, chapter 6.

24. These tendencies, *by comparison of course to the positions staked out here*, can be found to varying degrees in the following. Arendt, *Between Past and Future* stakes out a position anchored in the idea that the new science of quantum mechanics threatens human meaning and enactments. In rough agreement with her, Habermas argues in *The Future of Human Nature* that the advance of biology and its technologies squeezes out the space for human agency. He fails to explore how some complexity theories in biology, while multiplying the zones of micro-agency within and without, actually deepen our sense of human agency and creativity. Kateb in *Human Dignity* limits agency, dignity, rights, and creativity to human beings alone. Michaels in *Our America* attributes racism to those who include a biological element in human culture and philosophies of "difference." He omits reference to thinkers who refuse to identify the biological with fixity or to accept biological reductionism. I offer a critique of this stance in Connolly, *Neuropolitics*, though I would now say that the attempt to rethink nature-culture relations there insufficiently addresses a series of nonhuman, self-organizing processes that interact differentially with the human estate. I continue, however, to *think* the layered logic of difference in ways that transcend the limits Michaels discerns in our ability to *know* difference. He seems indeed to restrict thinking to knowing. Many others in their critiques of "affect theory" project a determinism onto such theories that misrepresent them profoundly. For most people indebted to theorists such as Deleuze and Whitehead pursue the theme of panexperientialism, where modes of feeling and agency flow well beyond the nonhuman world, and some of those agents also operate as micro-agents within human agency. Ruth Leys, for instance, in "The Turn to Affect" seems to skip over the theme of panexperientialism explored in such works. (I explore this theme in chapter 4.) There are several studies now

that contest these omissions in the humanities. For one that does so in a very thoughtful way see Morton, *Hyperobjects*.

25. For close and illuminating explorations of how these incursions have worked over the past several decades see Nixon, *Slow Violence and the Environmentalism of the Poor*; Klein, *This Changes Everything*. Nixon's thoughtful discussion of how "slow violence" works is discussed in later chapters.

26. Lewis and Maslin, "Defining the Anthropocene." In important posts Donna Haraway and Jason Moore have separately proposed *capitalocene* as the source and name of this phenomenon, saying that the takeoff was most dramatic during capitalism and arguing that *anthro* is too vague a term to cover the differential human sources and modes of suffering. See Moore, "The Capitalocene"; Haraway, "Anthropocene, Capitalocene, Plantationocene, Chthulucene." The latter two points are compelling, but not enough so in my mind to give the name *capitalocene* to the whole process. First, what might be called in its early stages "Eurocene" started before industrial capitalism was really off the ground; second, Soviet communism became a major contributor in the twentieth century; third, Germany and a few other capitalist states have recently taken a major lead in reducing carbon emissions; fourth, the United States, as a major outlier from at least 1980 to today, is so in part because of the formation of an evangelical/capitalist resonance machine in that country that differentiates it from other capitalist states; fifth, communist idealism has itself been a contributor to this phenomenon; and sixth, the term *capitalocene* may be too easily subject to the idea that nonhuman processes of climate, ocean currents, glacier flows, and the like moved at a steady, gradual pace until capitalism came onto the scene. They did not. That is not at all to say that extractive capitalism has been a minor player in this tragic history. It has been THE major player for a few centuries, aided and abetted by a variety of other cultural, technological, and spiritual forces. I am, however, more than happy to enter into a political assemblage with those who decide that, all things considered, *capitalocene* is the best term to use. The assemblage to come can be organized around a plurality of names.

27. For a thoughtful account of some of the forces involved, including Spanish and Catholic imperialism, added to an account of how a few maverick priests joined indigenous protests against these forces in the early period, see Todorov, *The Conquest of America*. That text in turn is engaged and criticized in "Global Political Discourse," chapter 2 of Connolly, *Identity/Difference*.

28. For texts that explore how both indigenous peoples and dissident traditions in the Euro-American world help us to come to terms with the contemporary condition, see Ignatov, "Ecologies of the Good Life"; Singh, *Poverty and the Quest for Life*; Viveiros de Castro, *Cannibal Metaphysics*. The authors make creative comparisons between the panexperientialism of "minor" Western thinkers such as Nietzsche and Deleuze and the "perspectivalism" or "animism" of living traditions in Africa, India, and the Amazon Valley. "Minor" does not here mean unimportant; it means a tradition of dissonant perspectives that challenged human exceptionalism, sociocentrism, and imperialism from inside Euro-

American thought in ways ignored or rejected by majoritarian theorists. Kafka, Nietzsche, Bergson, Butler, Whitehead, Bennett, Grosz, Massumi, and Deleuze form some diverse members of the latter tradition.

Chapter 2: Species Evolution and Cultural Creativity

1. My grasp of the later Darwin is indebted to the groundbreaking work that Elizabeth Grosz has done on it. See, for example, *Chaos, Territory, Art*, in which she places Darwin, Bergson, and Deleuze into several conversations. I admire and learn from the ways she does so, particularly her explorations of the aesthetic element in evolutionary processes. But my attention here is on a *minority* of contemporary biologists themselves who resist genocentrism and express (sometimes unconscious) affinities to the trio of thinkers Grosz draws upon. For a sympathetic review of an earlier book by Grosz see Connolly, "Elizabeth Grosz."
2. Mitteldorf, "Neo-Darwinism and the Group Selection Controversy," 88.
3. For some of these examples, see Sagan, *Cosmic Apprentice*.
4. For the perspective of the later Merleau-Ponty on this issue see *Nature*. Those lectures make contact with the work of Whitehead. For a phenomenologist who now calls upon biology and phenomenology to pursue movements back and forth as each perspective deepens, see Thompson, *Mind in Life*. I support such cross-fertilization in Connolly, "Experience and Experiment."
5. Nagel, *Mind and Cosmos*, 73.
6. Nagel, *Mind and Cosmos*, 33, 66–67, 87.
7. See Sagan, *Cosmic Apprentice*, 117.
8. Margulis and Sagan, *Acquiring Genomes*, 12, 20.
9. See Antrosio, "Denisovans, Neanderthals, Archaics as Human Races."
10. Oyama, *The Ontogeny of Information*; Kauffman, *Reinventing the Sacred*; Deacon, *Incomplete Nature*; Thompson, *Mind in Life*.
11. Thompson, *Mind in Life*, 189, my emphasis.
12. Thompson, *Mind in Life*, 196.
13. See Deacon, *Incomplete Nature*, particularly chapters 9, 11, 12, 14.
14. The example comes from Sagan, *The Cosmic Apprentice*, 66.
15. See Sagan, *The Cosmic Apprentice*, 215.
16. Quoted in Klein, *This Changes Everything*, 267.
17. See Taylor, "What's Wrong with Negative Liberty?" For a response to his recent position see Connolly, *The Fragility of Things*, "Third Interlude: Fullness and Vitality."
18. These themes of Nietzsche are presented in chapter 4 of Connolly, *The Fragility of Things*.
19. Nietzsche, *Daybreak*, #119, p. 118.
20. For Massumi's thought at this juncture, see *What Animals Can Teach Us about Politics*. That book explores the element of play in creativity in an admirable way. He provides yet another example of one who draws sustenance from complexity theory while opposing neoliberal capture of it. There are many.

21. Nietzsche, *Daybreak*, #382, p. 171.

22. The kind of political activism I embrace requires the mobilization of a complex pluralist assemblage. In such an assemblage there will be multiple onto-orientations, including participants committed to a salvational God, those committed to a morality of transcendental principle, those adopting an ethic of cultivation, those seeking contact with an impersonal, nonsalvational God, and more. In this chapter I now express the orientation I myself embrace in pursuing such a pluralist assemblage. What is needed for such an assemblage to work is that several parties come to appreciate, without existential resentment, how the source each engages is reasonably contestable in the eyes of others. So, as is made abundantly clear in other writings, the nontheistic ethic of cultivation I embrace is not advanced as a universal that all others must adopt; it is, however, presented in an invitational way for those who may find it tempting. The devil resides in the attractions. The same holds for the notion of creativity advanced here. The idea is to seek relations of agonistic respect with those who reserve creative power to a God or deny it to humanity for other reasons. Deep, multidimensional pluralism. If and when that fails, you seek to mobilize a pluralist assemblage to limit the damage produced by dogmatic, unitarian movements. See Connolly, *The Ethos of Pluralization*.

23. I explore the creative consolidation of the evangelical-neoliberal resonance machine in chapters 2 and 3 of Connolly, *Capitalism and Christianity, American Style*. Chapters 4 and 5 of that book explore how a new combination of tactics of the self, micropolitics, and militant macropolitics might be generated to respond to this machine—a machine that itself works on all of these intercoded levels. Indeed those three scales of action are always intercoded. Chapter 6 of Cooper's *Life as Surplus* covers similar ground; she adds a discussion of how debt imperialism has been joined to evangelicalism. We both use Gilder as a prescient founder of this still operative historical conjunction.

24. Nietzsche, *Will to Power*, #673.

25. See Whitehead, *Adventures of Ideas*.

Chapter 3: Creativity and the Scars of Being

1. Foucault, *History of Sexuality*, 2:8–9.
2. Foucault, *History of Sexuality*, 2:8–9.
3. Whitehead, *Process and Reality*, 7.
4. Whitehead, *Process and Reality*, 94.
5. Deacon, *Incomplete Nature*, 359.
6. For a critical comparison between Freud and William James see Connolly, *Neuropolitics*, chapter 5.
7. Marcuse, *Eros and Civilization*, 28.
8. Rizzolatti, *Mirrors in the Brain*.
9. Bennett, "Poetry and Posture in Leaves of Grass."
10. Rizzolatti, *Mirrors in the Brain*, 125.

11. Pitts-Taylor, "I Feel Your Pain." This is a superb essay that updates recent research on mirror neurons, emphasizes situated processes by which they become culturally organized, plays up their cultural plasticity, and places the research into conversations with recent work in feminist theories of embodied sociality.

12. Rizzolatti, *Mirrors in the Brain*, 192.

13. Baldwin, *The Fire Next Time*, 86, 92.

14. Nietzsche, *Thus Spoke Zarathustra*, #22, "The Gift Giving Virtue"; Nietzsche, *Twilight of the Idols*, 43–44.

15. For one attempt to see how such a binding operation has worked in the United States see the discussion of "the evangelical-capitalist resonance machine" in Connolly, *Capitalism and Christianity, American Style*, chapters 2 and 3.

16. Foucault, *The History of Sexuality*, vol. 1.

17. Whitehead, *Process and Reality*, 227.

18. Whitehead, *Process and Reality*, 226–27.

19. Proust, *Time Regained*, 419–20.

20. An earlier, less developed version of this section appeared in Connolly, "Freedom, Teleodynamism, Creativity," 70–73. The beginning paragraphs of this chapter about Foucault also represent rewrites of a section of that earlier essay.

21. Deleuze, *Cinema II*, 127.

22. I explore the relations of dissonance and interdependence between the Theorist and the Seer in chapter 6 of *A World of Becoming*.

23. Deleuze, *Cinema II*, 172.

24. Deleuze, *Cinema II*, 133, 133, 141, 147, 146.

25. I pursue some tensions and interdependencies between these two modes in Connolly, *Why I Am Not a Secularist*, especially chapter 6, and *A World of Becoming*, chapter 6.

Chapter 4: Distributed Agencies and Bumpy Temporalities

1. Zalasiewicz and Williams, *Ocean Worlds*, 47.

2. Zalasiewicz and Williams, *Ocean* Worlds, 50.

3. These summaries are taken from Steffen et al., "The Anthropocene." The authors consider the thesis advanced by some that the Anthropocene should be dated as starting 8,000 years ago; they conclude that the period from 1800 to today provides the most useful dating decision. As we have seen in chapter 1, others date the golden spike earlier, and I support the idea of several inflection points, each with its own triggering events.

4. For an illuminating piece on Cascadia see Kathryn Schultz, "The Really Big One," *New Yorker*, July 20, 2015, http://www.newyorker.com/magazine/2015/07/20/the-really-big-one.

5. Zalasiewicz and Williams, *Ocean Worlds*, 102.

6. A good summary of this process can be found in Spier, *Big History and the Future of Humanity*, last chapter. This book in general provides a fine touchstone for reviewing the timing of "big events."

7. Fagan, *The Great Warming*, 167. Fagan offers detailed accounts of the world-wide effects of the Medieval Warming Period, including the ones listed in this paragraph.

8. See Fagan, *The Little Ice Age*.

9. These examples as a set are taken from Fagan, *The Great Warming*; and Pearce, *With Speed and Violence*. The Fagan account is mesmerizing, as he joins an exploratory sensibility to modesty about the ability so far to explain the fateful processes studied. Pearce's interviews with a variety of climate scientists, in which he allows intramural debates to unfold, are excellent.

10. For one recent account that challenges the idea of a former era of pristine forests and so on and makes the case for "a new wild" see Pearce, *The New Wild*.

11. Quoted in Olson et al., "The Blood Red Sky of the Scream." The authors and others concur that this is a contested reading, since the painting itself was done ten years after the event. But they give reasons for thinking it is true.

12. See Connolly, *The Fragility of Things* and the postlude to this study.

13. See Deacon, *Incomplete Nature*.

14. Nagel, *Mind and Cosmos*.

15. Galen Strawson, "Why Physicalism Entails Panpsychism," 32. A thoughtful version of panpsychism is advanced in Shaviro, *The Universe of Things*.

16. Juarrero, *Dynamics in Action*, 127.

17. Whitehead, *Modes of Thought*, 151, 156.

18. See Viveiros de Castro, *Cannibal Metaphysics*, 56, 57, 58, 62.

19. Vivieros de Castro, *Cannibal Metaphysics*, 252.

20. For an insightful comparison of Nietzsche's version of panexperientialism (the core of his philosophy of will to power that too many have reduced to *human* perspectivalism alone) with the perspectivalism of the Gurensi in Ghana, see Ignatov, "Ecologies of the Good Life." The wonderful piece by Naveeda Khan, "The Death of Nature in the Era of Global Warming," tends to identify the inhabitants of the Jamuna River in Bangladesh as perspectivalists in the sense noted above.

21. Bressire and Bond, "Ontological Anthropology and the Deferral of Critique," 456.

22. Griffin, *Unsnarling the World Knot*, chapters 7 and 9.

23. Eddington, *The Nature of the Physical World*, 331.

24. Eddington, *The Nature of the Physical World*, 259.

25. I explore this side of Kant in Connolly, *The Fragility of Things*, chapter 3.

26. Zalasiewicz and Williams, *Ocean Worlds*, 100.

27. Zalasiewicz and Williams, *Ocean Worlds*, 96.

28. My description is drawn from Pearce, *With Speed and Violence*; Broeker, *The Ocean Conveyor System*; Orsenna, *Portrait of the Gulf Stream*; Zalasiewicz and Williams, *Ocean Worlds*.

29. Chris Mooney, "Why Some Scientists Are Worried about a Surprisingly Cold 'Blob' in the North Atlantic," *Washington Post*, September 24, 2015, https://www.washingtonpost.com/news/energy-environment/wp/2015/09/24/why-some-scientists-are-worried-about-a-cold-blob-in-the-north-atlantic-ocean/.

30. Lonny Lippsett, "A Newfound Cog in the Ocean Conveyor," *Oceanus*, March 23, 2012, https://www.whoi.edu/oceanus/viewArticle.do?id=132749.

31. Zalasiewicz and Williams, *Ocean* Worlds, 103.

32. See Mark Harris, "Waves of Destruction," *Scientific American*, May 2015, 67–71.

33. For a thoughtful review of this research see Roosth, "Screaming Yeast." I discuss the example and its import more extensively in Connolly, *A World of Becoming*, chapter 1.

34. "Wild in the Streets: A Guide," *New York Times*, July 5, 2015.

35. Whitehead, *Science and the Modern World*, 149, 150.

36. See Griffin, *Unsnarling the Knot*. Griffin argues that both dualism and blind materialism (the two dominant options in analytic philosophy) falter with respect to the issues of mind and body, the evolution from nonlife to life, and the account of human agency. His engagements with Searle, Nagel, McGinn, and others are salutary. The question remains, however, whether their problems provide enough support for Griffin's Whiteheadian vision of panexperientialism.

37. For a thoughtful comparison of my philosophy of becoming to the thought of an ancient Tantric Buddhist, see Biernacki, "Prabuddha Bhārata Abhinavagupta's Tantric Theology of Becoming and Contemporary Secularism."

38. See Malafouris, *How Things Shape the Mind*.

39. Reported in "Smell Turns Up in Unexpected Places," *New York Times*, October 14, 2014. The article starts by reviewing evidence of receptors in the skin and goes from there: Dr. Hatt "has since identified olfactory receptors in several other organs, including the liver, heart, lungs, colon and brain. In fact genetic evidence suggests that nearly every organ in the body contains olfactory receptors."

40. See Bennett, *Vibrant Matter*; Deleuze and Guattari, *A Thousand Plateaus*; Connolly, *Neuropolitics*; Massumi, *Event and Semblance*; Malafouris, *How Things Shape the Mind*. Malafouris offers some compelling examples to fix these themes, including two I discussed earlier: the one about the coordination between brain complexity, guitar, and finger dexterity and the one about flaking.

41. Whitehead, *Process and Reality*, 108.

42. Whitehead, *Modes of Thought*, 164

43. Kauffman, *Reinventing the Sacred*, 204. My discussion of Kauffman does not mean I concur with any tendencies he expresses to adopt a neoliberal model of economic organization. As discussed in chapter 2, there is a division within complexity theory between those who link creativity strongly to a neoliberal notion of linear advance through "catastrophe" and those who link multiple temporalities to what I call entangled humanism in a world deeply at odds with neoliberal and extractive models of life.

44. Kauffman, *Reinventing the Sacred*, 207.

45. Kauffman, *Reinventing the Sacred*, 209.

46. McGinn, "Hard Questions," 93.

47. I thank Stephanie Erev, a graduate student in theory at Hopkins, for calling the distinctive complexity of the octopus to my attention. Her essay is entitled

"What It Is Like to Become a Bat." Another essay on this topic is by Jennifer Tzar and Eric Scigliano, "Through the Eye of an Octopus," *Discover*, October 1, 2003, http://discovermagazine.com/2003/oct/feateye.

48. I explore the logic of an ethos of cultivation, with the notions of will, responsibility, presumptive generosity, and creative hesitation it supports, in chapter 3 of *The Fragility of Things*. That chapter is organized around a series of exchanges with Kant and is called "Shock Therapy, Dramatization and Practical Wisdom."

49. Pandian, *Reel World*.

50. For one geologist's review of how geologists, physicists, and paleontologists came reluctantly to a reading of such extinction events so late, see Benton, *When Life Nearly Died*. Benton also discusses how shocking this evidence was to his own preconceived sense of gradualism in geology and species evolution. For a fine journalistic study that links these issues to the effects of human-induced climate change today, see Kolbert, *The Sixth Extinction*. For a discussion of the implications of these findings for the human sciences, see Connolly and Grove, "Extinction Events and the Human Sciences."

51. Besides the example of Baldwin, noted earlier, Rob Nixon's book *Slow Violence and the Environmentalism of the Poor* explores a series of writer- activists and movements in India, Africa, South America, India, and the American West who do the same thing. Their positive attachments flow into the political fury they generate. Some of those instances will be engaged in the next chapter.

Chapter 5: The Politics of Swarming and the General Strike

1. I am delineating the dilemma of electoral politics in a neoliberal era as it finds expression in the United States. My sense is that its terms could be adjusted to fit several other countries as well. Here, for instance, is a formulation by Sankaran Krishna of a similar bind, with respect to a struggle in India between Dalits and tribals seeking to save their lands and Vedanta, a bauxite-mining company, driving to take those lands under the cover of eminent domain: "The activities of the State as land broker for large, hugely rich, and successful private corporations are difficult to legitimatize. . . . And yet the State has little choice but to act as land broker if it has to sustain an international image as an 'emerging economy' and one hospitable to foreign and domestic private investors. . . . The Indian state is literally caught between maintaining an external image as an attractive investment site . . . and the need to seem accountable to domestic constituencies that cannot withstand any more displacement in the name of development" ("Colonial Legacies and Contemporary Destitution," 94).

2. Nixon, *Slow Violence and the Environmentalism of the Poor*. One of the many achievements of the Nixon book is how it introduces those whose thinking does not yet range that far enough outside Euro-American zones to literary activists in Saudi Arabia, Nigeria, Kenya, India, and elsewhere who simultaneously publicize what is happening there, show how it escapes the conventional categories of those who have demarcated environmentalism as a white, middle-class issue separate from poverty, link it to transnational corporate collusions with

corrupted officials in decimated areas, and search for modes of dramatization that allow those outside the "peripheral" spaces to appreciate what is happening. The Nixon study can fruitfully be read in relation to Krishna, "Colonial Legacies and Contemporary Destitution."

3. I came across Seeley's *Honeybee Democracy* just when mine was going to press. While the notion of a politics of swarming preceded this engagement, I suspect that movement back and forth between that study and the image of political activism conveyed here can be further refined by exploring these affinities and differences more closely.

4. When I taught at Ohio University during the late 1960s the nonacademic employees protested very low wages and adverse working conditions by launching an illegal strike. The faculty were warned by the university administration not to cancel classes at the risk of being fired. A group of untenured faculty met to decide what to do. We soon set up a striker relief fund in the middle of campus. As we sat at the table a growing number of students and faculty contributed and volunteered to help. That strike eventually succeeded, and those who had been active in supporting it soon found ourselves playing a large role in organizing a faculty union. We were, in our modest ways, specific intellectuals avant la lettre, I suppose.

5. All these figures, with the exception of Singh, Tsing, and Klein, are discussed in Nixon's study. For pertinent references, see Carson, *Silent Spring*; Singh, *Poverty and the Quest for Life*; Tsing, *Friction*; Klein, *This Changes Everything*. The work of Tsing and Nixon is discussed more extensively in the next chapter in the context of a related issue.

6. Foucault, "Truth and Power," 126.

7. For a discussion, see Connolly, "The Zombie Syndrome." That post should be read in relation to posts by me and others on the blog *The Contemporary Condition* specifying modes of activism to break the zombie propensity.

8. Hansen, *Storms of My Grandchildren*; Foucault, "Truth and Power."

9. This summary and critique refers to themes in Sorel, *Reflections on Violence*.

10. My readings by Gandhi, to date, are drawn from *The Essential Gandhi*. The advantage of this large collection of his writings for a newcomer is that each stage and topic he writes about is prefaced with a review of the context and recent actions taken. I need to pursue these leads and texts further, clearly.

11. I explore several ways to support both in "Is Eco-Egalitarian Capitalism Possible," in Connolly, *Capitalism and Christianity, American Style*.

12. See Nixon, *Slow Violence and the Environmentalism of the Poor*, chapter 4, for one account of Maathai's writing and activism in Kenya. He calls her activism "intersectional" because it drew together environmentalism and the issues of poverty, democratic participation, and women's rights. Here is one comment: "The choice of tree planting as the Green Belt Movement's defining act, proved politically astute. Here was a simple, pragmatic, yet powerfully figurative act that connected with many women's quotidian lives as tillers of the soil. Soil erosion are corrosive, compound threats that damage vital watersheds, exacerbate

the silting and dessication of rivers, erode topsoil, engender firewood and food shortages, and ultimately contributed to malnutrition" (133).

13. Maathai, *Unbowed*, 173, 174.
14. Tsing, *Friction*, chapter 6.
15. I am indebted to Sankaran Krishna for calling this to my attention during a meeting at the University of Hawaii in February 2014. He also called my attention to an essay that engages this issue: Singh, "The Tagore-Gandhi Controversy. I." The way Gandhi pursued a soft race and class hierarchy that must be overcome today is powerfully elaborated by Krishna in "A Postcolonial Racial/ Spatial Order."
16. The text in question is Holland, *Nomad Citizenship*. His reading of a "minor" Marx, whose science of capital moves close to a Deleuzian understanding of interacting, open systems, is particularly pregnant.
17. Hirsch, *The Social Limits to Growth*.
18. See Eugene Holland, "To Believe in This World: Debt Strike," Academia, http://www.academia.edu/7022345/_To_Believe_in_This_World . . . _Debt -Strike_ (accessed, summer 2014).
19. See Margulis and Sagan, *Acquiring Genomes*, chapter 8.
20. See Massumi, *What Animals Can Teach Us about Politics*.
21. Francis, *Laudato Si'*, 71, 61–63, 74, 107.
22. I develop a critique of the "conceits of secularism" in Connolly, *Why I Am Not a Secularist*. The discussion of these issues is continued in an article on Charles Taylor, "Catholicism and Philosophy." In that piece I praise Taylor for folding his faith into the philosophy he embraces rather than pretending that the two can be bracketed from each other. I also criticize him lightly, and John Paul II more actively, for contending that those of us who do not profess a personal God tend to be nihilists. The pertinence of nihilism is discussed in chapter 6 of this book.
23. Francis, *Laudato Si'*, 54–55.
24. Francis, *Laudato Si'*, 55–56.
25. For a very thoughtful and provocative book that articulates a different take on democratic violence, as both threat and periodic reality, see Johnston, *American Dionysia*. We concur in adopting a tragic image of possibility; we both see the hidden violences in a hierarchical order; but we diverge on when and whether violence is tactically the way to go in resistance movements. Part of the difference, perhaps, is in the meaning of violence each adopts, since I am calling for a strike that is militant but not violent in the sense of being bloody. But it also goes beyond that.

Chapter 6: Postcolonial Ecologies

1. Nixon, *Slow Violence and the Environmentalism of the Poor*, 252.
2. For one recent study of how urban areas in the States are affected and how the recent turn in some sectors of black politics damages movements to respond, see Spence, *Knocking the Hustle*, especially chapter 2.

3. Nixon, *Slow Violence and the Environmentalism of the Poor*; Chakrabarty, "The Climate of History"; Singh, *Poverty and the Quest for Life*; Tsing, *Friction*; Krishna, "Colonial Legacies and Contemporary Destitution"; Ignatov, "Ecologies of the Good Life"; Khan, *Muslim Becoming*; Khan, "The Death of Nature in the Era of Climate Warming."

4. Tsing, *Friction*, 41.

5. For a rich review of these disparate stories and pressures that nonetheless formed a positive assemblage, see Tsing, *Friction*, 247–55.

6. See Tsing, *Friction*, 205–12.

7. Chakrabarty, "The Climate of History," 2.

8. Chakrabarty, "The Climate of History," 4.

9. For engagements with this dimension of Darwin's work see Grosz, *Chaos, Territory, Art*; chapter 2 of this book.

10. Bergson, *Creative Evolution*.

11. My knowledge of Alvarez is mostly derived from Benton, *When Life Nearly Died*. The next couple of pages bear the imprint of Benton's history of geology.

12. Jairus Grove and I posted a piece in *Contemporary Condition* in July 2014 titled "Extinction Events and the Human Sciences." My thinking about these issues remains intertwined with his. For a recent piece on the topic, see Grove, "On an Apocalyptic Tone Recently Adopted in Everything." I particularly appreciate his discussion of the event 2 billion years ago when a new proliferation of oxygen proved poisonous to most of the life that had heretofore existed.

13. Benton, *When Life Nearly Died*, 276–77, my italics.

14. See Barnosky, *Dodging Extinction*, chapter 3.

15. For discussions of different periods of human population change, see Spier, *Big History and the Future of Humanity*, especially chapter 5.

16. See Papagianna and Morse, *The Neanderthals Rediscovered*, chapter 4.

17. Finlayson, *The Humans Who Went Extinct*. The previous two paragraphs condense several chapters of that book. His own summary appears on 127–28.

18. See chapter 2, where the contributions of Lynn Margulis and Charles Deacon to a more teleodynamic rendering of species evolution are explored. The issue now is whether they push such notions of experience even more deeply into the world, and if not, whether they and we should do so.

19. This is a key theme in Taylor, *A Secular Age*. Taylor construes "exclusive humanism" to be the idea that the virtues and rewards of humanism can be secured without the grace of a loving God. I extend the idea to a mode that can be *either* theistic or nontheistic in shape: the attempt to secure human virtues and capacities without close attention to the efficacy of a variety of nonhuman force fields that have, to varying degrees, dynamic capacities of self-organization that enter into synergies with capitalism and other cultural processes.

20. For a superb review of how the fossil fuel corporate mode of locking in has been working for the past twenty years and now builds profit demands into the next twenty, see Klein, *This Changes Everything*, chapter 4. That book is superb in several other respects, including the way she pursues a broad-spectrum

strategy to challenge the extractive system. For my review of Klein's study, see Connolly, "Naomi Klein."

21. Nietzsche's account of passive nihilism seems to me to have some affinities with that of cruel optimism by Lauren Berlant. See Berlant *Cruel Optimism*. I thank Chad Shomura for calling this connection to my attention.

22. Nietzsche, *Will to Power*, #12, pp. 12–13.

23. Nietzsche, *Will to Power*, #36, p. 23.

24. For an excellent study of mimetic contagion see Lawtoo, *The Phantom of the Ego*, particularly the introduction and chapter 1.

25. For further discussion of the indispensability of dramatization to philosophy, specifically in the context of Kantian philosophy, see Connolly, *The Fragility of Things*, chapter 3.

26. For an excellent essay that delineates how messiness works in several venues of social life see Pahl, "What a Mess."

27. As earlier engagements in this text suggest, I find particularly promising in this respect Viveiros de Castro, *Cannibal Metaphysics*; Tsing, *Friction*; Ignatov, "Ecologies of the Good Life"; Singh, *Poverty and the Quest for Life*. All concur that critical movements in northern regions of the world need to make closer contact with those in southern regions; all identify modes of "perspectivism" in multiple species that break with Euro-American traditions of subject/object dualism and a human/nonhuman bifurcation; Singh, Viveiros de Castro, and Ignatov actively pursue creative exchanges between the "minor" tradition of Deleuze and Guattari on the one hand and indigenous movements in India, the Amazon, and Ghana on the other.

28. For a salutary and evocative exploration of negative theology in relation to these issues see Keller, *Cloud of the Impossible*. Negative theology acknowledges the mystery of divinity all the way down while drawing positive drafts of energy from its impossible pursuit, viewed from a merely representational point of view.

29. For a superb discussion of interspecies entanglements, including the entanglements of vulture, human, dog, anthrax, rabies, and rat noted here, see van Dooren, *Flight Ways*.

30. In this I concur with the valuable work by van Dooren, *Flight Ways*; Haraway, *When Species Meet*.

31. See Jamail, "Are Humans Going Extinct?"

32. See Pearce, *The New Wild*.

33. If radical action is not taken soon, my hunch is rather closer to that of Roy Scranton than to that of Guy McPherson. In *Learning to Die in the Anthropocene*, Scranton says, "Perhaps our descendants will build new cities on the shores of the Arctic Sea, when the rest of the earth is scorching deserts and steaming jungles" (109). The point is to act now so that neither scenario is enacted.

Postlude: Capitalism and the Planetary

This interview was pursued during the fall of 2014 and published as "Confronting the Anthropocene and Contesting Neoliberalism: An Interview with William E.

Connolly," *New Political Science* 37 (July 2015): 259–75. Bradley MacDonald teaches political theory at Colorado State University. His most recent book is *Performing Marx: Contemporary Negotiations of a Living Tradition.* I would like to thank Bradley for initiating the interview, for consenting to its reproduction here, and for posing such compelling questions. My definition of the Anthropocene, reviewed in the first chapter of this book, has changed a bit since that interview. The references to my earlier books are folded into the interview, to avoid unnecessary repetition. Two essays of mine and all other references are both noted here and included in the bibliography.

1. For a perceptive overview of the ideological and organizational positions associated with the Caucus, see Barrow, "The Intellectual Origins of New Political Science."
2. Connolly, "The Challenge to Pluralist Theory," 19.
3. Taylor, "Neutrality in Political Science."
4. Huntington, *The Clash of Civilizations and the Remaking of World Order.*
5. Connolly, "Voices from the Whirlwind."
6. The discussions in chapters 5 and 6 of this study draw planetary processes and postcolonial concerns more closely together than may be reflected in this interview.
7. MacDonald, "Review of William E. Connolly, *A World of Becoming* and *The Fragility of Things.*"

Alley, Richard. *The Two-Mile Time Machine: Ice Cores, Abrupt Climate Change and Our Future*. Princeton: Princeton University Press, 2000.

Antrosio, Jason. "Denisovans, Neanderthals, Archaics as Human Races." *Living Anthropologically*, 2012. http://www.livinganthropologically.com/anthropology/denisovans-neandertals-human-races/.

Arendt, Hannah. *Between Past and Future*. New York: Viking Press, 1954.

Baldwin, James. *The Fire Next Time*. New York: Vintage, 1963.

Balibar, Etienne. *The Philosophy of Marx*. Translated by Chris Turner. New York: Verso, 2007.

Barnosky, Anthony. *Dodging Extinction: Power, Food, Money and the Future of Life on Earth*. Berkeley: University of California Press, 2014.

Barrow, Clyde. "The Intellectual Origins of New Political Science." *New Political Science* 30, no. 2 (2008): 215–44.

Bennett, Jane. "Poetry and Posture in Leaves of Grass." Unpublished manuscript, 2014.

Bennett, Jane. *Vibrant Matter: A Political Ecology of Things*. Durham: Duke University Press, 2010.

Benton, Michael J. *When Life Nearly Died: The Greatest Mass Extinction of All Time*. London: Thames Hudson, 2005.

Bergson, Henri. *Creative Evolution*. 1907. Translated by Arthur Mitchell. Mineola, NY: Dover, 1998.

Berlant, Lauren. *Cruel Optimism*. 2011. Durham: Duke University Press.

Berlin, Isaiah. "Two Concepts of Liberty." In *Four Essays on Liberty*, 118–72. New York: Oxford University Press, 1969.

Best, Michael H., and William E. Connolly. *The Politicized Economy*. 2nd edition. Lexington, MA: D. C. Heath, 1983.

Biernacki, Loriliai. "Prabuddha Bhārata Abhinavagupta's Tantric Theology of Becoming and Contemporary Secularism." Unpublished manuscript.

Bressire, Lucas, and David Bond. "Ontological Anthropology and the Deferral of Critique." *American Ethnologist* 41, no 3 (August 2014): 440–56.

Broeker, Wally. *The Ocean Conveyor System*. Princeton: Princeton University Press, 2010.

Carson, Rachel. *Silent Spring*. New York: Houghton Mifflin, 1962.

Chakrabarty, Dipesh. "The Climate of History: Four Theses." *Eurozine*, October 30, 2009. http://www.eurozine.com/articles/2009–10–30-chakrabarty-en.html.

Connolly, William E. *The Augustinian Imperative: A Reflection on the Politics of Morality*. Newbury, CA: Sage, 1993.

Connolly, William E. *The Bias of Pluralism*. New York: Atherton, 1969.

Connolly, William E. *Capitalism and Christianity, American Style*. Durham: Duke University Press, 1980.

Connolly, William E. "Catholicism and Philosophy: A Nontheistic Appreciation." In *Charles Taylor*, edited by Ruth Abbey, 166–86. Cambridge: Cambridge University Press, 2004.

Connolly, William E. "The Challenge to Pluralist Theory." In *The Bias of Pluralism*, edited by William E. Connolly, 3–34. New York: Atherton Press, 1969.

Connolly, William E. "Elizabeth Grosz: The Nick of Time: Politics, Evolution and the Untimely." *Political Theory* 34 (2006): 663–67.

Connolly, William E. *The Ethos of Pluralization*. Minneapolis: University of Minnesota Press, 1995.

Connolly, William E. "Experience and Experiment." *Daedalus* 135 (2006): 67–75.

Connolly, William E. *The Fragility of Things: Self-Organizing Processes, Neoliberal Fantasies, and Democratic Activism*. Durham: Duke University Press, 2013.

Connolly, William E. "Freedom, Teleodynamism, Creativity." *Foucault Studies*, no. 17 (April 2014): 60–75.

Connolly, William E. *Identity/Difference: Democratic Negotiations of Political Paradox*. Ithaca: Cornell University Press, 1991.

Connolly, William E. "Naomi Klein: In the Eye of the Anthropocene." *The Contemporary Condition*, March 15, 2015. http://contemporarycondition.blogspot.com/search/label/William%20E.%20Connolly.

Connolly, William E. *Neuropolitics: Thinking, Culture, Speed*. Minneapolis: University of Minnesota Press, 2002.

Connolly, William E. "A Note on Freedom under Socialism." *Political Theory* 5 (1977): 461–72.

Connolly, William E. *Political Science and Ideology*. New York: Atherton, 1967.

Connolly, William E. *Political Theory and Modernity*. New York: Basil Blackwell, 1988.

Connolly, William E. *The Terms of Political Discourse*. Lexington, MA: D. C. Heath, 1974.

Connolly, William E. "Voices from the Whirlwind." In *In the Nature of Things*, edited by Jane Bennett and William Chaloupka, 197–225. Minneapolis: University of Minnesota Press, 1993.

Connolly, William E. *Why I Am Not a Secularist*. Durham: Duke University Press, 1999.

Connolly, William E. *A World of Becoming*. Durham: Duke University Press, 2011.

Connolly, William E. "The Zombie Syndrome." *The Contemporary Condition*, December 30, 2013. http://contemporarycondition.blogspot.com/search/label /William%20E.%20Connolly.

Connolly, William E., and Jairus Victor Grove. "Extinction Events and the Human Sciences." *The Contemporary Condition*, July 3, 2014. http:// contemporarycondition.blogspot.com/search?q=Extinction+Events+and+the+ Human+Sciences.

Cooper, Melinda. *Life as Surplus: Biotechnology and Capitalism in the Neoliberal Era*. Seattle: University of Washington Press, 2008.

Darwin, Charles. *The Descent of Man*. 1871. New York: Prometheus Books, 1998.

Deacon, Terrence. *Incomplete Nature: How Mind Emerged from Matter*. New York: Norton, 2012.

Deleuze, Gilles. *Cinema II: The Time Image*. Translated by Hugh Tomlinson. Minneapolis: University of Minnesota Press, 1989.

Deleuze, Gilles, and Félix Guattari. *A Thousand Plateaus: Capitalism and Schizophrenia*. Translated by Brian Massumi. Minneapolis: University of Minnesota Press, 1987.

Dumm, Thomas. *Michel Foucault and the Politics of Freedom*. Thousand Oaks, CA: Sage, 1996.

Eddington, Arthur. *The Nature of the Physical World*. New York: Macmillan, 1929.

Edelman, Lee. *No Future: Queer Theory and the Death Drive*. Durham: Duke University Press, 2004.

Erev, Stephanie. "What It Is Like to Become a Bat." Seminar paper. Johns Hopkins University, Fall 2014.

Fagan, Brian. *The Great Warming: Climate Change and the Rise and Fall of Civilizations*. New York: Bloomsbury Press, 2008.

Fagan, Brian. *The Little Ice Age: How Climate Made History, 1300–1850*. New York: Basic Books, 2002.

Feit, Mario. *Democratic Anxieties: Same-Sex Marriage, Death, and Citizenship*. Lanham, MD: Lexington Books, 2011.

Finlayson, Clive. *The Humans Who Went Extinct*. Oxford: Oxford University Press, 2009.

Flathman, Richard E. *Freedom and Its Conditions: Discipline, Autonomy, and Resistance*. New York: Routledge, 2003.

Foucault, Michel. *Discipline and Punish: The Birth of the Prison*. Translated by Robert Hurley. New York: Vintage Books, 1995.

Foucault, Michel. *History of Sexuality*. Vol. 1: *An Introduction*. Translated by Robert Hurley. New York: Pantheon Books, 1978.

Foucault, Michel. *History of Sexuality*. Vol. 2: *The Use of Pleasure*. Translated by Robert Hurley. New York: Pantheon Books, 1985.

Foucault, Michel. *History of Sexuality*. Vol. 3: *Care of the Self*. Translated by Robert Hurley. New York: Pantheon Books, 1986.

Foucault, Michel. *Security, Territory, Population: Lectures at the Collège de France 1977–1978*. Edited by Michel Senellart. Translated by Graham Burchell. New York: Palgrave Macmillan, 2007.

Foucault, Michel. "Truth and Power." In *Power/Knowledge: Select Interviews and Other Writings*, edited by Colin Gordon, 109–34. New York: Pantheon Books, 1980.

Francis. *Laudato Si': On Care for Our Common Home*. Vatican City: Libreria Editrice Vaticana, 2015.

Freeman, Anthony, ed. *Consciousness and Its Place in Nature*. Exeter, UK: Academic Imprint, 2006.

Gandhi, Mahatma. *The Essential Gandhi*. Edited by Louis Fisher. New York: Vintage Books, 1990.

Girard, Rene. *Job: The Victim of His People*. Stanford: Stanford University Press, 1987.

Gordis, Robert. *The Book of God and Man: A Study of Job*. Chicago: University of Chicago Press, 1965.

Griffin, David Ray. *Unsnarling the World Knot: Consciousness, Freedom, and the Mind-Body Problem*. Eugene, OR: Wipf and Stock, 1998.

Grosz, Elizabeth. *Chaos, Territory, Art*. New York: Columbia University Press, 2008.

Grove, Jairus. "On an Apocalyptic Tone Recently Adopted in Everything." *Theory & Event* 18, no. 3 (2015): 1–7.

Habermas, Jürgen. *The Future of Human Nature*. (Cambridge, UK: Polity Press, 2003.

Hansen, Jim. *Storms of My Grandchildren*. New York: Bloomsbury Press, 2014.

Haraway, Donna. "Anthropocene, Capitalocene, Plantationocene, Chthulucene: Making Kin." *Environmental Humanities* 6 (2015): 159–65.

Haraway, Donna. *When Species Meet*. Minneapolis: University of Minnesota Press, 2008.

Hayek, Friedrich A. von. *Individualism and Economic Order*. Chicago: University of Chicago Press, 1980.

Hayek, Friedrich A. von. *Road to Serfdom*. Chicago: University of Chicago Press, 1944.

Hirsch, Fred. *The Social Limits to Growth*. Cambridge: Harvard University Press, 1976.

Holland, Eugene. *Nomad Citizenship: Free Market Communism and the Slow Motion General Strike*. Minneapolis: University of Minnesota Press, 2011.

Honig, Bonnie. *Antigone Interrupted*. Cambridge: Cambridge University Press, 2013.

Honig, Bonnie. *Democracy and the Foreigner*. Princeton: Princeton University Press, 2001.

Huntington, Samuel P. *The Clash of Civilizations and the Remaking of World Order*. New York: Simon and Schuster, 1996.

Ignatov, Anatoli. "Ecologies of the Good Life: Forces, Bodies and Cross Cultural Encounters." PhD dissertation, Johns Hopkins University, 2014.

Jamail, Dahr. "Are Humans Going Extinct?" Interview with Guy McPherson. *Truthout*, December 1, 2014. http://truth-out.org/news/item/27714-are-humans-going-extinct?tmpl=component&print=1.

Johnston, Steven. *American Dionysia: Violence, Tragedy and Democratic Politics*. Cambridge: Cambridge University Press, 2015.

Johnston, Steven. *Encountering Tragedy: Rousseau and the Project of Democratic Order*. Ithaca: Cornell University Press, 1999.

Juarrero, Alicia. *Dynamics in Action: Intentional Behavior as a Complex System*. Cambridge: MIT Press, 2002.

Kateb, George. *Human Dignity*. London: Belknap Press, 2014.

Kauffman, Stuart. *Reinventing the Sacred: A New View of Science, Reason and Religion*. New York: Basic Books, 2008.

Keller, Catherine. *Cloud of the Impossible*. New York: Columbia University Press, 2014.

Khan, Naveeda. "The Death of Nature in the Era of Climate Warming." In *Wording the World*, edited by Roma Chatterji, 288–300. New York: Fordham University Press, 2014.

Khan, Naveeda. *Muslim Becoming: Aspiration and Skepticism in Pakistan*. Durham: Duke University Press, 2012.

Klein, Naomi. *This Changes Everything: Capitalism vs. the Climate*. New York: Simon and Schuster, 2014.

Kolbert, Elizabeth. *The Sixth Extinction*. New York: Henry Holt, 2014.

Krishna, Sankaran. "Colonial Legacies and Contemporary Destitution: Law, Race and Human Security." *Alternatives: Global, Local, Political* 40 (2015): 85–101.

Krishna, Sankaran. "A Postcolonial Racial/Spatial Order: Gandhi, Amdeker, and the Construction of the International." In *Confronting the Global Color Line*, edited by Robbie Shilliam, Alex Anievas, and Nivi Manchanda, 139–56. London: Routledge, 2014.

Latour, Bruno. "Facing Gaia: Six Lectures on the Political Theology of Nature." Gifford Lectures on Natural Religion. February 2013. http://macaulay.cuny.edu /eportfolios/wakefield15/files/2015/01/LATOUR-GIFFORD-SIX-LECTURES _1.pdf.

Lawtoo, Nidesh. *The Phantom of the Ego*. East Lansing: Michigan State University Press, 2013.

Lazzarato, Maurizio. *The Making of the Indebted Man*. Los Angeles: Semiotext(e), 2012.

Lewis, Simon, and Mark Maslin. "Defining the Anthropocene." *Nature* 519 (2015): 171–80.

Leys, Ruth. "The Turn to Affect: A Critique." *Critical Inquiry* 37, no. 3 (2011): 434–72.

Maathai, Wangari. *Unbowed*. New York: Anchor Books, 2006.

Macdonald, Bradley J. *Performing Marx: Contemporary Negotiations of a Living Tradition*. Albany: State University of New York Press, 2006.

Macdonald, Bradley J. "Review of William E. Connolly, *A World of Becoming* and *The Fragility of Things: Self-Organizing Processes, Neoliberal Fantasies, and Democratic Activism*." *Perspectives on Politics* 12, no. 2 (2014): 46–48.

Malafouris, Lambros. *How Things Shape the Mind*. Cambridge: MIT Press, 2013.

Marcuse, Herbert. *Eros and Civilization*. Boston: Beacon Press, 1955.

Margulis, Lynn, and Dorion Sagan. *Acquiring Genomes: A Theory of the Origins of Species*. New York: Basic Books, 2002.

Marx, Karl. "The Critique of the Gotha Programme." In *Karl Marx: Selected Writings*, edited by David McLellan, 610–19. New York: Oxford University Press, 1977.

Massumi, Brian. *Event and Semblance: Activist Philosophy and the Occurrent Arts*. Cambridge: MIT Press, 2011.

Massumi, Brian. *What Animals Can Teach Us about Politics*. Durham: Duke University Press, 2014.

McGinn, Colin. "Hard Questions." In *Consciousness and Its Place in Nature*, edited by Anthony Freeman, 90–99. Exeter, UK: Academic Imprint, 2006.

Merleau-Ponty, Maurice. *Nature: Course Notes from the College de France*. Translated by Robert Vallier. Evanston, IL: Northwestern University Press, 2013.

Michaels, Walter Benn. *Our America: Nativism, Modernism and Pluralism*. Durham: Duke University Press, 1995.

Mitchell, Stephen, trans. and ed. *The Book of Job*. San Francisco: North Point Press, 1987.

Mitteldorf, Josh. "Neo-Darwinism and the Group Selection Controversy." In *Lynn Margulis: The Life and Legacy of a Scientific Rebel*, edited by Dorion Sagan, 86–95. White River Junction, VT: Chelsea Green, 2012.

Moore, Jason. *Capitalism in the Web of Life: Ecology and the Accumulation of Capital*. New York: Verso, 2015.

Moore, Jason. "The Capitalocene. Part 1: On the Nature and Origins of Our Ecological Crisis." March 2014. http://www.jasonwmoore.com/uploads/The _Capitalocene__Part_I__June_2014.pdf.

Morton, Timothy. *Hyperobjects: Philosophy and Ecology after the End of the World*. Minneapolis: University of Minnesota Press, 2013.

Nagel, Thomas. *Mind and Cosmos: Why the Materialist Neo-Darwinian Conception of Nature Is Almost Certainly False*. New York: Oxford University Press, 2012.

Nietzsche, Friedrich. *Daybreak: Thoughts on the Prejudices of Morality*. Translated by R. J. Hollingdale. Cambridge: Cambridge University Press, 1982.

Nietzsche, Friedrich. *The Gay Science*. Translated by Walter Kaufmann. New York: Vintage, 1974.

Nietzsche, Friedrich. *Thus Spoke Zarathustra*. Translated by Walter Kaufmann. New York: Penguin, 1978.

Nietzsche, Friedrich. *Twilight of the Idols*. Translated by R. J. Hollingdale. New York: Penguin, 1968.

Nietzsche, Friedrich. *Will to Power*. Translated by Walter Kaufmann and R. J. Hollingdale. New York: Vintage Books, 1967.

Nixon, Rob. *Slow Violence and the Environmentalism of the Poor*. Cambridge: Harvard University Press, 2011.

Novak, Michael. *Catholic Ethics and the Spirit of Capitalism*. New York: Free Press, 1993.

Novak, Michael. *The Spirit of Democratic Capitalism*. Madison, WI: Madison Books, 1999.

Olson, Donald, Russell Doescher, and Marilyn Olson. "The Blood Red Sky of the Scream." *American Physical Society* 13 (2004). http://www.aps.org/publications /apsnews/200405/backpage.cfm.

Orsenna, Erik. *Portrait of the Gulf Stream*. London: Hans, 2008.

Oyama, Susan. *The Ontogeny of Information: Developmental Systems and Evolution*. Durham: Duke University Press, 2000.

Pahl, Katrin. "What a Mess." MLN, April 2015, 528–53.

Pandian, Anand. *Reel World: An Anthropology of Creation*. Durham: Duke University Press, 2015.

Papagianna, Dimitri, and Michael Morse. *The Neanderthals Rediscovered: How Modern Science Is Rewriting Their Story*. London: Thames and Hudson, 2013.

Pearce, Fred. *The New Wild: Why Invasive Species Will Be Nature's Salvation*. Boston: Beacon Press, 2015.

Pearce, Fred. *With Speed and Violence: Why Scientists Fear Tipping Points in Climate Change*. Boston: Beacon Press, 2007.

Pitts-Taylor, Victoria. "I Feel Your Pain: Embodied Knowledges and Situated Neurons." *Hypatia*, Fall 2013, 852–69.

Proust, Marcel. *Time Regained*. Translated by Andreas Mayor and Terence Kilmartin. New York: Modern Library, 1993.

Read, Rupert. "Why the Ecological Crisis Spells the End of Liberalism." Green House Think Tank, Summer 2011. http://www.greenhousethinktank.org/files /greenhouse/home/post_growth_commonsense_inside.pdf.

Rizzolatti, Giacomo. *Mirrors in the Brain*. Translated by Frances Anderson. Oxford: Oxford University Press, 2006.

Roosth, Sophia. "Screaming Yeast: Sonolcytology, Cytoplasmic Milieus, and Cellular Subjectivities." *Critical Inquiry* 35, no. 2 (2009): 332–50.

Rousseau, Jean-Jacques. "The Discourse on Political Economy." In *Jean Jacques Rousseau: The Basic Political Writings*, translated by Donald A. Cress, 111–40. Indianapolis: Hackett, 1987.

Rousseau, Jean-Jacques. *The Government of Poland*. Translated by Willmoore Kendall. New York: Library of Liberal Arts, 1972.

Rousseau, Jean-Jacques. *The Social Contract*. Translated by Judith Masters. Edited by Roger D. Masters. New York: St. Martin's Press, 1978.

Sagan, Dorion. *Cosmic Apprentice: Dispatches from the Edges of Science*. Minneapolis: University of Minnesota Press, 2013.

Scranton, Roy. *Learning to Die in the Anthropocene: Reflections on the End of a Civilization*. San Francisco: City Lights Books, 2015.

Seeley, Thomas D. *Honeybee Democracy*. Princeton: Princeton University Press, 2010.

Shaviro, Steven. *The Universe of Things*. Minneapolis: University of Minnesota Press, 2014.

Singh, Ajai R. "The Tagore-Gandhi Controversy. 1." *Indian Philosophical Quarterly* 19, no. 3 (1992). http://ajai-shakuntala.tripod.com/id45.html.

Singh, Bhrigupati. *Poverty and the Quest for Life: Spiritual and Material Striving in Rural India*. Chicago: University of Chicago Press, 2015.

Skinner, Quentin. *Machiavelli: A Very Short Introduction*. Oxford: Oxford University Press, 2001.

Sorel, George. *Reflections on Violence*. Translated by T. E. Hulme. Mineola, NY: Dover, 1950.

Spence, Lester. *Knocking the Hustle: Against the Neoliberal Turn in Black Politics*. Brooklyn: Punctum Books, 2016.

Spier, Fred. *Big History and the Future of Humanity*. London: Blackwell, 2011.

Steffen, Will, Jacques Grinewald, Paul Crutzen, and John McNeill. "The Anthropocene: Conceptual and Historical Perspectives." *Philosophical Transactions of the Royal Society*, January 31, 2011. http://rsta.royalsocietypublishing.org/content/369/1938/842

Strawson, Galen. "Why Physicalism Entails Panpsychism." In *Consciousness and its Place in Nature*, edited by Michael Freeman, 3–32, Exeter, UK: Academic Imprint, 2006.

Taylor, Charles. "Neutrality in Political Science." In *Philosophy, Politics and Society*, edited by P. Laslett and G. Runciman, 25–57. Oxford: Blackwell, 1967.

Taylor, Charles. *A Secular Age*. Cambridge: Harvard University Press, 2007.

Taylor, Charles. "What's Wrong with Negative Liberty?" In *Philosophy and the Human Sciences*, 211–30. Cambridge: Cambridge University Press, 1985.

Thompson, Evan. *Mind in Life: Biology, Phenomenology and the Sciences of Man*. Cambridge: Harvard University Press, 2007.

Todorov, Tzvetan. *The Conquest of America: The Question of the Other*. Translated by Richard Howard. New York: Harper and Row, 1985.

Tournier, Michel. *Friday*. Translated by Norman Denny. Baltimore: Johns Hopkins University Press, 1969.

Tsing, Anna Lowenhaupt. *Friction: An Ethnography of Global Connection*. Princeton: Princeton University Press, 2005.

van Dooren, Thom. *Flight Ways: Life and Loss at the Edge of Extinction*. New York: Columbia University Press, 2014.

Viveiros de Castro, Eduardo Batalha. *Cannibal Metaphysics: For a Post-Structural Anthropology*. Translated and edited by Peter Skafish. Minneapolis: University of Minnesota Press, 2014.

Wark, McKenzie. *Molecular Red: Theory for the Anthropocene*. New York: Verso, 2015.

Whitehead, Alfred North. *Adventures of Ideas*. New York: Free Press, 1967.

Whitehead, Alfred North. *Modes of Thought*. New York: Cambridge University Press, 1938.

Whitehead, Alfred North. *Process and Reality: Corrected Edition*. 1929. Edited by David Ray Griffin and Donald W. Sherburne. New York: Free Press, 1978.

Whitehead, Alfred North. *Science and the Modern World*. New York: Free Press, 1925.

Zalasiewicz, Jan, and Mark Williams. *Ocean Worlds: The Story of Seas on Earth and Other Planets*. New York: Oxford University Press, 2014.

Communism, 4; and Anthropocene, 190; and climate change, 34, 156, 202n18; and sociocentrism, 20, 25–27, 137, 184; types of consumption and, 27

Communitarian: and belonging, 19

Connolly, William: and agency, 109; and ethic of cultivation, 210n48; nature-culture relation, 203n24

Consumption, 136; and infrastructure, 4, 120, 132, 137, 144–45, 180–81, 185

Contestability: and ethic of cultivation, 58–59; and faith, 143; and surplus repression, 68

Cooper, Melinda: complexity theory and neoliberalism, 49–51; and evangelicalism, 206n23

Creativity: and activism, 134–35; and agency, 51–55, 60, 64–67, 78–81, 112; and Anthropocene, 83–87; and belonging, 81–87; and chance, 60; and culture, 51–56, 61; and drives, 10–11; of evolution, 10, 47–49, 61–62; and freedom, 21, 24; and pluralist assemblage, 144; and powers of the false, 81; and strike, 145–46, 174; and symbiogenesis, 45–46; and tactics of the self, 59; and the uncanny, 77, 82

Creed, and spirituality, 139–42

Crisis: and climate, 130

Darwin, Charles, 37–39; and gradualism, 118, 158

Deacon, Terrence, 10, 205n13; and emergence, 93; and teleodyanmism, 47–49, 66, 93

Debt, 13, 138; and Lazzarato, 192–93

Deep ecology: and bumpy planetary processes, 117, 153, 157, 183

Deleuze, Gilles, 11, 182, 184; and agency, 110–11; and belief in this world, 82–87; and creativity, 65; and events, 84; and extinction events, 115; and fascism, 60; and joy, 73; and

Lazzarato, 192–93; and Marxism, 190; and micropolitics, 186–91; and neoliberalism, 49; and nihilism, 167; and panexperientialism, 106; and perspectivism, 97; and powers of the false, 78–81; and receptivity, 72; and tactics of the self, 55

Dilemma of electoral politics, 122–24

Discipline: and activism, 129; and belonging, 15; and market, 23–25; and the nation, 16–19; and negative freedom, 19–20; and nonviolence, 131

Drives, 10–11, 13, 81; and creativity, 60–62, 65–67, 112; and entangled humanism, 171; and instincts, 67–70, 166; and Nietzschean self, 52–55; as purposive complexes, 53–55; and role experiments, 132–34; and tactics of the self, 56–60

Dumm, Thomas, negative freedom and normalization, 64–65

Eco-activists, 12, 126; and electoral politics, 123

Economic meltdown (2008), 3

Eddington, Arthur, 11, 106; and Kauffman, 111; quantum theory and panexperientialism, 99–102

Edelman, Lee, 203n20

Electoral politics: dilemma of, 123–25; and politics of swarming, 125–28, 185; and time, 123

Emergentism, 11, 93

Environmentalism: postcolonial and Euro-American, 12; and productivity, 181; and sociocentrism, 181–82

Ethic of cultivation, 210n48; and tactics of the self, 56–60. *See also* Role experiments

Evangelical-capitalist resonance machine, 6, 60, 143, 180–81, 186, 201n6, 204n26, 206n23

Evolution: and Anthropocene, 30; and creativity, 10, 44–51, 62; and Deacon, 10, 47–49, 66, 93, 205n13; and genocentrism, 38–39; 44; and gradualism, 158–59; and Margulis, 10, 45–50, 93; and Nagel, 10, 41–44, 93 205nn5–6; and neo-Darwinism, 38–40, 121; and planetary, 4; and symbiogenesis, 45–46, 93

Extinction events, 13, 32, 122, 158–63; and amplifiers, 161–62; and critique of planetary gradualism, 157–63; and Deleuze, 116; and geology, 210n48; and Nietzsche, 115

False, the: as source of power, 78–81

Flathman, Richard: and freedom, 19

Flint, Michigan, 176; and contaminated water supply, 152

Foucault, Michel, 197; and disciplinary society, 15; and events, 84; and Lazzarato, 192–93; and Marxism, 190–91; and neoliberalism, 60; and repressive hypothesis, 75; and sociocentrism, 29; and the specific intellectual, 125–29; and tactics of the self, 55

Fracking, 31, 122, 134

Francis, Pope, 12, 49, 129, 140, 173; and Anthropocene, 141–42; and pluralist assemblage, 143–44, 187; and poverty, 141

Freedom: and belonging, 24, 27; and collective politics, 74; and creativity, 21, 51–56, 61, 76–81; and domination over nature, 155; and futurity, 27–29; and market, 121; and nation, 16–19; and negative and positive, 19–22; and pluralist assemblage, 148–49; and socialism, 25, 181

Freud, Sigmund, 7; and necessary repression, 67–68

Futurity: and belonging, 33–34; and freedom, 27–29; and realism, 122

Gandhi, Mahatma, 12, 129; and nonviolent militancy, 131–35; and race, 134; and spinning wheel, 132

General Strike, as across world regions, 144–49; and Mahatma Gandhi, 132–33, 134–36; and Eugene Holland, 136–38; and Naomi Klein, 134; and Bruno Latour, 138–41; and Wangari Maathai, 133–35, 140–44; and Pope Francis, relevance of, 129–30; and Sorel, 130–32

Glacier flows, 4, 8, 11; and sociocentrism, 16–19

Goods: exclusive and inclusive, 180

Gradualism, 4, 24, 30, 32; and geological critique of, 90–93, 135–36, 158–63; and species evolution, 37, 118, 121, 157, 158–59

Great Acceleration: and carbon emissions, 30, 184

Green Belt movement: as cross-regional, 145; and local citizen action, 133–34

Griffin, David Ray: on panexperientialism, 97, 105

Grosz, Elizabeth, and new Darwinism, 205n1

Grove, Jairus: and extinction events, 213n12

Habermas, Jürgen: and sociocentrism, 29, 203n24

Hansen, Jim: and activism, 129

Haraway, Donna: and agency, 109; and critique of Anthropocene, 204n26; and sociocentrism, 182

Hayek, Friedrich, 10, 16, 27, 195; and belonging, 22–25; and self-organization, 136

Heterogeneous connections, 45

Hirsch, Fred: and consumption binds, 136–37

Holland, Eugene, 12, 129; and debt strike, 138; and Marxism, 190–91; and slow-motion strike, 135–38

Honig, Bonnie, and critique of anti-futurism, 203

Hubris, 8

Humanism: critique of exceptionalism, 10, 13, 16, 27, 29–30, 32, 50, 68, 97, 100, 108, 120, 163–64, 170–72, 182; entangled, 8, 12–13, 33, 39, 61, 121–22, 137, 156, 163, 168–74, 184–85; exclusive, 213n9

Huntington, Samuel, 177–78

Immanent naturalism, 40, 42, 139, 170; and Thomas Nagel, 42

Indigenous peoples: and perspectivalism, 204n28; and pluralist assemblage, 34

Ignatov, Anatoli, and Gurensi perspectivalism, 208n20; and "minor" philosophy, 204n28

Instinct: and drives, 52–56, 67–70, 166; and surplus repression, 69–70

James, William, 39, 182

Job. *See* Book of Job

John Paul II: and nihilism, 142, 212n22

Johnston, Steven: and democratic violence, 212n25

Judgment, 1; and evolution, 41; and powers of the false, 79–81; systems of, 83; and tactics of the self, 57–58

Juerrero, Alicia, and panexperientialism, 94–95

Kant, Immanuel: and freedom, 113, 116; and human exceptionalism, 100; and "royal" theory, 195

Karishna, Sankaran, and colonial exploitation, 210n1, Gandhi's limits, 212n15

Kateb, George: and sociocentrism, 29, 203n24

Kauffman, Stuart, 47, 48 205n10; and neoliberalism, 112, 209n43; and quantum brain, 111–12, 117, 209n43

Khan, Naveeda, and Bangladesh ecologies, 208n20

Klein, Naomi, 12, 25, 126, 129, 157, 213–14n20; and complexity theory, 50–51; and pluralist assemblage, 134–35; and spirituality, 140

Labor unions: Hayek on, 24; and slow-motion strike, 137

Latour, Bruno, 12, 129, 155, 182, 184; and Anthropocene, 138–40; and complexity theory and political economy, 50; and Schmittian division, 138–39; and spirituality, 141–42

Lazzarato, Maurizio, 13, 190–92, 195; and the planetary, 193

Lewis, Simon, and Mark A. Maslin: and golden spikes, 31

Lisbon earthquake (1755), 78–79, 87

Lyell, Charles: and planetary gradualism, 118, 158–59

Maathai, Wangari, 12, 126, 129; and activism, 133–35; and Martin Luther King Jr., 134

Macdonald, Bradley, 13, 175–97, 214–15

Malafouris, Lambros, 72; and agency, 109, 114 209n40

Marcuse, Herbert: and creativity, 11, 65; and surplus repression, 67–70, 75–76

Margulis, Lynn, 10, 45–50, 93, 159; and Gaia, 138

Market: and belonging, 22–25; and discipline, 23–24

Marx, Karl, 10, 16, 192; and alienation, 27, 190; "Critique of the Gotha Programme," 25–27; and freedom, 25; and labor theory of value, 26; and Lazzarato, 192–93; and primitive accumulation, 136, 190; and sociocentrism, 25–27

Massumi, Brian: and agency, 109; and creativity, 205n20; and included middle, 140; and Marxism, 190; and receptivity, 72; and sociocentrism, 182; and tactics of the self, 55